The
Kickass
Single Mom

The
Kickass
Single Mom

☆

Be Financially Independent,

Discover Your Sexiest Self, and

Raise Fabulous, Happy Children

EMMA JOHNSON

A TarcherPerigee Book

tarcherperigee
An imprint of Penguin Random House LLC
375 Hudson Street
New York, New York 10014

TarcherPerigee with tp colophon is a registered trademark
of Penguin Random House LLC.

Most TarcherPerigee books are available at special quantity discounts for bulk
purchase for sales promotions, premiums, fund-raising, and educational needs.
Special books or book excerpts also can be created to fit specific needs. For
details, write: SpecialMarkets@penguinrandomhouse.com.

ISBN 9780143131151

Printed in the United States of America
1   3   5   7   9   10   8   6   4   2

For Helena and Lucas.

May you always have the freedom and courage

to create the family that you want and need.

Contents

Introduction

TEN YEARS AGO, when I was married but not yet a mom, I attended a daylong book proposal workshop that required students to bring a two-page summary. My book proposal was about single motherhood. At the time I was thinking about becoming a mother, and reflecting on my own experience being raised by a single mom. I was also curious about how the divorce surge of the 1970s and '80s played out in our society, how that shaped my generation of kids and the decisions we were making as we became adults. After all, I was adamant *I* would never be a single mom! I would do better, get married before getting pregnant, *and stay married.* I'd do things "the right way." My interest in single motherhood was one part personal, two parts journalistic. The idea was nice, said the workshop leader. He smiled and was kind.

Like many projects I've considered throughout my life, after the workshop I parked this one in a digital file on my hard drive and forgot about it.

Fast-forward a few short years and my interest in single motherhood was reignited. This time it was zero parts journalistic, one thousand parts full-on personal. Despite every single proclamation to the contrary, I found myself as a single mom. For a long time, I was alternatively livid, confused, overwhelmed, accepting, and thrilling in that role—a process that I have seen countless women go through in my work, which is now committed to the empowerment of single mothers.

My story is unique. Yours is, too. Women come to the role of unmarried motherhood by way of divorce, breakup, incarceration, death of the other parent, unexpected pregnancy, and, increasingly, choice. Life as a single mother runs the rainbow, too. Maybe you have a beautiful co-parenting relationship with your ex, who lives a few blocks away and whom you consider your best friend, and you regularly go for mani-pedis with his new wife. Or, more statistically likely, your child's father is barely in the picture—or not at all. Perhaps you were the one who chose to leave a more or less decent relationship because you just weren't happy, or maybe your partner stunned you (and your family and friends) by admitting to having another family. Perhaps relations are amicable, or maybe you do weekend switch-off at the police station, owning to a restraining order (or two). Your journey may involve abuse, addiction, mental illness, or an insane court battle. If you were in a relatively happy relationship with your child's dad, there are also likely great memories of time together, shared hope, and plans for a future. Maybe you swore you never wanted kids, but found yourself pregnant—and really happy about it (or not—and that is OK!). Maybe you always dreamed of that great guy, the four-bedroom house, the dog, two kids, and the two-parent family vacations and holidays. But now you're doing it solo, in a one-bedroom apartment.

We all have one thing in common: Plan A didn't work out.

Single moms tend to have a lot more in common, too: money stresses. Gut-wrenching loneliness. Overwhelm. Social isolation. Feeling of shame for not giving our kids a "perfect" family. Family pressure to remarry yesterday. No (readily available) sexual outlet. Fear of messing up our kids. Fear of never finding romantic love again.

In this book, I share my own journey, as well as that of other women who have embraced their single motherhood on their own terms. This is a book of lessons on contending with the fact that sometimes in life your plan A doesn't work out. But plan B (or maybe plan C, D, Q, Z) can be really, surprisingly, stunningly amazing.

My plan A was looking pretty decent. So much so that in the spring of 2009 a thought flitted through my mind: *Everything is so good. What could go wrong?*

After all, my life seemed exactly as—no, *better than*—I had dreamed it would when I was growing up in the small Illinois town of Sycamore, raised by a smart and capable, but stressed-out, poor single mom of three.

Now, at the age of thirty-two, I was living my dream of being a writer in New York City. My ambitious, creative husband and I were drunk on adoration for our year-old daughter, brimming with plans for our family's future. Friends have since told me that from the outside, it all looked wonderful—and in many very real ways, it was. We had bought and remodeled a lovely, large prewar apartment. We traveled the globe. We threw dinner parties. We saved for retirement and college. We signed up for Mommy and Me music classes and had hung a vintage mid-century mobile above our daughter's crib. I discovered that I had married the type of guy who got up in the night with the baby and changed endless diapers.

Both my husband and I grew up in divorced families, raised by single moms. We both vowed to give our daughter more.

We were doing it!

We were winning!

I was winning!

In so many ways it was wonderful.

But then a call came.

I was at a writer's conference in Manhattan. The general number from the news network where my husband was a photographer was familiar. There were four missed calls. My husband was not in town; he was in Greece, on assignment. "There was an accident," my husband's boss said when I finally got through. "He fell off a cliff. They are trying to get him on an airplane to Athens. You need to get on a plane and go there now."

The words did not fully register. But I understood it was bad.

It was.

My daughter, then fourteen months, and I rushed to JFK airport and begged the gate attendant to open the closed plane doors so we could board the next flight to Athens. The next weeks were a blur of trying to be there for my husband and understand the severity of his brain injury, navigating the public hospital, and caring for my young daughter. My husband had fallen fifteen feet off a cliff while setting up satellite equipment. Because of the remote location, he had gone hours and hours without proper medical care. By all measures it appeared that his case was miraculous. The surgeon took me aside and showed me the X-rays: "See here, this butterfly-shaped mark?" he said, pointing to the central point of my husband's gray matter. "See how far to the left it is in this picture? That shows how inflamed his brain was when he arrived. This is a very severe injury."

On one hand, that severity registered. After being put into a medically induced coma intended to allow his brain to rest and heal, my husband spent days raging into consciousness. He had to be restrained to the bed, which only set him off into further fits of violent anger aimed at freeing himself from the hospital. In the public Greek hospital, I found that the care I assumed a nurse would provide—constant attention, bathing, food—was expected of the family, or a nurse paid privately. For days on end, his sister and I took the exhausting charge of physically handling a violent man desperately clawing his way out of a coma and brain injury.

Despite this, my husband awoke from surgery able to speak, walk, and move without any overt impairment. The contrast between his recovery and the severity of the injury was so great, the surgeon brought around his colleagues to show off the wonder. "In three months he'll be back to work—and in a year he'll be back to normal," said the handsome, gallant Greek doctor.

As my husband fought through the post-trauma blur of brain injury and regained his faculties, I saw a man who looked and smelled like my husband. His voice and most of his mannerisms were indeed those I'd known and loved for years. But the person I had married was not there. Not all the way there. I could not articulate it, but I could feel it in the marrow of my bones.

One day at the hospital, my husband's father arrived from his home on Crete to visit for the day. His dad made a comment, something that would have irritated my husband, something that we would have laughed about later in that deep understanding between two people who have known and loved each other for years.

I looked at my husband, tried to catch his eye to share our inside joke, something that would have come so easily, so comfortably and organically a few days before. I could not. His eyes were fixed on his dad, earnestly laughing along with my father-in-law. I could not connect with him. I panicked on a deep, visceral, female level. When I got back to the apartment where my baby daughter and I were staying, I googled "brain injury + divorce rates." The information I found confirmed what my intuition already told me. That night, as Helena slept next to me, she woke crying. I woke up finding myself in tears, too, having been sobbing in my sleep. "If you're crying and I'm crying, who is going to take care of us?" I wailed out loud.

A brain injury is a unique and horrifying trauma. The changes can be invisible, but they are devastatingly profound. Since no two brains are alike, no two injuries are the same, either. The medical experts offered little advice or support on how to contend with or mitigate the anger, confusion, warped perceptions, paranoia, and impaired judgment that plague someone who otherwise looks, moves, and speaks like a healthy person. There was hardly any advice for loved ones.

But our lives plowed forward. After being flown back to the United States and spending a couple more weeks in the hospital, my husband returned home to our daughter and me. He and I were both so eager for him to come home, start recovering, and find a way back to normal.

That didn't happen.

In the manic, angry, and often confused aftermath of his injury, life was constant chaos. I was living full time with a man who was a fraction of his former self—angry, constantly talking, trying to take control of every conversation and situation. He was always making plans: to run the New York Marathon; to travel to Peru and hike Machu Picchu (which he did a few months later), to become a New York City Police Officer (for which he took the exam). He launched a photography show, spending several thousand dollars without consulting me; booked himself a meditation retreat; rode his Vespa scooter around the city all night long, even though medically he was prohibited from driving.

He was perpetually furious with me, for whatever I did, always circling back to the weeks he spent in the Greek hospital and later in the New York hospital where he'd been transferred, accusing me of holding him hostage there. In reality, he had been in a New York hospital for about ten days, during which he kept trying to escape. I continually consulted the staff about when he should return and what I should do in the event he did something crazy. "Call 911," the social worker said, though she admitted that would do nothing. He was an autonomous adult, who, as her biological father married to me, had legal custody of our daughter, access to all our money, a driver's license, and a passport. It didn't matter that he was grossly unreasonable, or that I was terrified of him.

Brain injuries might be easier to understand if the affected people changed completely, but usually they don't. A brain injury takes a person's current personality and tweaks it, usually for the worse. In my husband's case, his ambition and work ethic were intact, and he was eager to return to his intense and successful career—one that included travel around the world, covering global events and interacting with celebrities and international leaders; not to mention the pride of being the breadwinner for our family.

But there were serious considerations at stake. If he returned to work too soon and was not able to handle it, he risked being fired without recourse. And since his employer had offered to pay his full (high) salary and benefits indefinitely, there was no financial reason for him to rush back.

I urged him to ease in, to start part time.

But my husband, who loathed being sedentary, who had so much of his identity absorbed in his career, wanted to return full force. He was adamant that he was already his old self and should return right away. Any suggestion, stance, expectation, or needs expressed by me were met with stone-cold apathy (at best) or enraged belligerence. There was no legal reason I should have a say over what he did.

This would be a tidy story indeed if I told you that we had been blissfully wed, he was my soul mate, and all was perfect until that horrible accident. That would not be true. Everything you just read is accurate, but also accurate is that ours was a difficult relationship, really since it started. Wonderful, fun, compatible, full of love, commitment, and adventure. Also full of contention, resentment, and loud, bitter fights.

Trauma brings people closer, or it tears them apart.

I tried so hard. I believe he did, too.

Yet after the accident, we fought—loudly, bitterly, crazily. Any troubles in our marriage were amplified a thousandfold, and with new, impaired twists brought on by his brain injury. Every argument turned into accusations. That I was trying to control him, I had kept him captive in the hospital on purpose, I had lied and manipulated him ever since the accident. I kept reminding myself of the maxim: *If you fight with a crazy person, no one can tell the difference*, and I vowed to myself over and over not to argue anymore. I promised myself I'd be the stable, well spouse who managed this health crisis for the sake of our family. I swore I would not take his words personally, that I

would not engage in an intellectual debate with someone who—
temporarily—was not my intellectual equal.

I succeeded sometimes.

Mostly, I failed.

We fought. Every single day, every decision, every interaction was
a battle. And when there were no battles, there were the daily impromptu sessions of blame that encompassed his every discomfort.
*Why didn't I get him out of the hospital sooner? None of this would have
happened if he'd been happier in the marriage and not trying to escape on
work trips. I did not straighten the throw rug in our bedroom, which made
him trip. The baby is crying—I'm a horrible mother.* And then, again
and again: He would kill himself, and it would be my fault.

The whole thing was so unreal, so unprecedented in anything I'd
experienced. Friends thoughtfully connected me with people whose
spouses suffered diseases such as cancer and multiple sclerosis. But
these tragedies did not alter their partners' brains. No one understood. No one I knew had ever been through anything like I was
going through. One day, in a fit of fury, as he lay on the sofa, I ran to
our bedroom, retrieved the manila folders full of the medical paper-
work and scores of appointments I'd diligently been tracking, and
chucked them across the room at him.

Through that whole year, I held tight to the Greek surgeon's
promise: "Within three months he will be back to work, and within
a year he will be back to normal." Because after an afternoon of desperate attempts to connect to my so different, so distant husband, I
found out that I was pregnant. The baby's due date was just shy of the
one-year mark I pathetically told myself would magically return our
lives to normal. Becoming pregnant amid this incredible turmoil
brought a layer of stress to the situation, and for me, a heap of guilt
for getting knocked up at a time when our lives and marriage were
so unstable.

Every day, I tried my best to put on my game face, care for my
daughter, manage the house, do some work, manage my husband's

medical care, and heed prenatal care, and we'd inadvertently have a blowout that would involve my husband's threats of divorce. My outlet was indulging in a big cry at night, after my daughter went to bed, sitting on the toilet lid of the tiny New York City bathroom, leaning over my growing belly to rest my head on the edge of the sink. Eventually, I grew so big that my head could no longer reach the sink, leaving me to wail aloud one evening, *"Oh my fucking God! Can I even get this one comfort?!"*

Within a year of the accident, he returned to work full-time. After nearly a year of relentless arguments, in which he threatened to kill himself or leave, he did the latter.

In the years since then, I have been timid about sharing the chronology of our story, and the detail that he left while I was pregnant. If someone hearing the story does the math quickly, his or her reaction is nearly always: "What an asshole to leave you when you were pregnant." That assessment is not unfair, but it is also not the whole story—and it is not the story I believe or tell. In the ensuing years, during which he has experienced remarkable recovery and perspective, my ex, after much hardship of his own, has apologized, saying what I already knew and understood: "I am so sorry for leaving when I did. Things were just so horrible, and I had to do something—I just couldn't think of what else to do, and so I left." I believe him, and I forgive him. I also have apologized for not being able to care for him in a way he needed.

At the time, however, huge with a baby, as unbearable as contending with the brain injury was, the thought of him leaving was worse. There was the terror of doing everything on my own. There was the disbelief that my husband—the one whose life's motivation was to overcome his own father's absence—was now leaving me pregnant and broke. I was overwhelmed with a sense of failure to care for my husband during his darkest tragedy and to keep our family intact. I worried and felt guilty about who would care for my children's father now, since he was still so unstable and clawing his way through recovery.

Looking back, I see what it would have taken to make him stay. I knew, deep down, that he really longed for me to beg. To tell him I loved him no matter what, that all I wanted was him, and our two-parent family. To plead. I knew him so well, and I know that would have worked.

I didn't say those things. I let him go.

It was pride, yes. But I knew on a cellular level (though not a conscious one) that I didn't want to be in that marriage. I also wanted—*needed*—to get out.

I received my first, telling glimpse of hope for the future on the very day he left. Despite my confidence that his departure would be a tragedy worse than what we'd already suffered, something else happened.

On the first night he moved out, I was alone again with our daughter, my back aching under the weight of pregnancy, and I stood in our—now my—kitchen. I was nearly paralyzed by shock. But through that tragic numbness was another emotion I was not prepared to feel:

Relief.

Calm.

Assessing these feelings, I felt even more shock. It took many years to learn to trust my gut again.

There was no child support, or arrangements for paying for childcare. At the time, I worked less than twelve hours per week as a writer, primarily caring for our daughter. My husband earned a six-figure salary with all the benefits.

I knew that my children and I would be entitled to child support, but I also knew that my ex's high-intensity, high-profile, high-paying job would not last in his impaired state. A low point was sitting on the wood pews of Queens County Family Court, in ugly downtown Jamaica, Queens (driving by the exit on the way to JFK airport still evokes a pit in my stomach), filling out a petition for child support, since I received none and the checking account was barreling toward zero. On one side sat my friend Carmela, who had driven me there because I didn't have a car. On the other was a baby carrier with my son, a few days old, whom I was nursing but struggling to hold or carry because I was recovering from a painful C-section. I planned for the promised long waits by packing peanut butter and honey sandwiches and a large bottle of water. Later, a judge would peer over her glasses at me and condescendingly ask me what I was doing to find full-time work, then hand me a photocopied worksheet to track and prove my job-search efforts. In that waiting room, I looked around me. The women were both familiar and alien. We were all mothers, all of us wanting—needing—to care for our babies, navigating the impersonal and antiquated court system in an effort to do so. All of us were up against men who earned money that they were not spending on their children. All of us scared. All of us broke.

Yet, I did not fit in there. Yes, I could barely make ends meet. Yes, I was terrified for myself and my babies. But this was not my future, I decided. I had blessings and gifts that other women in this world do not. I have an education. I have a Rolodex, contacts, a résumé, and a reputation. I have social skills and professional skills that can be leveraged. I had an obligation to not be in that courthouse seeking services and money—no matter how legally or morally my kids and I were entitled to that support. Because I *could* earn, I felt like I *should* earn. And if I was going to earn, why not earn a lot?

I would not give up on my ex's recovery—I could still see glimmers of my old husband, the one who could be reasonable and incredibly thoughtful, who was indeed committed to his family and was an adoring, playful dad. But I could not wait, either, for a version of that man that I could depend on.

I had to take care of all of us by myself. Now.

The fire in my belly was driven by pure necessity. For about a year we did receive child support, but of course that was not enough to pay the bills. I feared that if I didn't figure out how to make money, quick, we could be homeless, like so many educated women (an Allianz survey found that 49 percent of women fear becoming a "bag lady," including 27 percent of women who earn more than $200,000 per year).

But even more than that, I was determined to be better than my own parents. I absolutely could not repeat the shame, fear (again, of homelessness), or anxiety that I associated with my own childhood.

My mom did the best she could, I told myself, *but I have to do better.*

My mission became to earn as much money as I possibly could, while still spending lots of time with my tiny children. I adored mothering my kids when they were very small. I loved intimately watching the sweet and rapid changes that happen in those first few years of life—those first tiny smiles, and learning what it took to coax them out. Seeing their little motor skills develop—to explore their own mouths, then food, then toys, then reach for me, and my face, in innocent, loving curiosity. The early steps and words, and the daily routines of meals and playgrounds, neighborhood walks and bedtime rituals that were so sweet and new and ancient. I was driven not to lose that.

In order to do so, I needed to earn a lot of money in not a lot of hours and with lots of flexibility. For me, the consummate creative, the work had to be engaging. (I learned the hard way that highly paid but gruelingly tedious flat-rate corporate gigs would drag out into minimum-wage-rate hours, creating a grumpy mother indeed.)

I acquired a laser focus on precision time management and maximum hourly earnings with the goal of creating a low-stress, flexible life.

On the work front, I became a machine of hustle and productivity. I created my own system, based on Yahoo! e-mail folders, of cultivating and staying in touch with potential clients. I scheduled article interviews and client meetings back-to-back, in tight thirty-minute intervals, and became an expert at moving through the meeting with courteous yet assertive prompting. I also learned about marketing and negotiating, becoming a pro at charging top dollar for my services, and then delivering on my fees.

In my own informal way, I practiced manifestation to bring into my life the support, care, and income I needed—including a couple years of very steep New York City divorce attorney bills, the refinancing of a co-op apartment, and buying a car. I set and exceeded monthly income goals—something that was both logical, considering my hard work, and somewhat magical, considering this was in the midst of the recession, as well as the beginning of the end of decent fees for writing. A friend and I developed a daily e-mail gratitude practice, which kept me constantly focused on blessings huge and minute, attracting even more abundance into my life. Through it all, I never, ever told anyone, including myself, that any shortcoming in my life was attributed to my single-mother status. That was simply not part of my vocabulary.

But building a big career balanced with family life requires a lot of other skills and habits. I became a pro at outsourcing—first laundry and housekeeping (which, incidentally, was a huge source of contention in my marriage; my ex was vehemently opposed to paying others to do these tasks and expected me to do the bulk of them), which I committed to as a nonnegotiable budget item. I refused to waste time clipping coupons and bargain shopping for food (even though I cooked nearly all of our meals from scratch). And I opted for the most expensive day care in my neighborhood, not because I am a snob or even believe there is a discernible difference between most day care centers, provided they are clean and safe. No, both my children were enrolled in this Montessori program because the school is two blocks from our apartment. Every decision circled back to ease and efficiency.

I also learned to be emotionally vulnerable in ways that I had been unable to in the past. When girlfriends offered to fly across the country to be with me in the peak of crisis, I accepted. In better times, I would have defensively insisted I was fine. When neighbors in the elevator gave me knowing, loving smiles, or insisted on taking my kids for a few hours so I could rest, I luxuriated in their kindness. In earlier, less wise, less desperate times I would have proudly squared my shoulders and looked away, feigning oblivion. When a new friend, a neighborhood mom and divorce attorney, offered to review my family court petition, I let hang out all the financial and emotional horrors tearing me apart, and did not plaster my story with minimizing and Pollyannaism.

One of the greatest gifts of my journey toward embracing my new role as a single mom was in my relationship with my own single mother. I have always had a contentious relationship with my mom; no matter how much we love each other, or how much I appreciate the way she has always adored my children, there is usually a tension in our dealings. When my husband moved out, I shocked myself by asking her to come stay with me. "I was hoping you would," she said. "I can stay two weeks, or two years."

I scoffed. There was no way my mother and I could be in the same town for more than a few days without the threat of one of our homicides looming large! The idea of spending two years in a two-bedroom apartment was akin to the notion we would both be transformed into Disney princesses who raise a unicorn colony on the moon.

Instead, with mostly lovely memories (and to the shock of those who know us best), my mother did move in—and stayed for nearly a year as I gave birth to Lucas, acclimated to single motherhood, and braved the horrors of a contentious divorce. Today, when my mom is driving me nuts, I remind myself of the wee-hour cry from newborn Lucas, when I shuffled half-asleep to his crib only to find his grandma already there, having risen from her bed on the couch, insisting that I get some much-needed sleep while she lovingly rocked him back to bed.

The week my mother said good-bye and returned to the Midwest, I was so nervous, unsure of my ability to logistically manage two tiny kids on my own. This memory makes me giggle today, since of course moms manage situations like that all day, every day—married or single. Not to mention the fact that dozens of times over those months I had in fact had many outings with both my kids, all by myself.

Nonetheless, my first outing as an officially solo mom, with no backup at home, was initially overwhelming—nearly paralyzing. But I jutted my jaw, packed the diaper bag, stocked it with snacks for my toddler, and set off pushing one kid in the umbrella stroller and carrying the other in a Baby Bjorn on my chest. Off to the pool, fifteen blocks away, where we splashed in the shallow end, I jogged backward in the deep end carrying two little kids, one nursed, the other ate a Dreamsicle, and no one died. On the walk home, I was triumphant as the kids snoozed in their respective vehicles. *I am a mom! A single mom! I can keep all of us alive! And we can have a good time, too!*

My life was never the same.

In the five years since I launched my blog, *WealthySingleMommy*, I have heard from thousands of other moms going through their own uniquely horrifying and triumphant situations. There is Simran, who found herself as a very young widow in India, and despite her family's and culture's urging to move in with either her parents or her in-laws, she accepted a job first in Bangkok, then in New York City, and spent twenty years building an amazing career as a marketing executive, scheduling her weekdays around picking up her son from private school to spend evenings with him, and booking a nanny every weekend, so she'd have two days to come and go and enjoy a rich social and romantic life.

There is Victoria, a teacher in Philadelphia, whose intellectual and kind husband's minor depression erupted in a psychotic breakdown requiring supervised visits after their daughter was born. She tapped into support from close friends and family and has since built an education consulting practice in addition to her beloved teaching position, and spends summers traveling globally with her young daughter.

Then there is Christina Brown, who became pregnant while she was in a decent but not great-paying or satisfying digital marketing

position at age twenty-four. After having the baby and breaking up
with her boyfriend, she was inspired to take a big risk: quit the job
and focus full time on her blog, *LoveBrownSugar*, which empowers
women of color to embrace their natural beauty. She is now earning
more than ever while passionately serving hundreds of thousands of
women in a unique way.

In researching this book, I called friends who remember this time
with me. Morghan, a friend who, shortly after I did, became a single
mother herself, recalls: "You would do all these crazy things with
your kids—take them to the beach, hiking, to the theater, travel
across the country by road trip. It was like you decided that it was just
going to be awesome, and no one could tell you otherwise."

I laughed when she said that, mostly because it is true. I was determined. I wanted my kids to grow up going on vacation to the
beach without a stressed-out mom. Even more so, *I* wanted to go on
vacation to the beach and not be a stressed-out mom! Just because I
didn't have a spouse to help and enjoy those activities with didn't
mean they couldn't happen. Just because my plan A didn't work out
didn't mean plan B couldn't be really, really kickass. In fact, who was
to tell me that my life as a single mother couldn't be completely
wonderful?

I'm not so very special. I've heard so many inspiring stories from
equally determined single moms all over the world—like Leigh, who
decided, after a fantastic vacation there, to take her direct-sales business completely virtual and relocate with her tween son from Cali-
fornia to Costa Rica, where she would begin homeschooling him as
she'd always dreamed, all while running her six-figure business.

Back in my own story, within a year, the child support that had
indeed helped enormously suddenly stopped, as my ex—as I worried
would happen—became unemployed for several years. But by the
time those hefty deposits ceased, my business was thriving—and I
was, too.

A year after my separation, I started to date. After being practically forced on a few blind dates by wise friends, I fell into an intense yearlong relationship with a warm, older man. That relationship provided my first glimpse into how my sexuality intensified and blossomed in motherhood (an experience that is very common for women, most of whom happen to be in marriages when they have their children). This sexual awakening coincided with becoming single again, giving me untold freedom to explore, connect, and express myself. In fact, not a week goes by when I don't hear from a mom who echoes this Facebook private message I received from Marina last week: "Oh my god! The sex at this time of life is so amazing! Why doesn't anyone tell you?!"

In the years after that relationship ended, I have dated many men—for loving relationships, for casual arrangements, and for the occasional hookup. I found myself sexually and romantically free in a way I didn't know I was capable of. I felt newly powerful in my strong mother's body, and with no agenda for finding a husband, sire, or stepfather for my children. Instead, I found sex and relationships curious joys for their own sake—and that made me, I think, more attractive to men than ever before in my life.

Through trial and error and studying so many other women, I have developed rules for dating as a mom, which include being open and natural when it comes to talking about my romantic life with my children—and patently rejecting status quo, sexist notions that mothers should shield their children from all but the most very committed of relationships. Just as I share about my workday, my kids might hear about a date I've gone on. They sometimes meet men I'm involved with as they pick me up for a date or come over for a family dinner, and no major, mental-health-professional-required production ensues. I answer honestly and without shame all their questions about sex, relationships, and sexuality, and they have been home and informed when committed boyfriends of a couple of months have slept over—*in my bed*. (Did you just hear the universe implode? Me either.)

Other single moms around the globe are charting their own

unique romantic courses in ways that work for them and their fami-lies. There is Peyson, who found herself in love with her female best friend after her heterosexual marriage ended; Alaina, who, like me, enjoyed dating and sex thoroughly for several years, and decided she wanted to raise her son alone—until she happened upon a stunning single dad whom she quickly fell in love with and married, and now co-owns a seven-figure company with her husband. Still others find their own happiness, alone or partnered, in any number of configu-rations that suit their unique plan Bs.

Outside of a traditional marriage—especially one that did not particularly suit me—I found that I was thriving in every single ver-tical of my life. My business was blossoming in unprecedented ways. I loved the financial freedom, yes, but the creative work I did was intoxicating, and only fueled by no longer having to navigate the ego of a successful man. No longer constricted by working-mom guilt, and free to outsource as I saw fit, I prioritized self-care, including daily exercise, time with girlfriends, and my romantic life. In terms of dating, I have come to see single motherhood as the greatest gift, and learned to cast off shame for what I now embrace as a high libido, adoration of dating for dating's sake, and the freedom to explore partnerships in a way that is interesting, fulfilling, and meaningful to me.

One of the most surprising chapters of this journey has been my relationship with my ex-husband. For years his involvement with the kids could not always be counted on, and interactions between us were often tense, if not combative (the scene in *Girlfriends' Guide to Divorce* when the separating couple text each other brutal nastiness while smiling pleasantly in front of the kids rings painfully, hilari-ously true). It is now eight years after the horrible brain injury that set this story on its course. While I have been able to rebuild my life on my own terms, my kids' dad has faced challenges that few people can understand fully, including me, and maybe even him. I will say that in the ups and downs over the past few years, he has fought like no one I know could fight (remember—I have fought with him, a lot!), and worked incredibly hard to claw his way out of one of the worst medical conditions I can imagine. There have been highs and lows, steps and leaps forward and backward, and some verbal brawls along the way. But I can tell you that as I had hoped and expected, the best of my ex-husband has emerged. He has reclaimed a career and worked very hard to understand and address his challenges, and together we have worked through many of our differences, and embraced the fact that we are more or less on the same page when it comes to most things, including parenting.

Today I feel as though I do have a partner in parenting, one who is regularly involved with his children, who volunteers as the soccer league referee and at the PTA (the latter of which I owe him a huge debt of gratitude for taking one for the co-parenting team), and who backs me up when a certain kid back-talks or refuses to brush her snarly hair. I gladly concede his superiority when it comes to calming tantrums, cleaning ears, and completing homework. And as the years pass, sweet moments between the two of us are increasingly frequent. We have spent holidays together with our kids, enjoyed impromptu family dinners and sideline chats at sporting and school events. I adore that he can still make me laugh, and the warmth and familiarity that exists between two people who have known and loved each other for more than fifteen years has expanded my understanding of intimacy and how love can grow and change through time. Perhaps ironically, the evolution and endurance of my relationship with my ex-husband has given me an appreciation for long-term relationships that I didn't have when we were actually married.

My children are still young, and of course the verdict is still out on whether my unmarried status and unconventional parenting have caused them irreparable harm. But so far, so good. The kids are thriving academically, which of course is great. But what I'm most proud of is who they are becoming as people. Brilliant, hilarious, and curious, my kids are kind, caring people who stun me with how well they express their thoughts and feelings. I don't care to take credit for these qualities, as one of my many lessons from motherhood is that nature is so much more powerful than I assumed nurture to be. But I would like to think that caring for my own needs first, prioritizing their relationship with their dad, and living by my own rules has given me the energy to offer my children the best version of myself as a mother. I do know that the life I have created is one I am proud of, and one I hope serves as a model for both my son and daughter.

In 2013, four years after the accident, I began blogging. Wealthy-SingleMommy was intended to fill my weekends after a relationship ended very painfully. I initially focused on personal finance and single motherhood, merging my professional expertise as a business journalist with my personal experience as a second-generation, professional single mother. I noticed a gap in the market for content that spoke to professional single moms. At the time, my friends and I were having fascinating conversations about the unique challenges and joys of parenting without a partner in a time of such great opportunity for women. Certainly, I thought, there were countless other educated women around the world who would join the discussion, too—and I was right. In the months and years to come, I would be astounded by the onslaught of public attention to WealthySingle-Mommy as well as the A-list media attention it received from the very start.

While there was a ravenous response to this project in terms of traffic, engagement, and media attention, something else happened. For the first time in my life I started writing very—*scarily*—personally. Topics went far beyond posts about funding 529 college savings plans and refinancing a home after a divorce. I experienced a visceral creative burst, writing about the heartache of my divorce, the primal joys of motherhood, the hilarious hijinks of dating, the ancient necessity of sex. All of it came pouring out, unedited, in near real time on the WordPress posts of WealthySingleMommy and to my growing cadre of followers.

Despite writing millions and millions of words in my journalism career, this was by any measure my best work yet. More than creative satisfaction, this project became much bigger than me. The more personally I wrote, the more readers connected to my experiences and message. On one hand, my experiences were personal, but they were also universal: the very human experiences of women parenting alone in the social, political, and economic context that is unique to this moment in time.

I'm proud to say that my blog has grown and grown, morphing into a movement encompassing millions of women with stories like mine, including (hopefully) yours. There is a podcast, Facebook groups, video courses. The mission of WealthySingleMommy is not to show women how to get by as single moms. Nor is it to show them how to remarry or simply raise children who do not end up incarcerated.

Instead, my blog and this book are focused on changing assumptions about what single moms can achieve. It is about really, truly living life on your own terms. It's about learning how to tell society, your friends, and most important, *yourself* to go to hell when you are bombarded by messages that you cannot live a truly fulfilling and abundant life as an unmarried mother. This book honors how hard it can be to follow all of society's rules about what a family should be, and offers the space and wisdom for women to write our own paths. I offer suggestions for navigating the tough issues of single motherhood, as well as show you how and empower you to build a career, achieve financial wealth, raise children, and pursue your passions and romantic life by your own design, in a way that makes you a proud, strong, and thriving woman.

I share, truly and truthfully, *The Kickass Single Mom*.

PART I

Single Mom 2.0

---☆---

What Is a Kickass Single Mom?

I RECENTLY POLLED MY COMMUNITY of single moms (a Facebook group called Millionaire Single Moms, which I urge you to join. No income requirement; rules include big goals, no bitching or men bashing, and aiming for financial independence. It's my favorite hangout—virtual or otherwise. It is awesome.). I asked the members what their earliest memories were of a "single mom."

There were mentions of a few semi-empowered archetypes, including TV's original single-mom-by-choice, Murphy Brown (Dan Quayle could not keep her down!), Diane Keaton's entrepreneurial, gutsy role in *Baby Boom*, and the professionally competent but otherwise dopey and hopeless-in-love Angela from *Who's the Boss?* A few called out strong, competent real-life women, including their own mothers or neighborhood moms.

But many of these early messages about being a solo mom were—and for most of us, still often are—negative. Here is just a sampling of some of the messages women have received about single momhood, courtesy of members of Millionaire Single Moms:

- I always thought of them in a negative way. I hate to say this, but I thought that they had done something wrong to put themselves in that position. I saw single moms as disorganized, poor, uneducated, overwhelmed, exhausted, and basically needing someone to come in and save them.

- In high school a "popular and classy" girl got pregnant our senior year, so that opened my eyes to young motherhood encompassing all demographics. It was very scandalous in the Bible Belt.

- As a teenager, I only had the negative images of overwhelmed women howling at their children late at night in Walmart, where I worked.

- I grew up with a single mom. She was constantly stressed. She had no self-confidence, and she always told my sister and me that success would never happen to us because we weren't "those people." I thought being a single mother meant you'd struggle forever.

- My mom, with three kids, worked so hard there were nights she'd fall asleep before getting us fed. The oldest child (me) had to mind the others.

- I pictured struggling/poor/frazzled moms with kids, with an underlying theme of women who had made poor choices in men who didn't stick around. My family taught sympathy for single mothers.

- I was a single mom at 17. I was told single moms were whores and financial screw-ups destined for welfare and low-income housing. I was told I'd never amount to anything and neither would my kids.

- One of my neighbors was a single mom. She had a cool big house and her kids ran wild. She smoked. It all seemed very strange and a tad glamorous. In retrospect I think she was getting a boatload of child support.

- Growing up in Ireland, a single mother was either a "loose" young woman who got her just deserts—a life of shame, struggle, and hardship as a social pariah. Or, she was an unfortunate widow whose husband died too young, leaving her to struggle to valiantly raise her brood (and it was always portrayed as a brood) of underprivileged children.

- Couldn't keep a man.
- Poor, frazzled, and the kids are raising themselves because their mom is always working.
- As a child in the 1970s, my thoughts of single moms were either women who weren't good enough wives and their husbands left them, or they were loose women who had no morals and always made terrible choices, for which they suffered.
- And from Katherine: I always secretly wanted to be a single mom because in my eyes they can do everything and still look amazing. I don't know where I got this image from growing up, but I do remember thinking if I ever have kids it will be by sperm donor. But then I found alcohol and drunk sex. TMI?

My own impressions of single motherhood were complicated, and mostly informed by my own mom, who divorced when I was four. In many ways, my mother was very industrious and committed to giving my two younger brothers and me what we needed, and what she wanted to give us. Every day we ate home-cooked breakfast and dinner together as a family. We enjoyed music and sports lessons, had her help with homework projects, and were expected to attend college and succeed. There were sing-alongs on road trips, visits to museums and zoos, and lots of hugs and I-love-yous. I was so proud to watch my mom do whatever was needed around the house: hang shelves, lay carpet, give me a home perm (this was the '80s!)—and also volunteer as room mom at school. When we were all very little she enrolled our family in a sign language course at the local community college. In hindsight, it was really for adults, but she dragged a one-, three-, and five-year-old along each week, and together we practiced signing Neil Diamond's "Sweet Caroline," which we performed for the course final.

But we were always poor. Poverty creates stress and warps kids' perceptions of what is possible for their lives. My mother is a very educated, bright woman, and yet we always struggled financially—a stress that manifested in the tenor of our home. It was always so frustrating to me growing up to see my mother, who had more degrees than most of the moms in our small town, who grew up in an educated white middle-class family, struggle so much. There were always food stamps and free lunches. It was embarrassing, not just because we were poor, but because there didn't seem to be a good reason for it.

Looking back, I see that there were many factors that I didn't appreciate at the time. There was a lot of shame in my extended family about my parents' divorce. There was depression. And it was a different generation. Also, that is my mom's story, informed by her own limiting beliefs about what she was capable of as a single mom. As I came to terms with my own single parenthood, my own family, career, and *life*, I realized that I have the freedom and opportunities to write (literally and figuratively) my own story, including that of an unpartnered parent.

One of the biggest challenges we single moms face is defining ourselves—as parents, romantic partners, professionals, even as friends, daughters, or voting members of society.

I appreciate that it is hard for women to break out of the role of struggling single mom, as there are very few role models in media and popular culture for single moms that are not negative. Think about it. Outside of a welfare queen, a gold digger, an overworked corporate mom, or a depressed, horny divorcée, name one character on TV or in a movie who is a happy, successful single mom with a thriving romantic life and the full support of her family and society.

Yet in my life and work I connect with amazing, successful, beautiful, and dynamic unmarried mothers all the time. These women are killing it in their careers while being involved and present parents who enjoy dating, time out with friends, and contributing to their communities.

There is a gaping chasm between today's single moms and how the world perceives us—and more important, often how *you perceive yourself as a single mom*. After all, when every media message tells you that in your new role as unmarried mom, you are a broke, desperate loser, it can be nearly impossible to envision a different, empowered course.

I know from firsthand experience. When I was going through my own divorce, balancing my terror around not having enough money with my newfound thrill of making a lot of it, my own mother and I got into a full-on argument because I wouldn't apply for food stamps. She could not hear me when I told her that I was on course to earn six figures and not only didn't think I would qualify for public assistance, *I didn't want it*. Those words simply did not compute with the fact that I was a mother without a husband. As crazy as that sounds, it turns out this is not uncommon. Sarah, a very successful construction consultant who was making good money and had been the breadwinner when she divorced, heard from her sister: "You know, you are not above working at McDonald's in your situation." Others report charges to remarry right away, suggestions to decline medical school admittance and instead attend technical college, or to stop wasting energy on a master's program in order to focus on remarriage and parenting.

When the world tells you loser-dom is your destiny, you need to selectively choose your tribe in order to empower yourself with positive reinforcement and shut out the negative messages (from both the world and your own doubts). In the Wild West of the single mother family, we moms often need help to find the right tools to blaze our own paths and find the happiness we deserve. We need a definition of a successful single mother.

As I set out to define a *Kickass Single Mom*, I realized that the definition is not so different from what I would encourage my son to be as a kickass man, or my married mom friends to be as kickass people. But single motherhood, as we stand today, requires certain caveats and rules that other demographics do not.

Here is the framework by which I urge you to create your own definition of a kickass single mother:

The Kickass Single Mom Manifesto

A Kickass Single Mom believes mothers do not have to choose between professional and financial success and being an engaged and present parent. You reject any notion that stay-at-home moms are better moms, or that children require a parent home full-time in order to thrive.

A Kickass Single Mom seeks without guilt or shame work that is exciting, creative, and fulfilling.

A Kickass Single Mom strives for financial independence. Adult women do not choose to be financially dependent.

A Kickass Single Mom never plays victim. You are responsible for your life. You are not allowed to blame your ex (or his family, your family, your boss, the economy, your landlord . . .) when times get tough. You are never, ever, ever entitled.

A Kickass Single Mom sets giant scary goals for herself and her family, regardless of what her family looks like, or what other people think she is capable of. Because risk is the only way to grow and change—financially, professionally, and personally.

A Kickass Single Mom never makes professional decisions "as a single mom." Because statistically, single moms are poor. Don't decide to be poor!

A Kickass Single Mom is hopeful and positive about romance. You do not succumb to messages that there are no good men out there, or all the good guys are taken, or successful men don't want to date women with kids. Remember: You are rewriting the rules of romance, and being a positive role model for your children in all things in life—including dating.

A Kickass Single Mom does not need a man.

A Kickass Single Mom prioritizes her sexuality, and never denies her romantic or sexual needs in the name of being "a good mom."

A Kickass Single Mom forgives. Your ex did really horrible things during the relationship. You likely did, too. You forgive yourself, and you forgive him—and any lawyers, judges, in-laws, friends, and others whom you are angry at. It is impossible to build an incredible life for yourself and your family if you are stuck on anger and revenge for things that happened during a romantic relationship that is now over.

A Kickass Single Mom does everything she can to successfully co-parent with her kids' other parent. You support father's rights and do not presume that you are the superior parent just because you are a mother. You do everything in your power to facilitate a relationship with your child's father. Maybe he checks out of your kid's life for a time. But if and when he is ready to be involved, you welcome it and are never vengeful.

A Kickass Single Mom accepts responsibility for her children's well-being. Period.

A Kickass Single Mom puts her self-care first, per the oxygen-on-the-airplane philosophy: When you are fulfilled professionally, creatively, and in your health, spirituality, sexuality, and relationships, you are a better woman and mother.

A Kickass Single Mom will stumble, fail, and eff stuff up in the worst way. Then you will get back up and go for it again. As a Kickass Single Mom, you recognize that you might not have it all figured out right now, but you are taking steps to be financially independent, romantically fulfilled, and a confident, empowered mother.

A Kickass Single Mom relishes that she is a role model of professional, personal, and maternal success for her children, as well as for other women and moms.

A Kickass Single Mom gives back. Even—especially—when you feel like you don't have any more to give, you remember that you can give to others, and that gives you strength.

A Kickass Single Mom accepts help. You are just one woman, you are vulnerable, and you can't do everything on your own (that would be insane). As a Kickass Single Mom, you prioritize relationships that nurture and support you and your children.

A Kickass Single Mom appreciates every single day that she lives in a time of unprecedented wealth and opportunity for women, and it is her duty to honor both the people who fought for her to have these opportunities, as well as those who come after her.

A Kickass Single Mom knows: *I am capable of so much more than I limit myself to. I open myself up to the amazing and impossible.*

EXERCISE

Write down what you want your life to look like. You might choose to express this in a dream board, or in an audio or video recording of yourself on your phone. Your vision might include lots of time with your kids, a dynamic career you are excited to work on every day, a comfortable home you can afford easily, a loving romantic partner, ability to pay your bills without stress, a sense of being connected with your community and loved ones, international travel, a secure financial future, a warm relationship with your kids' father.

As you create this board or recording, focus on how you feel in these various scenarios. In each of your goals, what are you modeling for your children? What are you modeling for other women and mothers around you?

Your Single Mom Identity

WHETHER YOU'RE NEW to single motherhood or reevaluating your long-standing position as an unmarried mom, even the most casual, innocuous social situations can cause anxiety in your heart and mind, no matter how confident you are.

One friend of mine, a successful pharmacist, was in the process of breaking up with a toxic boyfriend, but found herself holding back from what she knew she needed to do. "I find it really embarrassing to tell people that I have three kids under age six with two different men, neither of whom I'm in a relationship with," she admitted. "I think that is part of the reason I'm having a hard time dating again, and one of the reasons I don't socialize much."

I completely understand her situation, as well as that of Cassandra, an attorney and mom of three teenagers in Birmingham, Alabama, who divorced her college sweetheart after an eighteen-year marriage. "*Single mom* just sounds so, so . . . not who I think I am or want to be!" she confessed.

The title you assign yourself is powerful. When I was a college student, we had a very glamorous professor who had been the chief foreign correspondent for the *Chicago Tribune*. "Get a business card,

with your name and 'Journalist,' on it. Not 'Student Journalist' or
'Aspiring Journalist.' Say what you want to be, and it will be."

"Single mother" of course comes with all kinds of connotations—
and, as it turns out, competitiveness.

Just as Dan Quayle derided Murphy Brown for choosing to have
a baby on her own, politicians and policy makers have consistently
blamed single moms for the ills of society.

In 1994, then-Senate candidate Rick Santorum said: "Most people agree a continuation of the current [welfare] system will be the
ruination of this country. We are seeing the fabric of this country fall
apart, and it's falling apart because of single moms." He later said:
"What we have is moms raising children in single-parent households
simply breeding more criminals." (Statistically inaccurate!)

Senator Marco Rubio, in a 2013 commemoration of the fiftieth
anniversary of the War on Poverty, told his GOP colleagues: "The
truth is, the greatest tool to lift children and families from poverty is
one that decreases the probability of child poverty by 82 percent. But
it isn't a government spending program. It's called marriage."
(Twisted facts.)

When national leaders shame single mothers, it is no wonder you
may squirm when probed about your family status. Later, in the parenting section of this book, I arm you with all kinds of renowned
research that confirms that single motherhood is far from a sentence
to the state pen for children. Ultimately, though, it takes a healthy
dose of not giving a fuck to overcome your own insecurities and face
the judgment of others.

I get it.

When I was a newly single mom with a toddler and a newborn,
I'd cringe when meeting new people, especially other young parents,
none of whom seemed to be anything but blissfully orbiting in their
nuclear family unit. I'd dance around any pressures (perceived or
real) to reveal my marital status, until I'd burst, and a flood of un-
prompted details would pour out: "I'm-separated-yes-your-math-is-

right-my-ex-moved-out-while-I-was-pregnant-but-he-had-a-brain-injury-and-destabalized-so-it-is-an-unusual-situation-a-medical-crisis-he's-actually-a-very-good-person-I'm-not-angry-about-that-we-are-all-fine!"

It was mostly true (except the anger part. And the fine part.), and 100 percent not at all what the other person asked for—or was their business. My verbal barfing was an expression of my own insecurity, the fact that I was barely managing to get everyone (myself included) out of bed in the morning, much less own with any sense of confidence who or what I was.

If you're skittish about declaring your family status, just try it out. Perhaps with a stranger you'll likely never see again, practice your new intro. "These are my three kids. . . . Yeah, she's the only one with light eyes because she has a different dad."

Try it on for size. Tweak the message. Just get used to it, like a bad haircut that will eventually grow out: In the process of accepting it until it grows out, you learn to love it.

As for your moniker, most unmarried mothers stick with "single mom" as their family status. But be warned: This title is far more contentious than you may assume. Which leads us to examine what "single mom" really means. Yes, you are unmarried and romantically available. Fair enough. But "single mom" is a heavily loaded term with lots of social and political connotations. Depending on how you vote, a single mom is responsible for bearing fatherless criminals and living off of the taxpayer's dime; or she is a saintly martyr for her children and a victim of a chauvinistic society that tells men it is OK to abandon their children, and a male-dominated court system that lets them way, way off the hook. The term also doesn't specify if you are widowed or a single mom by choice, straight or gay, with or without a boyfriend or girlfriend.

While calling yourself a single mom may be a bitter pill to swallow, the term carries with it at least a twinge of status in many circles—if not serious street cred. Being a single mom can be inherently hard, and in the United States, we uphold *hard* as a virtue. In most of the country, bragging rights belong to the person who put herself through college, saved up for the down payment on her condo, and never took a cent from her parents after graduating high school. Likewise, single moms often have the lock on the hard-times card when they can legitimately claim that they—usually with grace and success!—run a whole household without the financial or logistical assistance of another parent. In fact, I googled "street cred + synonym" and the number two result was an Urban Dictionary entry that offered up: "born to a single mom home"!

As can only happen in our class-obsessed society, women in this great nation can be heard vying—scratching eyes out, even—for the right to refer to themselves as a single mother. It is an interesting and relevant debate—one that speaks to how unmarried moms move forward with our lives as individuals, but also how we collectively define our place in the world. One of the most trafficked and commented-on blog posts I've written is "Who deserves to call themselves a 'single mom'?" in which the comments spiraled into a vehement debate.

Before I help you figure out what you will call yourself, let's get out of the way all the broads who are *not* single moms:

Ladies, if your husband is away on a hunting trip for a weekend, you are not a single mom for a few days. Or, as Michelle Obama (bless her as she withstood the ensuing public flogging) did a few years ago, if you call yourself a single mom because your husband is really, really busy with his fabulous career, you are out. Even if you make all the money, do all the house and childcare, are totally miserable but don't have the courage yet to leave—not a single mom. And FYI, when you refer to yourself as a single mom but are actually married or in a committed, live-in relationship with your kids' dad, you piss off a whole lot of people—people who have little or no financial help to raise their kids, and no partnership that provides the emotional and logistical support that all families need. Not that you meant anything by it, but if you are married and casually call yourself a single mom, real-life single moms want to kill you.

On forums and in casual conversation, I hear people (usually men who pay lots of child support) grumble about women (usually their exes) who define themselves as a single mom. "She has no right to say that—I pay for her manicures and weekends in Cancún with her twenty-six-year-old personal trainer boyfriend!" is the usual gripe. Moms without involved co-parents or outside financial support often claim that unmarried mothers who do have these resources are disqualified from the "single mom" club. These critics, in essence, believe that unless you are raising your children 100 percent on your own, you do not get to call yourself a single mom.

But what if you fall somewhere in between? What about families in which custody is civilized and shared fifty-fifty? What if you get a fat support check every two weeks, but your kids' dad barely sees them? Or you are saddled with 100 percent of the responsibilities, but you remarry into a supportive relationship? Or you get no financial support, but lots of logistic and parenting cooperation? What if you're doing it all on your own, but have the financial means to hire extensive help with the kids and house?

I say: *Whatever.* If you are not married, are a mom, and do not cohabit with your kids' other parent, you are a single mom.

A Breakdown of
Single Mom Monikers

CALL MYSELF A *SINGLE MOM*. If you want to get technical about it, I mostly float my family financially and am the primary caretaker of my kids. If my ex's situation were different he would gladly participate in a different way, and he very well may in the future, and I'd still be a single mom. It is a fact, no matter how you argue it, that I am a single mom.

However, I mainly use "single mom" because it is easy, and it is discreet. I respect your choice to call yourself whatever you wish. But the more obscure the term, the more questions others will naturally ask. That is fine, but you must be prepared to deal with these intrusions. Perhaps you welcome frequent opportunities to educate people you meet about different types of families, or maybe you are seeking out other divorced people with whom to bond. But I find it easiest to stick to a nonchalant, smiling, "I'm a single mom," when a school mom is trying to commiserate with me about how little her husband does around the house.

The more you practice using your title, and the more practice you have as a single mom, the more you will find a natural confidence, and that communicates far more than the moniker you choose. Unlike in my early days, when my stammering over-sharing let the world know that I was a hot mess and elicited a zillion questions and puzzled, pitying looks, today, when I let others know in as few words as possible (maybe the editor in me) that I am not married and am the mother of those two wild monkeys over there, my actual peace about my life is translated wordlessly. Today, the only kind of reaction I typically get are confessions about a miserable marriage, or expressions of the desire to have a baby without having a partner.

As you navigate this self-definition, consider the connotations evoked by your options (or if you've come up with another title that works for you, please reach out and tell me!):

Solo parent. This is uncommon, thus confusing to others.

Not married. This can be challenged if you are in a committed relationship with your kids' other parent or someone else. Maybe it matters to you whether you once were married, or maybe it doesn't.

Divorced mom. This term may carry a tinge of elitism, suggesting that because your child was born in wedlock, you are superior to mothers whose children were not. Or perhaps it underscores your romantic availability, though of course many divorced women are in relationships.

Choice mom or single mom by choice. This may mean you were inseminated through a sperm bank or asked someone you knew to be a donor, with no commitments attached. Or you may use this title to describe an unplanned pregnancy that you chose to carry to term and beyond, knowing the father would not be involved. These distinctions are muddied and debated, especially if a father has been held financially responsible.

EXERCISE

Practice using your single mom title and telling your story. Take your time, and explore sharing your family status with new acquaintances. "I'm an adoptive single mom," or "Yes, I have kids. No, I'm not married." Try sharing a whole lot of gritty details. Or when someone presses you for the 411, give "I'd rather not elaborate" a whirl. Try it with a smile, and try it with the stink eye. Also, see how it feels to respond to inquiries about why you have kids but no wedding ring with a wry smile, lowered eyelids, and nothing more. Remember, this single mom business is revolutionary. You can do what you want, and I urge you to push the limits of what you think is acceptable. This is your title, your story. Own it in a way that works for you.

☆

Single Mom Support Network

SINGLE MOTHERHOOD is a funny thing. There are 10 million of us in the United States, and unmarried mom status applies to every age, race, geographic area, and religion. There have been single mothers en masse since the dawn of time. (Though historically parents found themselves unmarried by way of death of the other parents. War and plague were to blame. In recent history in the United States, the biggest surge in unwed motherhood, contrary to popular assumption, was not during the divorce boom of the 1970s and 1980s; it was in the period between 1940 and 1958, when premarital sex was common and abandonment of women and children by fathers was prevalent. Does that blow your mind? It does mine.) Despite the fact that there are *millions* of us, and there have *always* been millions of us, one of the most common challenges of single moms, after finances, is loneliness.

Yes, moms crave romantic partners (and fabulous sex), but like every other human, single mothers need community and companionship: friendship and support from your family, however you define your family, and a sense of belonging, ideally where you live. That is nearly always a challenge for women I meet who have become single moms: They either can't relate to the people in their lives, or they are actively ostracized by their communities.

In the research about how single motherhood affects children, one of the metrics is how much social support the mother has. Needless to say, the more logistical help and emotional and social connections moms have, the happier and healthier they are, and their children reap those benefits.

One of the most important tenets of successful single motherhood is accepting support, and that includes social support. Moreover, you must actively cultivate a community. This can be hard, especially if you are an introvert or do not historically have a lot of social or family connections. Nevertheless, I cannot emphasize enough how important it is that you surround yourself with positive, successful people who believe in you, and whom you can rely on for practical matters (watching your kids in a pinch, say) and to serve as a sounding board during both good and challenging times. If your family-and-friends set is already filled with amazing people who are living up to their full potential in their professional and personal lives, who believe in your potential, regardless of what your family looks like, then give a giant shout-out to the universe, and relish your network. However, that does not mean you could not stand to add some new fab members to your tribe. Even good things can be improved.

If you are like most people when they go through a major life transition, you may need to tweak your social circles. You may find that your newfound quest for mind-blowing fulfillment and success in your career means you no longer identify with moms in your neighborhood who stay home full time with their kids or are content in low-paying jobs. Perhaps your family is pressuring you to find a husband, tries to shame you when you say you are happy with casual dating, or simply does not understand your decision to have a child without a partner. Members of particularly religious or conservative communities can be met with active hostility upon divorce or pregnancy outside marriage. Maybe your new vision of a big, exciting life for your kids and yourself means that chatting about a recent trip to Central America at the bus stop is met with alarm, then snubs. Or you may be painfully stunned to find you've been shut out of your social circles now that you are the only member without a spouse.

The loss of family and friend relationships can be just as painful as a romantic breakup, especially if these losses occur during a time when you need support the most. These breakups or drifts are necessary molting to make room for new, positive relationships that will guide you through the next phase of your success. I acknowledge it is no small thing to lose connections that you have previously enjoyed and depended upon. Loss of a loved one sucks, no matter how necessary.

Even if you do not suffer actively toxic people in your life, it is still critical to take a harsh assessment of the people in your midst, and do some serious editing. There is a lot written about brutal weeding out of people in your life. The message is: *If a person does not add to your life and bring you joy when you are together, he or she must go.*

I don't always agree with directives to cut out everyone who does not bring you joy all the time. Not only do all relationships ebb and flow, but completely ceasing to speak to a close friend or relative can result in even more anxiety than simply seeing the other person less and adjusting your own expectations of what you can get from the relationship. For example, if you and your mom were always close while you were with the father of your children, whom she loved, maybe you feel abandoned by her now that she lays on the guilt trip after you broke it off. That doesn't mean you should never speak to your kids' grandma again. It just means telling your mom: "I am having a hard time with my breakup, and talking to you about it only makes it harder. I need to surround myself with people who support me right now, so I don't want to talk to you about it, and this means we will probably see you less than before." That doesn't have to be forever, and let your mom know that.

But if your social and professional network are not meeting you halfway in your new journey, you do need to cut some ties and move forward.

One of my favorite single mom success stories is Leanne Ely, who launched Saving Dinner, one of the first online meal planners, in 2009, as a newly single, homeschooling mom of two. At the time of her divorce, Leanne was the breadwinner in her marriage, though her family "lived hand-to-mouth, and I was tired of thinking that was all I deserved." Leanne's network was the other families in her very religious community, with other homeschooling moms who did not work outside the home. "I had this crazy idea that I should have a retirement account, and a lifestyle that I loved, and I put the pedal to the metal in my business. The other moms in my neighborhood told me to put the brakes on, to focus on my kids and enjoy this precious time while they were young. They all had husbands who supported them, and they had no idea what it took for me to pay the bills. I put my kids in private school, stopped trying to connect with my old friends who were suddenly 'busy' all the time, and built a new network through health conferences I'd attend around the country. That was a *huge* game changer."

By making friends with other successful entrepreneurs, many of them moms, Leanne could see what she wanted to become in the people who now believed in her. Today Saving Dinner is a seven-figure business that prioritizes work-life balance for its employees, many of them parents. Her advice for single moms looking to build a new, kickass life? "Leave the church, run for your life, light your town on fire, and *go!*"

Regardless of how content you are with your current personal and professional network, it is important to tweak and strive to improve on this part of your life. There has been a lot written on this subject in recent years, including academic research that proves the power of your peers. A few examples: Peers have a big influence on whether teens engage in smoking and other wayward behavior. You are far more likely to divorce if your good friend split from her spouse. Finally, whether you will be overweight or fit depends on who your peers are. In other words, you become what you believe, and you believe what you surround yourself with. So, surround yourself with people whom you aspire to be like.

One of the most important things I've done in my life is move to New York City. Growing up in a small Midwestern town, I found NYC intoxicating, with its allure of so much opportunity and interesting, successful people. When I moved here in my midtwenties, the city did not disappoint. I found it easy to network with successful people for friendship, professional connection, and later in my New York experience, dating! The most important thing this city has afforded me is face-to-face access to incredibly successful people. Simply finding myself chatting comfortably with people I admire and aspire to be like tells me that I am capable of their same greatness. One of the moms on my daughter's soccer team is a world-famous painter. I count in my close circle best-selling authors, producers of national television shows, film directors, and founders of multimillion-dollar start-up companies. I'm not interested in painting or producing a TV show, but spending time with other people—many of them moms, including single moms—inspires me to greater things.

One of the most important relationships in my single-mom journey is my friendship with Morghan, a mom in my neighborhood who divorced about the same time, and whose kids are the same ages as mine. Just as I was launching my blog, she was starting her family-law firm. We talked often about parenting and navigating dating, but mostly discussed business and supporting each other's big goals for professional and financial success. It was a constant, organic reminder that my family status was in no way a detriment to my professional potential.

Of course, you don't have to move to New York City, or even another town, to fill your life with support and inspiration that validates your own inclination to greatness. One of my favorite interactions from a reader came last year, some months after I returned from Copenhagen, where I'd spent a month of child-free traveling, meeting new friends, and enjoying a hot affair with a Danish dad. The newly single mom wrote to share that she'd been struggling with whether to accept a professional opportunity to travel to Europe for three weeks. She was thrilled at the prospect, but her family was highly critical of the idea, since it would mean leaving her three-year-old daughter behind for that time. "Your guilt-free travel adventures gave me permission to accept the opportunity, which has resulted in a promotion and raise. Plus I had a great time!" This mom needed outside validation for her ambitions, just like we all do. Since she didn't get support from those closest to her, she found it elsewhere.

Find yours.

This might be a fabulous new circle of single mom girlfriends you connect with in your apartment building, but it may look like something else. Your tribe may consist of friends and mentors from all walks of life. For example, my professional network has zero boundaries when it comes to gender, age, and marital status. Most of my very closest longtime girlfriends are married, and in some cases I am also close friends with their husbands. At my kids' school, or on the playground, I find it easier to connect with immigrant working moms than I do the American-born stay-at-home variety. When it comes to finding like-minded people to discuss dating, gay men and single dad friends have been my go-to sounding boards. One of the biggest supporters of my romantic life is the Trinidadian grandma in my apartment building who always tells me how beautiful I am, and roots for me when I tell her about a recent date when I bump into her on the elevator. I need more of her in my life!

If you need a new network but are not sure of where to turn, consider these options:

- Go online. There are countless forums and Facebook groups where you can find peers for whatever your needs.
- Join my closed Facebook group Millionaire Single Moms. No income requirement, only positive, big-dreaming mind-sets, a

sense of humor, and no man bashing. There are thousands of professional single moms of all ages, backgrounds, and personal stories, and we chat all day and night about everything from career and financial strategy to dating shennanigans to parenting advice.

- Focus on professional goals. If you are passionate about your career, you are likely to connect both professionally and personally with people in that field. These people will encourage your drive to earn and succeed, and not give you a guilt trip for not being a stay-at-home mom, or for investing time and money in work travel. Positive colleagues, clients, and vendors are likely sources of inspiration, commiseration, and support in work. They are also likely to become personal friends who get you.

- If you need support when it comes to dating—whether people to chat openly with about your latest exploits, or to hit happy hours in the tech or financial hub of your town (because, for better or worse, those sectors are dominated by men), find your single tribe. That might be much-younger single colleagues, or gay male friends.

- If you feel ostracized by your religious community, find another. Or take a time-out from organized worship.

- Date. If you feel like you're the only single person in your town, hit up Match.com, Bumble, Tinder, or OkCupid—all single people (well, *mostly* single people). Whatever your dating needs are, dates with people you meet online can offer a sense of support among other singles in your area. I have gained very good platonic friends and several acquaintances from online dates that did not have romantic potential.

- Invite people for dinner. One of my tricks for making friends and creating community is to invite people over for weeknight dinner or Saturday brunch. It seems that what was commonplace in my grandparents' day is becoming an obsolete practice. About once per week my kids and I host dinner guests. These might be close friends or family, or a new acquaintance, a business contact, or someone I hope to be closer friends with. People love this. It is far more relaxed than meeting at a restaurant, people feel touched you invite them into your home and offer to cook for them, and it creates so many great, warm feelings. It's also ripe with lessons for the kids: how to be a good host, greet new adults, and participate in grown-up conversation.

Your house doesn't have to be perfect, and the meal doesn't have to be fancy or even home-cooked. It is perfectly fine to order in, toss burgers on the grill, or ask your guests to bring a dish—and always, always ask they bring the wine (or whatever you don't feel like cooking). Keep it fun and simple. The goal is to be relaxed and welcoming and nuture a relationship with new or old friends.

Another tip: Sometimes friendships can be maintained if you limit what you discuss. No relationship is built to be your everything, all the time. If you're fielding snide comments about your co-parenting relationship from your sister, let her know that you won't be sharing that part of your life with her for a while. If your colleagues are aghast that you went on a date instead of tucking your kid into bed once last month, keep your romantic life to yourself. Prudishness is the problem of the beholder.

One thing to watch out for: Careful with the divorced mom tribe. I often hear from women who magically find other moms who find themselves single around the same time, and they form tight bonds, weathering the heartbreak of divorce and the hijinks of dating. These relationships can be beautiful, but they are also high risk of being toxic. Make sure that all your relationships ultimately connect on a mutual devotion to positivity, honesty, and striving for a light at the end of the tunnel. In other words: There are a lot of perpetually bitter people out there. Don't be one, and don't hang out with them, either.

EXERCISE

Who is your tribe? How do those people make you feel? Who do you need to drop? Where will you find the support you need? Make a list, and be creative! Revisit and revise frequently.

☆

Single Mom Self-Care

WHEN THE (NOW TIRED) discussion of *balance* for moms comes up, it is always about the tension between work and life, a.k.a. kids. To this, I say: *Fuck that.*

You are a whole woman who has far more dimensions of yourself than just work and kids. You have romantic and sexual needs. You have a gorgeous body and your health, which require exercise and care. You are a social being who needs friendship, companionship, and community. You are an intellectual, a creative being, a spiritual vessel, and a generous member of society who thrives when you give back.

It can be tough to prioritize these parts of yourself and get out of the work-kids tunnel vision. After all, there is so much pressure to over-parent your kids *because they already have the short shrift because they come from a broken home*, and you likely, at least at the beginning of your single mom journey, struggle financially.

The more you nurture each and every part of your being, the happier, healthier, more energetic, and *truer to your authentic self* you will be. The more joyful and abundant you are, the more you will have to give to your children and work, which will only energize you more, and your life becomes a self-generating loop of vibrancy.

Single moms are prone to going down the slippery slope of entitlement when it comes to self-care. Self-care has nothing to do with massages or clothes or cosmetics, no matter how much Oprah (I love me some Opes, but we part ways when she urges viewers to buy, buy, buy) tells you to treat yourself, or entices you to indulge in her list of "Favorite Things." While you may find you can very much afford the time and money for these splurges, they are not something that anyone owes you, until you earn them yourself, and have budgeted them into your life in a way that you can afford and enjoy.

Self-care means being in touch with who you are and what you need, and recognizing that prioritizing these human parts of yourself is part of living your very best life.

A note about time management for single moms:

One of single moms' biggest challenges is finding time to do it all. If you have a co-parent, it can be tempting to use those hours and days your kids are with their dad to catch up on housework or professional work. Don't go down that rabbit hole. Use this time to prioritize self-care. Later, you will read from several women who so appreciate the time afforded by co-parenting to exercise, build businesses, catch up on TV and movies, nurture their social and dating lives, or just read a book. Do not squander those hours by doing laundry!

Despite how full (and crazy) your days can be, there are always pockets of time you can dedicate to self-care. Here are some ways to find that much-needed time to care for your whole self:

- Your commute. If you drive or take public transportation to and from work, plan to make the most of that time. Listen to audiobooks. Catch up with your most hilarious friend on the phone. Read the news. Plan ahead and make it count. If you are self-employed, take thirty minutes before your kids are due home from school or their dad's to recharge with a cup of tea and the Sunday paper, a jog around the neighborhood, or meditation on the deck.

- You can find thirty minutes to exercise every day. Worst-case scenario, download a seven-minute workout app and do it four times in a tank top and panties in the family room after your kids go to bed. Whatever it is, get some cardio and tone up. Look and feel your best, and set a great health example for your kids. Plus, statistically, as women live longer and are more likely to be single in their older years, it is important to show your kids you are making your best effort to take care of yourself now, so they will not have to take care of you later.

- Plan your evenings ahead. Those hours after the kids go to bed can be lost in scrolling your Facebook feed. Instead, schedule in your Google Calendar a movie you will watch, books or magazines you will read, or a friend you will catch up with, or invite a neighbor over to share a glass of wine.

- Set a schedule for going out regularly. I suggest at least once every two weeks. This might be a date, an evening with girl-friends, or a professional networking or community event. The goal is to spend time having adult conversations with adults. Single motherhood is prone to social isolation, since you likely do not have another adult living in the house. Be proactive and get out.

- Focus on *investing in yourself*, as opposed to "getting a break from the kids." I understand that babysitters are expensive, and when your kids are not with you, the pressure is on to make the most of the time being productive. You likely feel guilty for wanting to do a whole lot of stuff other than spend more time with your children, even though you feel guilty that you don't spend enough time with them as it is. It is very easy to be *freaking exhausted*! But the whole equation changes when you frame it as: "I am going out tonight to reconnect with my girlfriends, which will give me laughs and energy until next week, when I spend the evening at the pottery class." The other way to frame

Single Mom Self-Care **31**

it is: "I need a break from my kids, who are driving me *nuts*." One is positive; the other, negative.

EXERCISE

Here are five areas of life that you must attend to. Write down three to five activities you will do to fulfill these parts of yourself.

- **Health and fitness.** How can you be active and improve your health?
- **Creativity.** Crafts, writing, home decorating, gardening, cooking (beyond basic feeding of the gremlins), or expressing yourself through music.
- **Social life.** When and where will you regularly spend time with loved ones (whose company you enjoy) or meet new people?
- **Spiritual life.** This might include being active in a house of worship, or attending meditation classes in person or at home, or developing your own spiritual practices.
- **Give back.** Humans are happiest when they give back. This shifts your energy and thoughts away from what you *don't* have, and refocuses your energy toward gratitude. Regardless of where you are in your single mom journey, you have something to give. This might be informally by being a good friend who listens, or by volunteering at local charities or scheduling a medical mission trip with your children.

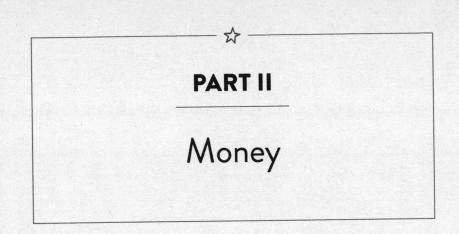

PART II

Money

☆

Single Mom
Money Management

THE NUMBER ONE CHALLENGE single moms face is money. In survey after survey of my single mom followers, finances is the most pressing challenge, the one that creates the most stress and the most conflict with exes, and what holds single moms back from being the parents, romantic partners, and *women* they want to be. If your bank account is low, your credit is a mess, you are miserable at work, and you are stuck in your stressful money situation, you are far, far from alone.

Also, you're not materialistic or greedy for prioritizing money. Money, even more than health, it can be argued, is the most important part of life. Make no mistake: More does not automatically mean more, and extreme affluence is not the goal (though it is a very good goal, and if that is yours, *go for it with abandon*. Then invite me on your private jet, OK?). However, *not having enough*, or not *feeling* like you have enough, affects your emotional and mental health. In turn, this stress affects your ability to thrive as a person, enjoy motherhood, and be an effective parent. Fear of poverty can interfere with wise career choices, and keep you stuck in a low-paying job that you hate. That further sucks your energy and well-being. Buying into pressure to work all the time can warp your priorities, get in the way of an exercise routine, or keep you back from investing in self-care, like the occasional evening out with cherished girlfriends or a trip to invest time with your extended family. If you feel broke, you likely don't feel great about yourself, and that will impact the types of men you attract and date. And if you are poor, you are likely not to have access to quality health care or healthy food, which increases the chances that you will be sick now, and dependent on your children sooner than later.

So, never, ever be ashamed about prioritizing earning, saving, and growing your money. In fact, I urge women to own their love of making, saving, and growing money.

Say it out loud: *I love making money! Having money is fun and important! Building wealth feels AWESOME!*

If you spend about forty-five seconds on Google, you will find very accurate statistics about single moms and money. Fact: Single mothers are poorer than married mothers, and poorer than women without children, and poorer than pretty much all men.

More facts: There are 10 million single mother–headed families with kids at home in the United States. That is a quarter of families, and 40 percent of babies born today. Those figures are about to explode, as a full 57 percent of millennial moms are not married. And they are not all broke and uneducated. Far from it.

Of the 64 percent of millennial moms who have babies outside of marriage, two-thirds are college educated, and a third have four or more years of higher education. That is far from surprising if you consider the strides women overall have made in the past half century. Today, women make up the majority of college undergraduate students, our participation in the labor market is closing in on men's, and 40 percent of families are headed by breadwinner women. In a single generation, the pay gap has narrowed significantly, and more and more women are leading businesses large and small. Thank you feminism! Yay women!

As women overall enjoy more professional and financial success, so, too, do single moms. No one said it would be easy, but it is getting easier every day—from a logistical and financial standpoint—to raise a child without a romantic partner. It is no wonder that the fastest-growing type of single mom is the single mother by choice, women who tend to be older and more professionally established than unmarried moms overall, and who have the financial means to consciously choose a single mom family.

In sharing these facts I do not intend to minimize the very real challenges of raising children without a spouse or committed partner. Rather, I share them to put into perspective exactly what those challenges are for single moms, and to urge you to be very conscious about where you put your energy. It is true that in the United States we lag behind many developing countries when it comes to affordable child- and health care, parental leave, and paid time off. Generational poverty and education inequality are no joke. Spend any time researching the embarrassment that is our social welfare system and you will find yourself in tears.

But one of the tenets of being a Kickass Single Mom is to focus your energy on what you can control. You and I alone, today, cannot change policy and reallocate federal spending to prioritize affordable health care or stagnant wages. The Democrats and various advocacy groups have been on this mission for decades! Universal, affordable, quality childcare will not happen in the foreseeable future in the United States, as much as you and I want to see it, and as much as we must continue to fight for it.

However, there are three critical components to thriving financially as a single mom, all of which *you can control*:

1. Use the time + money + energy = abundance formula in every part of your life. More on this later.
2. Create a lifestyle that you can afford *now* (not when you were married, or where you hope to be in two years. Now.). This includes a savings plan for emergencies and retirement.
3. Focus on earning.

Here I want to note that money ranks in the top three reasons couples fight or divorce in any survey or study. So, if you are reading this book, you are likely in or have left a relationship, and chances are you did not agree about personal finances with your partner. Those arguments took lots of time and energy, and there is a good chance that your relationship held you back from your full career and financial potential. In this single mom phase of life, you are now free to earn, save, spend, and invest however you like. Women often find that this newfound control is one of the most empowering parts of single motherhood, one that is the foundation on which you can build your entire, fabulous life.

Money was one of the biggest sources of conflict in my marriage. He loved to shop and spend: music, concert tickets, clothes, travel, shoes. I hate shopping and love living a frugal life with few possessions. It didn't help that I grew up with a broke parent who loved to shop—which left me feeling vulnerable, scared, and out of control, making finances a real trigger for me. Marital strife ensued. After my divorce, my newfound control over 100 percent of my budget, never worrying about what charges might appear on my bank accounts, and watching my income and savings grow was so unbelievably freeing— and empowering. One day, when packing up some outgrown kids' clothes to give to a girlfriend, I looked under the kitchen sink, where shopping bags had always been stored. Throughout my marriage, crowded next to the plant fertilizer and tile cleaner were always heaps and heaps of folded shopping bags, evidence of shopping sprees and my related anxiety. This day, some months into my single mom journey, there was not one shopping bag: confirmation that spending and money were now firmly within my control. This newfound power to live as frugally as I liked freed up untold sums of energy, which I then used to rebuild the rest of my life.

Running a frugal financial ship is just one part of a much larger equation. The other two keys are time and energy. Often, single as well as married moms consider professional changes based on the hours they must work to pay for childcare. This is an incredibly limiting mind-set, one that will keep you stuck in barely-scraping-by mode.

Recently, Shana, who lives in a small Northwestern city, asked me for advice on whether to take a new position. Her current job, as a manager of a floral shop, required a ninety-minute commute. Her boss was very difficult to work with, which made her dread going to work every day. Meanwhile, a former boss, whom she adored, offered Shana a job very close to home and her kids' school, which would all but eliminate the commute. Even after saved gas and childcare, the new job would pay fifteen thousand dollars less than her current one.

To me, the decision was obvious: Take the new job! With all those extra hours—about thirty per month!—Shana could now invest in any number of activities that bring her joy. She could launch the interior design business she'd always dreamed of, which could bring in much more money on the side and eventually become a full-time, lucrative enterprise. She could now exercise regularly, spend more time volunteering at her church, or develop a hobby—all of which would make her a happier, thriving person and mother. Plus, her energy would no longer be leached each and every day by going to a job that made her miserable.

To make this career decision, Shana factored in the money, which was significant and important, as well as the time and the energy involved. In this case, the energy equation included the negative energy she spent on her old job, and the potential positive energy she would gain from her new job, plus all the positive things she could do with her newfound free time, including starting a new business that could boost her income infinitely.

The SAHM Fantasy That Holds Women Back

BEFORE YOU CAN REALLY BUILD a full, amazing life as a single mother, it is important to understand what I believe is the single biggest factor that holds women of the United States back in career and money:

Working mom guilt.

The general assumption is that in the United States, women earn seventy-nine cents on the male dollar because white men in C-suites arbitrarily decide that women do not deserve equal pay, and the male-dominated halls of government fail to fund family-focused policies.

Instead, many studies find, it is women's decisions about career, marriage, and children that retard our ability to earn and build wealth on par with men.

Every single day I am grateful to the women and men responsible for the enormous strides in passing and implementing policy and programs that do equalize the gender playing field. Nonetheless, the social and internal pressures that women face to create the *Leave It to Beaver* nuclear family with a stay-at-home mother and breadwinning father are real and powerful forces that shape attitudes and major life decisions. To successfully navigate your life as someone clearly outside that "perfect family" paradigm requires an understanding of just how powerfully that paradigm influences our lives and beliefs.

First, here are the facts about working moms in the United States: A full 70 percent of mothers with children under age eighteen work outside the home, and 40 percent of these moms are the family breadwinner. Yet whether mothers work because they want to or—far more likely—because they and their kids need to eat, they usually feel bad about it, or at least about how many hours they spend earning. It's no wonder why. Society teaches us that when mothers work outside the home, children are hurt. A recent Pew Research Center survey found that 60 percent of Americans believe children are better off when a parent is at home, and 37 percent of people in this country believe it's *bad* that mothers of young kids work outside the home.

When you believe you should be doing one thing (in this case, spending all your waking hours with your children), but do another (like earning a living), guilt ensues.

It's no surprise that Pew found that 38 percent of full-time working mothers say they spend too little time with their kids, compared with just 11 percent of stay-at-home moms. A *Working Mother* poll found that 57 percent of respondents feel guilty every single day, and 31 percent feel guilty at least once a week.

Where does all this guilt come from?

American moms feel guilty for working outside the home because collectively, as a society and as individuals, we idolize a fictitious notion of a world in which the norm is a classic nuclear family: The father worked outside the home, earning the money, the mother stayed home all day, caring for a house and nurturing children's frontal lobe development.

The problem with this fantasy world is that it was never, ever the norm.

In 1960, 73 percent of families with children at home consisted of that nuclear, "traditional" family, and in these families a quarter of the mothers worked outside the home (though that figure does not account for women who worked on family farms, or in family businesses). In 2014, headlines blared that at 46 percent, nuclear families were now the minority of households with children. Today, the majority of "nontraditional" families with children consist of mostly single-parent households, as well as gay parents, multigenerational families, and other configurations that have existed since the dawn of time, though historically in smaller numbers.

Our collective point of reference for a "healthy" family often goes to a contrived golden era of the 1950s and 1960s, when television shows and newspaper and magazine advertisements blasted this stereotype into millions of American homes. But that model has never existed in history, now or then. The number of mothers who work (for our purposes here I define *work* as paid labor) is difficult to accurately track. Some recent headlines declared that based on US Census figures, the number of working mothers has ballooned by 800 percent since 1860, bolstering arguments from traditionalists who equate the decline of stay-at-home moms with the surge of social ills. In reality, in 1860, and for most of the years since then, women were unpaid laborers on the family farms that supported the majority of Americans, or unpaid workers in family businesses. The increase in the number of mothers in the workforce coincides with the Industrial Revolution, when it was easier to determine who worked for pay, and more people earned a living by being employed by others. In other words, women's labor was not compensated or recorded until recently, so those headlines are not accurate, and only perpetuate the *Leave It to Beaver* fantasy.

Until those postwar years, women had always been financially critical to their family's survival, typically working on the family farm or alongside the men in the family business. Homemaking was labor, requiring hard physical work: growing, harvesting, preserving, and storing food, cooking entirely from scratch, spinning, weaving, sewing, chopping wood, and other time-intensive and physically grueling tasks. Yes, childcare was women's work, but with scant and recent exceptions, children have been raised in communities where grandmothers, aunts, and other older women cared for young children while their mothers' valuable labor was maximized. This was the standard until just a couple of generations ago, before women made personal choices to stay home full-time and devote themselves to infant sign language and baby playdates while a Roomba whirled around their tiled floors, Crate & Barrel china was quietly scrubbed by a Bosch dishwasher, heaps of barely worn clothes whirled under the easy care setting in the washer, and honey-garlic pulled pork simmered, hands-free, in the Crock-Pot.

In other words: Humanity has thrived despite the fact that women's prime earning years coincide with our childbearing years. It is no wonder that survey after survey has found that mothers want to work, and those who do work report less depression and anger and are overall happier than moms who do not work for pay. This was true in the 1960s, too. Just read the culture-shifting 1963 blockbuster *The Feminine Mystique*, in which Betty Friedan details how millions of educated housewives were prone to depression, two p.m. cocktails, barbiturate abuse, and not spending so much time with their kids (moms in 1965 spent an average of ten hours per week with their kids, less than the eleven hours working moms spend today—and far less than the eighteen hours stay-at-home moms today devote to childcare, according to Pew). These housewives' discontent with the "problem that has no name" was so widespread that women launched a full-frontal bra-burning feminist revolution a decade later, in the 1970s. People happy with their stations in life, after all, do not revolt.

Stephanie Coontz, a well-known academic who studies family and gender dynamics (and on whom I have a total professional girl-crush on), shared in *Time* magazine that it wasn't until the 1920s that just over half of US children were raised in a family with two married parents and a stay-at-home mom, and for the first time in history not working in a factory or field. Post–World War II, the economy paired with government veteran benefits meant that the average thirty-year-old man could buy a house on less than 20 percent of his own salary—a fleeting equation. Writes Coontz:

> That era is gone—for good. And yet the U.S. formulated its work policies, school hours and social-support programs on the assumption that this kind of family would last forever, that there would always be someone at home to take care of the children and manage the household.

The Feminine Mystique documented the many serious pitfalls this stay-at-home mom idealization had for women—a message that struck me as remarkably fresh today. What did we learn from *The Feminine Mystique*? Nothing, as far as I can see! In a *New York Times* op-ed, Coontz writes:

> For their part, stay-at-home mothers complained of constant exhaustion. According to the most reliable study of all data available in the 1960s, full-time homemakers spent 55 hours a week on domestic chores, much more than they do today. Women with young children averaged even longer workweeks than that, and almost every woman I've interviewed who raised children in that era recalled that she rarely got any help from her husband, even on weekends.
>
> Not surprisingly, these social norms led to widespread feelings of inadequacy and depression among stay-at-home mothers. . . . Study after study found that homemakers had lower self-esteem than women who took paid employment, even when it came to assessing their skills as parents. They experienced higher levels of stress and greater vulnerability to depression than women with paying jobs.

Thankfully, the stay-at-home mom is being challenged in significant ways. One of the most exciting antidotes to working-mom guilt has been the recent slew of scientific research that finds that children with mothers who work outside the home thrive.

A Harvard Business School study of fifty thousand adults found that in twenty-four countries, daughters of working mothers finished more years of education, earned higher salaries, and were more likely to be employed and in supervisory roles than their peers raised by moms who never worked. In the United States, daughters of working mothers earned 23 percent more than daughters of stay-at-home mothers, and sons spent seven and a half more hours a week on childcare and 25 more minutes on housework. "In other words, when mothers work outside the home, the pay gap narrows, and the labor gap inside the home narrows," the study's lead author, Harvard Business School professor Kathleen McGinn, told me. In further good news for working-mom guilt: Sons of mothers who had paying jobs earned just as much as their peers who had stay-at-home moms, and both groups of adult children were not more or less happy than their peers.

It makes sense that women who were raised by earning moms have both a positive attitude and professional acumen afforded by their maternal role model—not to mention that sons are also positively influenced to respect working women, and to do more of their share at home.

But what about all those poor babies neglected by their ambitious mothers? And what about all those working single moms whose babies are abandoned to childcare?

First, a history lesson: Today, moms spend an average of 14 hours per week with our children—40 percent *more* than mothers did in 1965, according to Pew. For three- to eleven-year-olds, mothers spend an average of 11 to 30 hours each week either fully engaged in activities with them or nearby and accessible when needed. In 1975, moms spent just 7 hours per week with their kids. And today, working mothers spend the same number of hours stay-at-home moms in the 1970s spent with their kids.

Meanwhile, thanks to technology (dishwashers, Swiffers, easy-to-clean kitchen floors and countertops, snow blowers, leaf blowers, and George Foreman grills that will give you a sizzled steak in four easy-clean minutes flat—need I go on?) and perhaps more lax expectations of sparkling clean homes, we now spend on average far fewer hours on housework than our grandmothers and mothers did—and seemingly have shifted those efforts to intense parenting.

To what end? Not a whole lot, according to the most liberating of all research when it comes to working-mom guilt: University of Maryland's awesome meta-study "How Does the Amount of Time Mothers Spend with Children Matter?"

The answer to that academic question? It doesn't! That's right, with few exceptions, it matters zero how many hours you spend with your kids. For children ages three to eleven, it makes no difference at all the number of hours a mother spends with her children when it comes to their academic or psychological success. In fact, the pressure to spend hours of quality time with children creates so much stress in moms that it may actually make us worse parents than if we just focused our time on making more money, as a mother's education and financial achievements have a greater impact on her children than sheer hours spent together, the researchers found. Meanwhile, an increasing number of studies show the importance of unstructured playtime, and of bonding with caring adults—like grandparents and babysitters—in addition to the primary caregivers.

If the University of Maryland researchers found that stressed-out moms are a negative influence on their kids, is work the antidote? What about those very first months and years? Shouldn't mothers be full-frontal then? Isn't it traumatizing for the *moms* to be torn away from their babies? Science says, not so much.

A recent study looked at families in the United States, United Kingdom, and Australia, and found that when the children entered school, kids of mothers who went back to work before the child was two years old showed cognitive and behavioral skills similar to those of children whose mothers stayed home full time during the first two years after birth. For poor families, children actually fared better when their mothers returned to work before babies turned nine months.

Further, a multiyear study by University of Akron sociologist Adrianne Frech and coauthor Sarah Damaske found that women who worked full time following the birth of their first child had better mental and physical health at age forty than women who did not work. With the exception of high-stress, low-wage jobs that come with inflexible time demands, moms who work long hours during the first year following childbirth—even low-earning moms—experience less depression than those who cut back to fewer hours, which ties right back into the previously mentioned findings that women's life-time earnings are compromised when they step off their career paths or downshift to part-time work, not to mention the giant survey that found that working moms are simply happier than their stay-at-home peers.

This history lesson, and addressing the fallacy that is working-mom guilt, is critical if you are to build a huge, full life as a single mom. If married mothers who earn a living contend with bad feelings for developing professionally and caring financially for themselves and their families, that pressure is a bazillion times worse for single moms, who already face social ostracization for not having a husband.

I often hear from women who are facing professional or financial decisions, who ask: "Which is the better road to take when I reach a fork?"

My answer: *Never make a money decision as a single mom!* Hidden in these queries are questions about how to spend the maximum amount of time with your kids, be at home, and replicate a wifely, stay-at-home persona while eking out a living.

That is not an option. The only reason to consider your family status in single mother career planning is to expect the absolute most from yourself. Without a romantic partner to hold you back from your maximum success and earning, or to buffer financial and career risk, you have no excuse not to put the pedal to the metal and go for the career you've always wanted.

After all, I have never read advice from a respected financial expert who supported the notion of parents staying home full time to care for children. Affordability aside, depending solely on one income and one career is simply too high a risk to take. You and I know that couples have a 50 percent chance of divorce. Most adults will face unemployment during their lifetimes, and the chances of disability, illness, or death are also significant. I have heard from several recruiters and career experts who say that stepping off the career ladder for more than two years more or less guarantees starting over again, thanks to the rapid-fire changes in every industry that technology has facilitated.

My heart breaks for women who were fed the message that stay-at-home moms are better moms and made big, life-changing decisions as a result. Jo told me, in desperation: "I haven't had a job outside the home for twelve years. I really, truly believed that staying home with my three kids was the best thing I could do for them as a mom. I am an educator, and assumed in a worst-case scenario I could always find a teaching job. My husband up and left last year, and education has changed so much that I can't even find a part-time job, and I'm desperate. Leaving my career was the worst decision I ever made, even if it was made with the best of intentions."

If there is one thing that I want to leave you with from this chapter, it is to abandon all guilt about working and earning a living. Work and money are not luxuries, and your children benefit in countless ways by having a proud, successful, financially comfortable mother. Go earn, and never look back.

☆

Identify Your Money Mind-Set

MOST SINGLE MOMS are faced with a million negative messages about single moms' financial realities. But when we address these fears head-on—as we'll do in this chapter—it's easy to see why these messages are outdated, irrelevant, even complete bullshit. You're not going to become a bag lady anytime soon, I promise! It is possible, however, to become financially independent—faster than you might think.

Money mind-sets are simply your beliefs about what is true and possible with money. These can be negative or positive, but whatever you believe will manifest. You have a choice about what you believe, and therefore what will manifest in your life.

We all come to adulthood with our unique sets of experiences and attitudes about money and what is possible for us. Growing up, I bought into my mother's belief that life is inherently really, really hard, and just to get by you have to be a special snowflake. Starting out as a young newspaper reporter, I would work crazy long hours, believing that the only way to succeed was to clock long days and hope to scrape by. My belief became my reality as I drove my twenty-year-old rusted-out Honda Civic station wagon around the Georgia country roads, reporting articles and racking up credit card debt just to pay bills. I no longer believe that survival requires snowflakiness. Yes, work ethic is important, but now my recipe for abundance includes being very smart with my time and energy, focusing on relationships, and nurturing my talents and passions that give me the greatest joy and serve the world with the greatest impact. But to achieve that sense of abundance and ease, I had to first identify the money mind-set that held me back, and consciously choose to adopt a new one.

When it comes to the label "single mom," it can be very easy to slip into assumptions about what your financial situation will be. It is completely human to assume your life will conform to stereotypes or other ideas that informed your concept of what your life would be like in this stage.

The most common single mom archetypes, all related to money, are:

Welfare mom: This mom is down and out, on public assistance, or is supported by a family member, and has no professional skills and no hope of changing her situation.

Gold digger: This woman can't make it without a man, is manipulative, and has all kinds of tricks for finding and keeping a guy with money.

Works hard for her money mom: Refusing anyone's help, this mom works two or three jobs to make ends meet. She prides herself in sacrificing for her children. A martyr.

Princess mom: This damsel in distress doesn't need to be proactive about taking care of herself now, because a knight in shining armor will come rescue her soon. Plus, real men are intimidated by successful women, right?

Man mom: She has a professional job that consumes eighty hours of her week. This single momma replicates a 1950s model of fatherhood: sacrificing family time for financial security.

Hippie mom: This crunchy momma rejects all things establishment, including material comforts. Deep down she just doesn't know how to make the money she needs to have a secure financial life—or feel she deserves one.

Of course, your limiting beliefs are uniquely your own. Maybe you are a combination of these archetypes, and your beliefs are informed by your own childhood messages about money and success, and by people you've known. Maybe you've made financial mistakes in the past, and are resigned to the idea that you're just not good with money, so that is how it will always be. Perhaps you've accepted that you must work very long, grueling hours, survive a nightmare commute in order to replace the income of a second parent, maintain an expensive lifestyle that you and your husband designed, or miss out on important moments in your kids' lives.

These are all just ideas—stories that you tell yourself, and have assumed to be true. So, they become true.

But you can change your truth by changing your story.

EXERCISE

Take some time right now to dig into your own limiting money beliefs. Ask yourself:

- What are you, as a single mom, capable of when it comes to your career and money? What is the first thing that comes to mind?
- Where did you get that idea? Was it something you were taught growing up? A message from the media or your family? What money messages did you receive from your parents when it came to finances and career?

Write these answers down. Own them. Your assumptions about what you are capable of are not good or bad. This is just information. You are understanding where you are on your single mom journey, and where you want to go (because really, you can go anywhere you want. Anywhere!).

Later in this book, I will share with you my tricks for career management, since unbridling yourself from your single parenthood when it comes to your earning power is one of the most critical things you will do in your life. But first, there are some personal finance basics you must prioritize, right now, today. I mean it—unless you totally have your financial act together, read this and make some changes today.

☆

The Kickass Single
Mom Money Rules

ARGUABLY THE MOST IMPORTANT SKILL I possess as a single
mom is my productivity. I was chatting with some moms at the
playground. One stay-at-home mother, who quit a big fashion job
when, in her words, her husband said it "didn't make sense for me
to work," was sharing about how her typical day included spending
forty-five minutes handwashing the dishes and an hour or two doing
laundry; warming up three frozen meals; and spending time over-
seeing her kids' homework after the bus dropped them off in the
afternoon—then collapsing in exhaustion the minute they went to
sleep.

I thought about what I would do that day: wake up to make my
kids a hot breakfast, work out at the gym, record three podcasts,
write a blog post, take two client meetings, and have lunch with a
girlfriend. Oh, and make those same meals (brag: from scratch), do
the bedtime snuggles, and read a chapter of *James and the Giant Peach*
before tucking my kids in. Then I'd get ready for a date, which looked
like it would include hot sex in his car while the sitter read on my
couch.

That, I thought, is a day I'd enjoy spending—one that was productive and fulfilling and included making great money doing what

I love, spending time with people I love, and enjoying an evening with a handsome man—all while creating a healthy life I am proud to model for my son and daughter.

This scene didn't happen by magic. It takes a ton of coordinating, self-discipline, and the creation of and investment in efficiencies—all of which are important for any person to succeed, especially unmarried moms who do not have the financial or logistical support of a partner. This kind of productivity is a basic skill that can be taught and learned, which is what this chapter is all about.

In a previous chapter I mentioned my three keys to thriving financially as a single mom:

1. Use the time + money + energy = abundance formula in every part of your life.
2. Create a lifestyle that you can afford *now* (not when you were married, or where you hope to be in two years. Now.), including a savings plan for emergencies and retirement.
3. Focus on earning.

This is a recipe for wealth that affects all areas of life and nearly every decision you will make. All three elements—resources spent, budget, and earning—are intimately intertwined. Before I show you how, first let's look at the last key.

Focus on Earning

When you're going through a life change, whether divorce, death of a loved one, new baby, job change, or relocation, in the likely event that money, time, or human resources are reduced, the natural impulse is to tighten up and hunker down. Frugality is a wonderful, powerful thing—one I urge you to cultivate and maintain throughout your life, even when you have money coming out your ears. Frugality has nothing to do with how much you earn or spend, and everything to do with being conscientious about your resources—money and otherwise—and managing them with a sense of gratitude and abundance to make your life and the world around you better.

Frugality, however, can be a slippery slope to a scarcity mentality. Scarcity mentality is the belief that all your resources—money, jobs, love—are limited and must be hoarded. A sense of scarcity, especially when everything seems to be falling to pieces, is primal, normal—and potentially crippling.

Here's a classic example: Your husband announces he's having an affair, and leaves within a week. He earns more than half the household income, all of which he takes with him when he moves out of the house he shared with you and your two kids and into the apartment of his mistress. You, understandably, *panic*. Your bills are beyond what you can afford on your own. The payment on your house is huge. Your name is on the mortgage, which puts your credit at risk.

You quickly go through the monthly expenses and start slashing like mad. That is exactly what you should do! Cable, gone. Gym membership that you never use, canceled! Tell the kids that this time you will indeed enforce the household rule that the thermostat will not go above sixty-six degrees in the winter, commit to doing your own nails, and cancel the Christmas trip to the Bahamas.

Is this you? I'm loving this story, and it is exactly what you should be doing (though, sixty-eight degrees, maybe?).

However, let's look at the math. Aside from the vacation, those cutbacks add up to a few hundred dollars per month. That is not going to make a significant difference in your ability to afford what was a two-income household, much less a large mortgage that was financed with two salaries.

A common mistake is that when people panic—and moms are especially prone to this—they focus on how much they can *save* each month. Savings and frugal living are passions of mine, and come with all kinds of residual benefits aside from immediate cost savings. But you can save only so much. You can clip only so many coupons. I understand the temptation to focus on savings—budgeting, discount shopping, and cutting back can indeed add up to significant dollars, but remember: What you focus on becomes your reality. If you focus all your energy on fifty-cent coupons for toothpaste, and one-dollar discounts on paper towels, at the end of the month you will be left with discounted oral hygiene products and paper goods.

In fact, I argue you should *not* clip coupons. Clipping coupons requires hours per month with very little return on investment of that time. Instead, the absolute best, proven way to get ahead financially in the short and long term, build wealth, take control of your time, and have the freedom to create a life for yourself and your kids is to focus on *earning*.

Let's say that in addition to slashing the fat from her budget, renegotiating her phone plan, and swapping in a few Crock-Pot dinners lieu of takeout each month, that newly single mom commits to a plan to earn more money. The residual benefits are astronomic.

In the preceding example, if after receiving the "peace out" bomb from her kids' dad, the mom devotes her lunch hour and Saturday afternoons to overhauling her résumé, turbo-charging her network, applying for new positions, and strategizing with her boss about her career goals. Within a few months she could very reasonably increase her income by five figures—income very much needed immediately—and have residual financial and professional benefits for the rest of her life. Plus, by focusing *not* on the Sunday clipper but on big goals and investing in her own worth, she would actually gain control over a chaotic situation.

Many women find that single motherhood is a fantastic motivator for driving them to risk going for their professional goals—and earning a lot of money along the way. Christina Brown, age twenty-eight, launched *LoveBrownSugar*, a lifestyle blog for women of color, as a hobby project while she earned about fifty thousand dollars per year working in public relations in New York City. When she became pregnant, and a single mom, Christina jumped full time into her entrepreneurial endeavor. "I had to kick it into high gear when I found out I was having a baby, and it was a big motivator to earn to take care of her." Motherhood drove Christina to increase her blog's advertising rates, double down on strategy, and button up her processes. Within three years, *LoveBrownSugar* went from zero to a hundred thousand dollars in revenue, while Christina works from home and spends lots of time with her daughter, who often models toddler fashion on her mom's websites.

Rachel was a homeschooling mom of teens in a small town in Minnesota when her husband left. With a thirteen-year career gap, she was earning ten dollars per hour at a part-time customer service job. Her marriage now off the rails, and facing financial catastrophe, Rachel consulted with numerous people about writing her résumé, then quickly applied to as many openings as she could, before landing a forty-thousand-dollar sales job with a local cable station. There, she "networked like crazy," with everyone she met, focusing on the CEOs and other business leaders in her community. "I kept my ears open for what they needed and what was important to them: a phone number, seed money for a nonprofit they were starting, an answer to a problem." She listened to their stories to learn about their success, and took their advice when it was offered.

A year later, Rachel landed a recruiter position with an insurance company, which netted her a $100,000 income, and was on track for $250,000 the following year when I met her. "After such a long time out of the professional world, I knew I needed to relearn many of my skills," she says. "I focused on meeting and learning from people in power, which ultimately was the best networking strategy."

Money, of course, isn't just about surviving, paying the bills, securing a future, and enjoying nice things. Building a great career that you love and modeling that passion and success for your children is incredibly satisfying—especially when you accomplish it in the face of what you believed was impossible.

Jessica, a finance executive in Arkansas, went after a director-level position at her bank after separating from her husband. She got it. "I never would have sought that out during my marriage," she says. "I was afraid of earning more than him because I knew he would be threatened, and our relationship was already so rocky."

Jessica's story resonates with me, and with so many women. My own marriage to a fellow journalist was largely rooted in our shared professional passion and, as the years went on, success. By outward appearances, I did very well in my career, succeeding first as a newspaper and Associated Press reporter and then as a full-time freelance writer. Two years after beginning to work for myself, I'd earned more than a hundred thousand dollars and had bylines in some of the biggest publications in the world. Yet, after my marriage ended a year later, my career skyrocketed far beyond any previous goals I could have set for myself. My income eclipsed what my husband had earned, and I was forced to reevaluate my earlier presumptions about my own potential and the role my marriage played in my not expressing that potential.

As happens during a divorce, my now-ex and I let it all hang out. We said the meanest things, those things that you keep inside (because they really should be kept inside), and because everything has gone to shit and all guards are down, those horrible things come out. What each party has really, truly believed all those years, but has been too timid or decent to say—we said them. I called him fat. He said the sex was boring. He said: "You are such a *loser*! You only earned a hundred thousand dollars *one year*. You're so scared! I can see it! You can't afford to stay in our apartment *that I pay for*."

There, in that mean truth of his feelings about me, were his feelings about himself, which reflected on my feelings about all of it. The truth was this: Despite his feminist politics and progressive beliefs, and outward appearances of celebrating and encouraging my career, the man I chose to marry was a macho guy. I liked that he was macho, that he had a big and glamorous job, held the door and pulled out the chair, and could fix a car. He liked that role, and I liked that role. With his masculine, dominant personality came financial dominance—even though it was never significantly more, he earned more. In that equation he felt powerful and I felt cared for. It wasn't until my life fell apart and my pent-up desire to succeed burst to the surface that I realized I knew very well, though entirely unconsciously, that my marriage would not have survived had I earned a nickel more than my husband.

It hit me like a bomb: *I held myself back so I could have the marriage I thought I wanted.*

Needless to say, I am so grateful that life thrust my breadwinner status upon me, because without this turn of events, I have no idea how or if I would have been able to express my full professional potential. Never mind that my professional success happens to be contingent on writing about my single-mother life, which doesn't work if you have a husband!

This story is far more common than has been reported. There is increasing research about what happens when the woman is the breadwinner in a romantic, heterosexual relationship, but I suspect that many, many women hold themselves back professionally for the sake of keeping their marriages intact—whether that decision is made consciously or not.

In her book *When She Makes More*, my friend, financial journalist Farnoosh Torabi, details studies that find that marriages in which the wife earns more than her husband are 50 percent more likely to end in divorce, and wives are most inclined to drop out of the workforce at the career point when their income is about to eclipse their husbands'. One Cornell University study of both married and un-married couples found that a man is more likely to cheat on his part-ner if she earns more than he does, and men who are completely dependent on their girlfriends or wives are *five times* more likely to cheat than men who earn the same amount as their wives and girl-friends. This dynamic is tough on the women, too. Studies find that breadwinning wives do far more housework than women who earn less than their husbands, and one study of two hundred thousand married couples in Denmark found that when women make more than their husbands, they are more likely to use antianxiety medica-tions and suffer from insomnia.

In other words: Jessica and I have a lot of company in women who know that they cannot pursue infinite success and also stay married to their current partners. Breaking free of those limiting relation-ships and finding their own professional, creative, and financial suc-cess is often one of the most empowering, exciting things that single mothers do in their lives.

It's normal to feel a deep, unashamed gloat in your newfound, bigger-than-his success (I won't deny that I have!). The dynamics of your relationship have very likely required you to mute your bril-liance, and limited what you believed you were capable of. We're only human. But far more critical is my message to you:

If you are struggling financially and professionally, and unsure of how to make ends meet without a romantic partner, you have to let that idea go. That very idea is likely holding you back not only from more money, but from a career that you love, one that fills you with joy and passion and nurtures the most beautiful, creative parts of yourself. It is normal in a time of change or when facing financial difficulties to go the safe route: Go back to teaching because that is what your degree is in, or stay in a stable, if boring, job. But these are the times you should take more risk—measured, smart risk—because the upside of risk is so much more abundant and *fun* than safety. In finance, higher-risk investments generally pay off much more hand-somely over the long term than sticking with safe, conservative in-vestments. Plus, risk leads you to the good stuff in life. As the famously modest, ukulele-playing billionaire investor Warren Buffett said: "There comes a time when you ought to start doing what you want. Take a job that you love. You will jump out of bed in the morn-ing. I think you are out of your mind if you keep taking jobs that you don't like because you think it will look good on your résumé. Isn't that a little like saving up sex for your old age?"

Often, by simply hustling up new work and being open to amaz-ing opportunities, you will find you magically manifest amazing ca-reer opportunities—which often come with a fat paycheck.

Jennifer, a hospital translator in Wyoming, was a married stay-at-home mom for five years, then tried to reenter the workforce. When she was married, her husband refused to help with caring for their son, and she did not assert her need for childcare. So her employer was reluctant to schedule her during her limited availability. Jenni-fer's career floundered.

When her marriage ended, Jennifer booked childcare for her son, and asked her manager for as many hours at the hospital as possible. A raise ensued. Then came a surprising request to do voice-over work in Italian for a cosmetics company at three hundred dollars per hour—a thrilling new revenue stream that inspired her to seek out formal training—in which Jennifer is thriving. "I always wanted to work in voice-overs, but lacked the courage," she told me. "I thought I was too old, that as a mother I didn't have time to try a new career. Boy, was I wrong! My coaches say I am a natural and they are brand-ing my voice for luxury products. I could never have opened myself up in this way if I had still been married and feeling so trapped. It was scary and empowering. I could kick myself for how I used to be, but I prefer to kick ass today and pat myself on the back for regaining control of my career and my life."

EXERCISE

What are three things you can do *today* to increase your income? This might include: Polish your résumé, make plans to meet with an old boss or colleague who can give you insight on job opportunities, or sign up for a class to learn a new, income-boosting skill. Write all three things down, then *do them*!

What are three things you can do *this week* to blow up your career? What are five things you can do *this month*? Write them all down, then *do them*.

Repeat every day until you have more money than you know what to do with. Then, keep going.

Outsourcing = the Secret Formula for Single Mom Success

As you just learned, it makes far more sense to focus on earning than on saving, while also focusing on frugality and minimalism. It's a balancing act, one that you have to constantly evaluate and tweak. All good things can be overdone, after all.

Now, I want you to reconsider all your household chores. Every single one of them. Make a list: cooking, cleaning, laundry, yard work, home repair and maintenance, cleaning the dead squirrel out of the gutter, painting the basement, washing pigeon poo off your car.

How much time do you spend each week on these tasks? How many hours each month, or year?

Do you enjoy these activities? Do they bring joy and energy into your life? Or do you just do them because *that is what people do*? Or do you do those things because *that is what good mothers do*? Or is it that you do them because you never really thought about it, and assume that you can't afford to hire those tasks out, because *you're a single mom for crying out loud*?

One of the three most popular blog posts (out of more than one thousand) on *WealthySingleMommy* is a piece I wrote called "You are stupid if you do your own laundry." Harsh, yes, but I stand by my point: If you are going to thrive, you must outsource. No one has ever built a successful business without outsourcing. In my business, I am thrilled to pay skilled and hardworking people (usually self-employed moms) very good money to help my business grow by doing what they do best: taxes, bookkeeping, website design and programming, video and podcast production, tech consulting. There are not enough hours in the year for me to be competent at maximizing my tax returns, and the thought of doing that makes my brain melt. So I happily pay my very competent and friendly accountant three thousand dollars each year to handle my taxes. I guarantee you, I get that investment back manifold, as I don't spend foolish time trying to understand thousands of pages of tax code (that would be insane), and Harry, weirdly, is passionate about this topic. I use the hours I would otherwise spend trying to do my own taxes in parts of my business I am passionate about: writing, speaking, networking, and sending big, fat invoices to clients. No-brainer.

Spending time, energy, and headspace on activities you hate sucks your energy, fosters resentment, and steals time, energy, and head space from things that give you joy and energy and possibly earn you more money. Laundry is a great example, but it clearly challenges women on a visceral level, as evidenced by the 157 comments on my post on the topic, including these nuggets:

> This is a post for being lazy. I work 50+ hours a week and my husband works 40+ but we still get home after getting the 2 kids from school, he goes and makes dinner, I help with homework, by the time dinner is ready homework is done. We then eat and the kids do the dishes, one is 8 the other is 11. If it is a laundry night which is only 3 nights of 7 then I do the 1 to 3 loads we might have depending on activities and by this time it is only about 8. None of this requires any "outsourcing" of my personal responsibilities. That is what having and building a family is about, not paying someone else to do it for you. If you pay someone $25 every week just to come out once or twice to

get your laundry that is $1,300 more I save a year than you because I take care of my family and myself.

Or:

The attitude expressed by this "blog-writer" reflects more than just snobbery and ignorance, but a dangerous and self-serving attitude. Sadly, this attitude is rewarded in consumer society; it allows individuals to feel entitled to a life of comfort and ease, usually achieved through spending patterns (purchasing either products or someone else's labor). Her position on this subject is the product of decades of marketing and advertising initiatives—so in a way, it's not her fault that she is part of this gross trend, though at the same time, it's always disappointing to witness such a lack of critical thinking.

The arguments for outsourcing—laundry or otherwise—from this "blog writer" (why the quotes?! Do you need to see my state-issued credentials for this illustrious title?) are based on simple math. Let's say you find a way to outsource the washing, drying, and folding of all your dirty clothes. Maybe there is a service in your community at a local laundromat, or someone who does this out of his or her home, or you pay your house cleaner, or find someone via Care.com or TaskRabbit. If you spend thirty dollars per week doing a chore that takes you three hours per week, then doing your own laundry costs you ten dollars per hour. Do not forget about other costs, including water, electricity, detergent, wear and tear, and the purchase of a washing machine and clothes dryer—plus likely a large table to fold it on (no trivial matter if you live in an apartment like I do, or other small home). Those three hours are just for the labor. They don't account for the energy and mind space it takes to think about when and how you will do the laundry, being annoyed with yourself when you forget to move the wet clothes to the dryer, and whether they got moldy, or the irritation you feel when you leave the dry clothes in the dryer and have to fluff them because they're now wrinkly. You also don't have to remember to buy detergent or dryer sheets, or mess around with finding a repair person or warranty in the event one of your machines makes thumping noises or spews soapy water around the house. No, none of that time or energy are spent on the menial task of laundry if you outsource it. You are now free to spend many more hours and countless more kilowatts of energy on other things.

If I could give you 12 hours per month, what would you do with that time? If you want to increase your income, do some simple calculations. How much do you earn per hour? If you work 2,000 hours and earn $50,000 per year, that is $25 per hour. Can you work a few more hours each month to reach some personal finance goals—say, save for a vacation, put more toward retirement investments, or pay down debt? Or what if you invested those hours in earning a second degree, taking on freelance or consulting work, or building a side business that you're passionate about? Suddenly, those 12 hours of laundry that seemed like "just something you're supposed to do," or something you were certain you couldn't afford to outsource, have become something you simply can't afford *not* to outsource.

I received this message from Nessandra:

> I took four giant bags of dirty clothes and linens to my local laundromat on a beautiful spring day, prepared to spend the afternoon washing, drying, sorting and folding. When I walked in, I thought of your message about outsourcing. So I rummaged through all four bags to pick out my panties (too shy to let a stranger handle them), then told the worker that I wanted to pay for wash-and-fold service. I spent the rest of the day at the park having fun with my kids, and it only cost me a little more than doing it myself.

Why are women so hung up on taking care of laundry and the house? Women—usually unconsciously—simply repeat childhood and media models of what it means to be a mother, wife, and woman:

"My mother and grandmother scrubbed the refrigerator every week; that is simply what women do." This notion is evidenced in the research about men and women and housekeeping. Studies show that women spend far more hours on household duties than men do. The presumption in reading these reports is that men are dogs and women do it all, and guys need to step the eff up already!

I read it differently: Just because a woman arbitrarily decides to do all that cooking and cleaning and laundering doesn't mean that housework needs to be done! Further, studies find that the more professionally successful married women are, the *more* household work they do, suggesting that on some level women worry that their feminine duties are not being met because they are bringing home the bacon, and that their relationships with their spouses require they up their domestic game in order to secure their marriages. This is powerful, hindering stuff, even more evidence that the pressure to mimic the dutiful stay-at-home, married-mother model is real and debilitating.

All of us—myself included—battle notions ingrained in us since birth about how to do things—raise children, care for a home, be a romantic partner. But as adults it is up to us to take a step back, examine our own behavior and beliefs critically, assess what is really important to us, and use our time accordingly. For example, if you feel guilty for outsourcing yard work, consider all the things you already outsource: produce production to farmers, food preparation to restaurants and packagers, clothes to factories, and probably laundry to sophisticated washing machines and dryers. Why the existential crisis about taking all this outsourcing one step further?

Effective delegation of tasks you are overqualified for or can outsource is critical to getting out of poverty, moving from middle to upper-middle class, and growing a small business or giant corporation. To start: If you want to get off of welfare you need to gain professional skills through formal education or training, or start a small business—all of which require hiring childcare for those with young children. If you want to grow your career, you need to spend time at networking events or conferences, in continuing education courses, or taking on big projects that will get you noticed at work. Again, you will likely need to hire childcare. You also may need to hire a career coach, résumé editor, or other professionals to help you up your game. Again, no one has ever become wealthy without outsourcing!

If you love laundry, or lawn mowing, or toilet scrubbing—knock yourself out. But I'll bet there are lots of other things you also love doing even more and wish you had more time for. Really examine why you are doing those things. Do they really bring you joy and satisfaction? Then classify them as hobbies. Or do you do them out of guilt for outsourcing ("My family would think I were such a snob if they found out I hired a cleaning person!"), or a sense of failing your family ("My kids deserve home-cooked meals every day. That is what good moms do.")?

I've struggled with my own identity as a mom, as it pertains to household tasks. For example, my own single mom, as her (married) mother before her, a farm wife and teacher, rose each morning and cooked her children a hot breakfast. Some of my fondest memories are of waking up on a cold Illinois morning on a school day, and leaving my dark and chilly bedroom and coming into the warm light of our kitchen, where a hot and tasty breakfast waited. Without considering it, I did the same for my own kids, delighting in the fact that they started their days with bellies full of homemade blueberry pancakes, ham-and-cheese scrambled eggs, apple muffins, or healthy smoothies. I typically relish our morning routine (which I categorize under "hobby" and not "necessity"). I rise before my kids, turn on NPR, and make a pot of French-press coffee while whipping up some variation of one of a half dozen breakfast recipes I've mastered, then wake my sleepy monkeys.

As you get into your outsourcing groove, you will falter. On one especially insane morning, when I was rushing around to get the kids off to school and myself out the door to a conference, where I would spend a few days, I decided that I would make my kids a breakfast of French toast with homemade blueberry compote. As the fruit and sugar simmered on the stove, I ran around the apartment, packing, yelling at my kids, and blow-drying my hair. As I applied a second coat of mascara in the bathroom, I smelled something sweet and burnt wafting from the kitchen. The sticky, boiled-over blueberry mess was evidence of my irrational assumption about what a good mom does, mimicking what I knew, without much thought. Next time I tossed out bowls of Cheerios and a banana and called it a guilt-free, low-stress morning, and considered it a win. Meanwhile, I hire a weekly house cleaner, and have a handyman on call for broken faucets and closet shelves in need of building. These professionals are part of my team, and they free me to use my time to build a business, enjoy my kids, invest time in friendships and dating, or just chill out and watch *OITNB*.

As for the argument that our consumerist culture suggests we all feel entitled to a life of comfort and ease: NO SHIT. Humans have been seeking safety, comfort, and ease since the dawn of time. Now that it is accessible to so many people, including single mothers, who until recently were sentenced to lives of poverty and struggle, it challenges people's ideas about what is fair and just. But you have to decide for yourself: Do you deserve comfort, ease, and a life of your own design? I really hope your answer is a resounding *yes*. What do you want your children to remember about their childhoods? A mom struggling to make ends meet, staying up late cleaning and folding laundry, stressed and tired all the time? Or a mom who made her own rules, kicked ass at work, and came home energized and enthused about sharing her day with her family? No one on their deathbed ever says, "You know, I am so glad I spent all that time scrubbing the house," or "The one thing I'm really proud of is conquering the folding of fitted sheets." A friend's mother—who just turned eighty—recently said to her, "I wish I'd been a more fun mom—I was always so worried about keeping the house clean!"

A Note About Childcare

The very real pressures of working-mom guilt go hand in hand with guilt over paying for childcare. The messages in the world are loud and clear: *You are paying someone else to raise your children. Babies need their mommies. You are missing out.*

You know what? All of that is correct. Historically, throughout the world, extended families and villages helped raise babies, while moms worked. Today, extended families and villages help raise babies, while moms work. You have the luxury of freedom to choose who your family and village are. You choose the childcare center, nanny, or babysitter, and have a lot of control over which friends and family are part of your support network. You have a lot of control over which schools your kids attend and even which teachers they have. Embrace this freedom. Hire, without guilt, as much childcare as you need to create the lifestyle that you want. There is nothing worse than leaving your kids in the care of people you don't feel great about, or who make your children unhappy. But it is wonderful (if bittersweet) to drop your children at preschool, have them leap out of your arms and into their class, then pick them up to hear them chatter about all the fun they had. This is great for children, and it is a fantastic investment for single moms.

The takeaway of this chapter on outsourcing is that when you feel the financial pinch that nearly every single mom faces at some point, be very critical about your urge to do it all yourself in the name of saving money. Instead, take the logical route and pay someone else to do what holds you back. Invest in outsourcing.

Build a Lifestyle You Can Afford—Today

I F SINGLE MOTHERHOOD is new to you, I will tell you the hard truth: In the short term, you are likely to be poorer than when you lived with your spouse or partner. Or if you have been single all along, you know that adding a new baby to the mix is expensive (i.e., water is wet). Basic math: Two adults' income and household labor are nearly always more than one adult running that show on his or her own, and two homes cost more to run than one. Also: Kids are expensive.

It can be easy to focus on these facts and lose sight of other, more powerful facts.

One, that adult who no longer lives in the same house? He was expensive. He needed his own car, clothes, lots of food and wine, health insurance, a plane ticket and amusement park admission on vacation, and his favorite premium cable stations. He also probably required you to own a bigger home than without him. In other words, his income didn't go as far as you might have assumed.

Two, that relationship wasn't working out. Maybe you are glad that the relationship ended, or maybe you are devastated and would prefer to have stayed together. It doesn't matter. It wasn't working, and whether you realized it or not at the time, the arguing, discord, or tension were draining you.

Now you are free to funnel that energy into anything you want, including a great career and untold earning. Plus, while household income may be lower, so is the overhead.

If you were never in a relationship with your kids' father, I don't need to tell you that kids are expensive, and the thought of raising one without a live-in partner and second income can be overwhelming. After all, look at any media message and you are 99 percent likely to be faced with images of a smiling (white) nuclear family. Even if intellectually you know that family construct is a statistical minority, and you have embraced your mission to earn and build wealth like crazy, it is completely normal to feel crippled with worry about money and finding enough time to earn it while also raising a child in a meaningful way.

If finances are indeed a challenge, you first need to reconcile your bank account with your lifestyle. There are no shortcuts here. You must live within your means now, if you want to thrive. That may very well include downsizing—your home, your wardrobe, car—to one that you can afford today.

Social pressure is a very real thing, one that has played an important role in society since forever. Social pressure is not always bad. After all, if fear of embarrassment in front of the people at church or at the town pub keeps men from beating their wives, or abusing their kids, or smoking, who cares what works, right? You are statistically more likely to smoke if your friends smoke. You are also more likely to feel really bad about yourself after perusing gorgeous filtered Instagram and Pinterest images of your friends at Disney World with their toddlers, or showcasing their recently renovated, all-granite-all-the-time kitchen, or freshly gel-manicured toes and fingers each week.

Researchers suggest that social media amps up this equation to degrees never before experienced. Numerous studies find that people simply feel worse about themselves after spending time looking at the perfectly coiffed feeds. A 2014 survey conducted by the Manhattan-based marketing agency Current found that 61 percent of millennial moms felt overwhelmed and annoyed after spending time on social media.

When creating a full life on your own terms, you must live within the very real parameters of that life as it is now. *Living within your means* is defined as comfortably being able to pay your bills each month, having a cash cushion of at least three months' living expenses for emergencies, and having savings for future goals, including retirement.

Living within your own financial parameters does not mean keeping up with the families in your neighborhood. It does not automatically mean you can stay in the house in which you currently reside. It does not include financing your lifestyle now, with plans (and hopes and prayers) that you will earn enough to afford that lifestyle at some future date, and pay off that debt. Living within your financial parameters means you enjoy life, but it precludes any and all overspending in the name of "treating yourself." Debt is not a treat. Straying from your financial goals is not a treat. Sacrificing your financial stability or freedom is hardly a deserved splurge.

Budgets are not very fun or sexy, but they are critical to financial solvency. An astonishingly few Americans have a budget. In the following chapter is my easy, realistic recipe for creating and sticking to a budget. Remember: This is your budget for now. As your income grows, and you pay off debt and create and meet savings goals, you will upgrade this budget.

Quick and Dirty Kickass
Single Mom Budget

IF YOU ARE HAVING A HARD TIME making ends meet—much less planning for the future—the very first thing you must do is get a grip on your monthly spending. As we've discussed, your real focus must be on *earning* more. After all, when it comes to income, the sky is the limit!

But you're not there yet. We will talk about the critical nature of dreaming big and aiming high. But you can't thrive professionally and financially if you spend all your energy worrying about making rent. You need to stabilize first.

This is where a budget comes in.

The very first thing you must do is sign up on Mint.com. This is a totally free online tool and I have been using it for about ten years. I love it (and no, they don't pay me to say that—though don't you think they should?). Plug in all of your financial information and get a clear, honest snapshot of your money: bank and savings accounts, credit cards, mortgage, car loans, student loans. Those numbers don't lie. Tweak the settings so that you can see how much you spend each month in different categories, such as transportation, restaurants, clothes, and entertainment.

Now, get real with yourself. You may estimate you spend a hundred dollars monthly on takeout. But Mint might tell you a different number. That is the real number. This is about getting real.

You can use Mint's category feature, which allows you to group expenses into different categories (utilities, clothing, auto, etc.). Alternatively, go through your credit card and bank statements and tally the damage. Write down:

- Your income
- Debt (student, credit card, medical, back taxes, money you owe friends and family, auto)
- What is the absolute minimum you need each month to get by?
- How much do you *want* to earn to create a lifestyle you want, as well as save for the future?

Now that you see where your money is going, it is time to get brutal and start slashing. Start with these:

- **Car.** Nothing makes me crazier than when a mom who confesses to me that she is struggling financially posts on Facebook a pic of her "new" 2003 BMW she saved up for to "treat" herself. Gah! Unless you really, truly can afford a luxury vehicle, your car should be nothing more than a ride. A reliable, gas-efficient, affordable way to get you and your kids places you need to go. Ideally, you have no car payment, of course, but if you do finance a vehicle, an affordable annual payment plan should be roughly the equivalent of your monthly income. So, if your net monthly income, after taxes and benefits, is four thousand dollars, don't finance a car for more than a $333 monthly payment. And for the love of all things holy, do not buy an old luxury brand car as a "treat" for yourself.
- **Cable TV.** I know, you love it. The kids love it. But this is serious business, and the whole family must get on board to make important changes. And it doesn't have to be forever. You can

watch tons of stuff on your computer (or stream Netflix and Amazon videos to your TV, which is what I do). Also: Read, play games, and do other stuff you keep telling yourself you'll do with the kids but don't get around to.

- **Gym membership.** I really hope you're getting exercise and taking care of your body. But if you haven't been to the gym in more than two months, you must cancel that membership. Get real. Also, there are zillions of ways you can get and stay fit for free, including jogging, yoga, and training and aerobics at home.
- **Subscriptions.** Go through all the subscription and automatic-renewal services on your bill. Upon close inspection I realized I was paying for *two* monthly Netflix subscriptions. At $9.99 per month, that was costing me nearly a hundred dollars per year. Sneaky on their part! Lazy on mine! You may pay for membership to professional organizations that you're no longer interested in, or access to publications or online services you don't use. Cancel, cancel, cancel.
- **Phone.** If you have a landline and a cell phone, cancel the landline. Then call your cell phone carrier and ask them to analyze your usage and suggest a more affordable plan. I did this and saved twenty dollars per month, effective immediately.
- **Utilities.** Get serious about using less electricity and gas:
  - Set the thermostat at a few degrees cooler in winter.
  - Raise the AC a few degrees in the summer.
  - Keep blinds closed in the summer and unplug electronics when they're not in use.
- **Food.** It can be very tempting for a busy working single mom to splurge on restaurant food and prepared meals. Use these as special treats, or when a discount makes them a great deal, and keep your monthly food budget to around 10 percent of your take-home. To save time and money:

- Focus on cooking in bulk. I like to make a giant pot of stew, roast, or pasta sauce—eat a third that night, freeze a third, and eat the rest for lunches and dinner leftovers.
- Avoid purchased lunches, and instead pack sandwiches and leftovers.
- Remember: Generic and bulk products tend to save you big bucks.
- Eating healthy can be the least expensive way to eat. Replace meat with lentils and beans a few days per week. Focus on fresh fruits and vegetables. In many parts of the country, farm shares are very affordable ways to get local, fresh produce, while also supporting area farmers.
- If your kids are age eight or older, they can cook full meals by themselves. This cuts down on pressure on you to cook three full meals each day, which can lead to last-minute, exhaustion-saving, expensive takeout.

- **Insurance.**
  - Call your auto insurer and ask about lowering your rate.
  - Ask about bundling your car, life, and homeowners policies for a discount.
  - If you own an older car, don't carry more than your state minimum, and note if you drive fewer than ten thousand miles per year, which could mean savings.
  - Research other car insurance policies.
  - For health insurance, if your family is generally healthy, downgrade to the least expensive policy. Your co-pays and deductibles may be higher, but you will save overall on this expense. PolicyGenius is where I go to comparison-shop for health insurance.

- **Holidays and birthdays.** Christmas, Passover, birthdays, Valentine's Day . . . these special days can be especially stressful for single moms (they are for me). Co-parenting arrangements tend to implode during these events, and special times can feel extra empty without another parent to share them. The financial stress can make them anxiety ridden for everyone involved. It's no wonder that overspending plagues the holidays—and single moms are particularly vulnerable. To tackle this financial land mine:

- Set a budget in August for the holidays.
- Stick to it.
- Establish on January 1 a budget for each family member's birthday celebration and gift.
- Stick to it.
- Get the whole family on board. Tell the kids: "We are on a family mission to stay on a budget and get wealthy! Everyone has to participate, and that includes really thinking about what we buy and give to one another."
- Focus on activities instead of things. Instead of toys, make part of the Christmas gift a family trip to the water park or a favorite museum (especially if you were planning to go to these places anyway). Studies find that experiences bring more and lasting enjoyment than things.

■ **Stop shopping.** Sure, kids grow out of clothes all the time, and you may find that your thighs have rubbed holes through all your jeans (true story, happened to me). But many women believe that shopping is a legitimate hobby. If you are independently wealthy, maybe. Otherwise: Do. Not. Shop.

Want something new to wear? Dig into your closet and drawers. Swap with a friend. Mix up tops and bottoms that you otherwise never pair. Do not buy new clothes. Just don't. Not until you can afford it.

One trick that I use during really tough times is to always, always give to charity. Times when you feel broke are exactly when you should give. Even a ten- or thirty-dollar monthly donation to your favorite nonprofit is incredibly empowering. Seeing that deduction on your bank or credit card statement each month is a reminder of your blessings, and of the abundance of the universe and your own power. Giving even a modest sum now—with the goal of giving more later—is an exercise in gratitude.

Get Out of Debt for Good

Divorce is one of the top predictors of bankruptcy and home foreclosure. People simply get in over their heads financially during times of major life change. Debt in the United States is a big problem, no matter a family's makeup. According to Federal Reserve data, US households have on average $15,863 in credit card debt and $33,090 in student loans.

Debt is bad for all kinds of reasons, the most obvious of which is interest on that debt is expensive. If you have $15,000 in credit card debt, at 15 percent interest, and make a $300 minimum payment, it will take you 6.5 years to pay off that debt, at a cost of $8,687 in interest!

That is just the beginning. Debt compromises your credit score, which can limit your choices when it comes to where you live, jobs, and access to credit for a car, mortgage, or business loan.

Most of all, being enslaved to banks and creditors is *stressful*. You know having debt is a bad thing and not having debt is a good thing. This affects your relationships, mental health, and career choices. Scraping by to make loan payments prevents many families from ever building wealth. That is a stressful, exhausting way to live. I know— there have been times in my life when I had as much as $10,000 in credit card debt, and I left college with $20,000 in loans (in 1998—$29,300 in today's dollars).

The upside to the personal debt crisis is that there are tried-and-true methods for getting rid of it—and plenty of analog and tech resources to help. Here is my step-by-step guide to getting out of debt, once and for all:

1. Be brutally honest with yourself. Collect statements for every one of your debts: credit cards, medical bills, student loans, car note, mortgage, home equity line, personal loans from your parents or cousin. If you are married or live with your partner, get him or her involved. Lay these out on the kitchen table. In paper. Feel them in your hands. Look them in the eye. I'm talking 100 percent transparency.

2. Get your free AnnualCreditReport.com credit report to double-check the accuracy of your debts, including notes of missed payments and credit limits. Get your credit score—that three-digit number that is your ticket to good financial times. Check your student loan information in the National Student Loan Data System.

3. Create a list of all your debt, including interest rates, monthly minimum payments, and any deadlines. Mint's monthly goals feature is a good place to start, though I recommend Ready forZero, a free app and website that connects to all your debt accounts and helps you create and execute a payoff plan. It even alerts you when you reach goals. Hooray! Other good debt repayment apps include Debt Payoff Assistant and Debt Free.

4. Create a monthly budget, and figure out how much you can afford to pay toward your debt. It is time to get serious, cut out any extra spending, and lower your overhead. Remember: Overspending is how you got in this pickle in the first place.

5. Research lower rates. Depending on your credit score, you may qualify for credit cards with lower rates. Call your current

credit card companies and ask if they will lower your rate based on a good repayment history and solid credit score. Bankrate and Credit.com are also great places to search for cards with competitive terms.

6. Call the holder of any outstanding medical bills and negotiate. Research student loan consolidation through StudentLoans .gov. Also, private banks are starting to offer student debt consolidation and refinancing.

7. Decide: Debt snowball or debt avalanche? These terms are lingo for the two main methods for paying off debt.

   ◆ *Debt snowball:* Pay off credit cards or loans with the lowest balances first. The advantage is that you get the psychological and emotional thrill of paying off accounts quickly.

   ◆ *Debt avalanche:* Pay off accounts with the highest interest rates first. The big perk of this method is that you save more money by depleting high-interest debt sooner.

8. If you're totally overwhelmed with this process, or truly believe that you cannot dig out of debt on your current income, get professional advice. A credit counselor will help you create a debt repayment plan, which may include debt consolidation— in which case the credit counseling agency will consolidate all of your debt into a single payment that is at a lower interest rate than all of your debt combined. Two places to start your search for a reputable credit counselor include the National Foundation for Credit Counseling and the Financial Counseling Association of America.

9. Set up automatic payments. If you are going the DIY repayment route (and not using a counseling agency), set all the payments on autopilot.

10. Use tricks to pay down debt even faster. These include:

    ◆ Put tax refunds toward your debt.

    ◆ Allocate any salary raises toward the principal.

- Sell off unused furniture, clothes, electronics, books, or household items and put all proceeds toward debt.
- Start a side hustle—work as a virtual assistant, babysit, line up freelance gigs in your industry—and commit that income to paying off debt.

11. Celebrate! You did it! You paid off that effing debt! YOU ARE DEBT-FREE!
12. Don't think you're too cute. Now is not the time to go shopping! Now is the time to focus on saving and other financial goals.
13. Stick to that budget!
14. Keep monitoring your credit score. Mint automatically updates your credit score for free and displays it in the app. Or, use AnualCreditReport.com's score monitoring service, which updates monthly.

☆

Superhigh Priority: Your Credit Score

THERE IS A REASON divorce is cited as one of the leading factors in bankruptcy: Your finances are in upheaval, income per household is down, expenses rise with lawyers' fees and financing two homes and furnishings, and no one's mental space is focused on FICO scores. Plus, joint bank accounts, credit cards, and car and mortgage notes mean that each party may assume the other is making payments, while their own credit history crumbles under missed payments.

Identity theft is incredibly common during breakups—both by disgruntled exes, who know your date of birth, social security number, and address and can go on a spending spree, as well as by strangers, who can more easily access your information when you are opening and closing financial accounts. Relocation and new babies are other scenarios that trigger credit problems.

Single moms cannot thrive financially without a solid credit score. When you're going through a divorce or breakup with a significant other with whom you have joint accounts, you're so vulnerable financially. The better credit you have, the more options you have. Many women don't realize that credit affects your whole life.

Bad credit can make it more difficult or impossible to:

- Rent an apartment
- Refinance or buy a home
- Buy or lease a car
- Get a credit card
- Get a job (almost half of employers run credit checks on job candidates)
- Start a business
- Get a man (true: people who pay attention to their own financial health look for the same when dating)

I reached out to my friend Gerri Detweiler, credit expert, for tips on navigating divorce and credit:

How big a problem are credit scores for people facing divorce or a big breakup?
Your credit scores can take a big hit when you divorce, usually for one of three reasons: One, your income may drop, and your expenses may increase since you are no longer splitting them with a spouse. This may mean it's harder to keep up with bills. The second is that most couples have at least one joint account when they split. If the debt isn't paid off right away it will usually end up being the responsibility of one spouse, and if he or she doesn't pay it, both credit reports (and by extension credit scores) will suffer. The third problem is identity theft. It's surprisingly common for an ex to "borrow" the other person's information in order to get new credit, utility services, etc.

Why is divorce so often cited as a reason for bankruptcy?
Again, after divorce, many people find their finances stretched. Some have to pay alimony, others find they're paying for new expenses such as childcare, and most will find their expenses increased because they're no longer splitting bills with their now-ex. Some people are pushed into bankruptcy by their former

spouse. Let's say they owned a house together but they either don't want to sell it (because they want the children to keep living there) or they can't sell it because it's upside down. One of them agrees to pay the mortgage; it might be the spouse who lives there, or it might be the ex who is supporting him or her. But the mortgage doesn't get paid. Maybe that spouse eventually files for bankruptcy, and the other one ends up having to file in order to keep the house and catch up on payments, or to discharge their responsibility for the remaining loan.

Why is it so important to make your credit score a priority if you're splitting with your significant other?
Divorce is usually very stressful, and even if you are glad to be splitting up, there are a lot of details that have to be taken care of. This means that it's easy for bills to slip through the cracks. One late payment can cause an otherwise excellent credit score to drop by 50 or 75 points or more. So it is important to try to make sure that bills are paid on time.

In addition, after divorce you will often need good credit to rent or buy a new place to live, or get utility services without a deposit. You may decide to hunt for a higher-paying job or start a small business, both of which may involve credit checks. And let's face it: If your credit does take a nosedive, it's not going to be fun having the reminder of that time in your life coming back to haunt you several years later when you're filling out applications for credit.

What should everyone—regardless of credit history—do when it comes to their credit when facing divorce?
Get your credit reports so you know exactly what bills appear there and so that you understand your responsibility for them. If you are an authorized user, you're typically responsible for the balance but you may want to get removed from the account if you are

worried about whether your ex will pay it on time. For any joint accounts, they should be closed from future purchases, and balances should be paid off as soon as possible. Keep in mind that you are legally responsible to repay the joint debt until it's paid off. Your divorce decree doesn't change that.

If your ex is abusive or vindictive you may want to place a fraud alert on your credit report, or even freeze your credit so that no one can access your credit report information without a PIN you provide.

If you are facing divorce and have bad credit, what can you do to rebuild it?

The good news is that when it comes to your credit, you can always get a fresh start. While you may not be able to change the past, going forward, if you are meticulous about paying your bills on time you can see significant improvement in your credit scores. Recent information tends to have the greatest impact, so make sure that you have open, active accounts that are paid on time. If you don't already have one, get a credit card in your own name, even if it's a secured card.

Of course, you can't fix your credit if you don't know where you stand, so get your credit scores to monitor your progress.

In the short term, if you have no or poor credit, what are the best ways to get a loan or cash to finance a needed car, a family lawyer, or even daily expenses, which is common for people in the midst of a split?

What types of financing you'll get will depend in large part on how good or bad your current scores are. If you don't have a lot of credit, it may be easier to get a loan than if you have a lot of debt or very poor payment history. Some consumers find they are able to get a personal loan; others may turn to credit cards, even if they have a fairly high interest rate. Watch your mail; if you get an offer for a low-rate balance transfer, you may want to take advantage of it. Another option that doesn't require a credit check is a loan against a retirement account such as a 401(k). It is not ideal by any means, but it's usually better than cashing in a retirement account early and paying taxes and penalties. Finally, you may be able to get a loan from family members or friends. These loans don't appear in your credit reports, so that can be an advantage. But it's best to put details in writing so everyone's clear on how and when this loan will be repaid.

What if you start hearing from debt collectors about debts your ex didn't pay?

If the collector is trying to collect from you, you have the right to ask him or her to put it in writing and I recommend you do so. If you don't believe you owe the debt, or you don't believe it's correct, you have the right to request the collector verify the debt. Put your request in writing.

If the collector calls about a debt your ex owes, you don't have to discuss it with this person if you don't want to. You can explain that you can't help and ask him or her not to call you again. That generally should stop those phone calls. If it doesn't, you can file a complaint with the Consumer Financial Protection Bureau.

Steps to take to manage your credit in the face of divorce or separation:

- Check your credit score. Face your reality and go to Annual CreditReport.com for a free check of your scores. It's free, people. You don't have an excuse.
- Get a credit card in your own name, and use it responsibly. There is no such thing as joint credit. If your mortgage, car note, and credit cards are held in your husband's name, you may have terrible credit—even if your husband runs a hedge fund

and gets Visa Platinum offers in the mail daily. Further, if you
have no income of your own, you may have trouble getting a
credit card.

- If you do have cards in your name, figure out who is an authorized user. Is it your husband? Are you 100 percent sure he will
not use it to run off with the babysitter to Cancún? Even if
you're married to a wonderful person, remember that divorce
brings out the worst in people. Even if Mother Teresa had divorced God, there would have been moments of nastiness and
regrettable spending. Protect yourself—remove yourself from
any cards in his name, and remove him from any cards in your
name. This gives you protection and control over your financial
future.

- Pay your bills on time. Electric, phone, and insurance all count
toward your credit score.

- Get a job. Even if you don't think you need one, you do for lots
of reasons, including that credit cards often require a source of
income from applicants. You need your own credit card to get
around in this world.

- Watch the balance-to-credit ratio, and keep it below 30 percent.
This means if you have a ten-thousand-dollar limit on your
card, don't carry more than a three-thousand-dollar balance.
This ensures a good credit score, and gives you a line of credit if
you need it to establish your new life.

- If you have no credit or terrible credit, get a secured credit card.
These require a minimum security deposit and are the easiest,
quickest way to rebuild credit (if used responsibly).

- Then, decide that your new life will be one of good credit. Set
up automatic payments and text alerts to assure your bills are
paid on time, only charge when you absolutely need to, and set
goals for boosting your score with an eye toward other goals:
buying a home, retirement, family vacations, and peace of mind.

The House

FOR MOST PEOPLE, housing is the biggest monthly expense, and if you own your home, it's your biggest investment. Real estate is also often one of the biggest sources of financial mistakes, especially for people going through a divorce or breakup in which the home is at stake. For a variety of reasons, women tend to make the poorest decisions when it comes to this matter. The most common mistake is holding on to a home you cannot afford, for purely emotional reasons.

I completely understand this impulse, and real estate is part of my own single mom story. I have been very lucky in real estate. My husband and I bought a dump of a co-op right after we got married, remodeled it into a beautiful, modern yet charming home, and saw the property value in our neighborhood skyrocket. Icing on the cake is that the home is indeed a true home, in a lovely building where we are surrounded by a mess of loving friends and supportive neighbors who have looked out for me and my children.

The bonus: I can and have always been able to afford this apartment, including buying my husband out in our divorce settlement. For me, it made sense to keep my home.

This may not be your story, and that is OK. Moving or selling is not a sign of failure. Your life simply changed, and as a sign of grace and financial maturity, you moved to a home that makes sense during this new phase of life.

On the flip side of that coin, desperately holding on to the family home at all costs may be the biggest mistake you make during this time. Attorneys often tell me that the number one mistake of divorcing couples is spouses who want to keep the big marital home and sink every ounce of savings they have into it. Reasons include:

- Inability to let go of the past or their vision for their life.
- Desire to take revenge on the other spouse by arguing the need for more money to pay the mortgage on a large house for the benefit of the children.
- Failure to understand tax strategy. A financial professional can help you understand the tax benefits of home ownership that include the ability to write off property taxes and mortgage interest, and capital gains caps.
- Belief the kids will be traumatized if they're relocated.
- Failure to calculate the time and cash it takes to run a house.
- Sense that selling the family home is a sign of failure or defeat, even if it makes financial sense.

When splitting assets with a spouse or partner, there are three things to consider:

Monthly cash flow. Can you afford this house on your own, each month and year, without going into debt, and while staying on track for retirement and other investments? To calculate your actual monthly housing expenses, tally up:
- Mortgage.
- Property taxes.
- Homeowners insurance.
- Association fees.

- Maintenance. Includes everything from the occasional paint job to cleaning gutters to lawn maintenance.
- Repairs. This might include spending fifty dollars to buy a new bathroom faucet, or five thousand dollars to replace a roof. You need a sizable savings account to anticipate these repairs. Do you have one?
- Utilities. The bigger the house, the more you'll pay to heat and cool it. Older homes typically come with pricier electric, gas, or oil bills.
- Furniture. The bigger the house, the more furnishings you'll need to buy, clean, and repair.

Holistic financial planning. In most states, marital assets are split fifty-fifty in divorce. That means it doesn't matter how much each spouse earned during the marriage—any real estate, retirement accounts, or other investments made during the marriage are tallied and divided by two, and each party gets half. But let's say that during the marriage your ex-husband has assumed $100,000 more in his employer's 401(k) plan than you, and the house you own together has $50,000 in equity. That means you each are entitled to $75,000 in assets. One way to do this is to sell the house and each take $25,000 cash profits, which you could then put down on a home that you can afford on your own, and he would transfer $50,000 into your retirement account, which would grow into a great security for your future.

Often, moms are tempted to take a lesser settlement in a desperate effort to keep the house. I understand why. A house is also a home, and a home is, of course, much more than an investment. A home is where you raise your children, create memories, mark the kids' heights on the hallway wall, and host neighborhood families to play in the backyard sprinklers. Also, listing your home for sale is a very public act, while no one in your life has to know about how much money is transferred from one brokerage account to another. The act of selling a house may feel like twisting the knife when you're already roiling in hurt and humiliation. Now you must relocate your children and forge a new identity in a different neighborhood or town. Not only will you be the new family on the block, but you will be making this adjustment as a single mom—a title you may not yet be comfortable with.

These are all very real, often devastating facts and worries. Do not dismiss how you feel. But when considering what is likely your largest financial asset, keep your feels in check. Listen to your lawyer, accountant, financial adviser, some friends who aren't insane, and your brother who doesn't want to punch your ex in the throat. Your home, and your kids' home, is wherever you live. And you must live where you can afford—and will be able to afford in the future. That might mean a house or apartment that is different from the one you currently own. Otherwise, that charming, memory-stocked bungalow will be a strangling albatross that could very likely ruin your life. Again, divorce is cited as a top precursor for both foreclosure and bankruptcy.

Money and Your Feels. That said, personal finances are rarely black-and-white, simple math. Part of making sound financial decisions is assessing the emotional backstory of your decisions. For example, if you are hell-bent on keeping the house, spend time, perhaps with a therapist, digging into the roots of that. Is it that your property feels like a way to hold on to your plan A, nuclear family? Is the decision rooted in any revenge or malice toward your ex? Perhaps you wanted to buy the home more than he did, and staying in it and using his child support payments somehow validates an old marital rift. Or is staying put feeding into ancient ideas about tradition, and creating a family homestead that will be the foundation for generations of family to come?

All these feelings are completely understandable and human. I've had my own love affair with a house. About a year after my own divorce, my grandfather died. He was ninety-two, and had lived a very full and healthy life, and his passing was clearly expected. Though my grandmother was healthy enough to stay in their home, she decided to sell it and move into a very nice local retirement community. We all supported her decision, as the value of the house afforded my grandmother a very comfortable life. Still, I grieved the loss of this lovely house furnished with good early-American antiques and a large walnut table with half a dozen leaves that would be put into place for the many family gatherings. There were a couple of extra bedrooms, where I spent many nights as a child, as well as into adulthood, including after I became a mother myself—I would bring my small children to visit, and show them where I had grown up, since there was no such homestead from my parents' generation.

The sale of that house felt like a huge loss for me in the midst of settling into my own, newly single life—it left me feeling shaken, further uprooted. But it also helped me come to terms with my own home. I realized that I had unconsciously been thinking about my apartment as a "forever home"—a family base for eternity. In reality, it is a piece of real estate that has a lot of equity in it, and at any point should be considered a financial asset that should be treated as such—and not a sentimental heirloom.

Natalie made a common real estate mistake in her split, holding on to the family house despite any sound financial reason. "It was such a beautiful place, and I had so many great memories with the kids there, I didn't want to let it go," she said. Instead, she found she had to make an investment of $180,000 in the property to make it flood compatible, then wound up selling it at a loss when she was finally forced to come to terms with her new financial reality. "I was making emotional decisions about a financial matter, without the financial information," Natalie told me. "I regret it every day."

Also, about all those great memories with the kids, the neighbors, the Shabbat dinners and birthday mornings? There were also probably plenty of bitter marital arguments in that bedroom (the same bedroom you now hope to invite the cute soccer dad to), that time you threw wine in his face in the cozy kitchen, and those hours you'd sit in your car in the garage instead of coming inside and facing your unhappy marriage. Many moms are stunned to realize that moving out of the house they shared with their now-ex helped the whole family move forward much quicker and easier than had they stayed.

Stacy had loved the large brick colonial she shared with her husband and two small kids. "Initially, I dreaded the thought of selling that beautiful home, and considered fighting to keep it," she said. Ultimately, Stacy realized that all the great memories she cherished of the house included her kids and her mom, and not her husband, who was often away on business. She agreed to sell the home, and relocated with her kids across the country to New Mexico, where she had gone to college and had friends, and her now-ex would follow. "It was so great for all of us to have a new start, in a new place, with a new home. It has made the whole divorce so much easier for all of us, including my ex-husband."

Commit to Frugality

I F YOU FEEL broke, it is easy to lose sight of just how many material blessings you have. Face it: If you live in the developed world, especially the United States, you have a lot. The typical American home has tripled in size in the past 50 years (yet 1 in 10 still rent a storage unit), and is outfitted with more televisions than people. The average American woman has 30 outfits (compared with just 9 in 1930), yet throws away 65 pounds of clothes each year. As a mom, it is hardly surprising to learn that British researchers found that the average 10-year-old kid owns 238 toys, yet plays with just 12 daily.

Downsizing your home, buying a car you can afford, and getting rid of the heaps and heaps of *stuff* that likely crowd your closets, basement, and garage (which, according to federal statistics, is likely to be too crowded to park your ride inside!) will change your life. Decluttering is a divine exercise, one that forces you to reevaluate your past, cast aside bad memories, revisit the lovely ones, and make room for a new existence—exactly the functions required for building a new and powerful life as a single mom.

Plus, getting rid of all that crap—and yes, even if someone pays you for your stuff, it is just stuff, and stuff you don't actually use is almost always crap—makes life easier. Simpler. More elegant.

Unload the storage unit and you rid your monthly budget of that bill. The memories locked behind the rolling door are no longer lurking in the back of your mind, avoiding confrontation. The energy you spent thinking about what to do with the storage unit (or those boxes in the basement, garage, or attic), and feeling overwhelmed at the thought of dealing with it, no longer occupy head space.

By ridding your life of clutter, you free yourself to build a life that you want and deserve.

When she split from her wife, Rose moved out of a three-thousand-square-foot home with a huge yard and pool and into a modest twelve-hundred-square-foot three-bedroom townhouse: "My ex took out more loans to settle her share of the divorce attorney bills, while I used my settlement money to make a large down payment so my mortgage would be low. I also decluttered and have adopted a minimalist philosophy. Now, I think twice about what I buy and whether it's going to add to my happiness and serenity—or create more work to keep it clean or maintained. The money I save goes toward investing in myself. I just hired a personal trainer and I'm attending a motivational seminar, which I wouldn't have been able to afford before. I love my new lifestyle!"

Your home is wherever you and your children are. A house that is just big enough for you, your kids, the pets, new memories, and guests who will join you in the breakfast nook for lasagna dinner—*that* is an abundant life. That is a home.

Ohio mom Wendy, together with her teenage daughters, moved out of a four-thousand-square foot spread with five bedrooms and four bathrooms and into a three-bedroom, one-bath rental that was one-third the size. She took very few things from her previous home, which had been largely decorated with gifts and heirlooms from her ex-husband's parents. "Starting from nothing was daunting, but it was also completely liberating. I didn't have to ask anyone else their opinion. My choices were mine, and mine alone. It was a huge adjustment for my kids moving from a fancier home into a quite spare rental house. But it was a very valuable lesson in what actually makes a home: people, feelings, and memories, and not granite countertops and spiffy bathrooms. A year ago, I purchased a condo just a few blocks from our rental house. We had grown to love our neighborhood and neighbors. Our new home is still small, and we still have only one bathroom, but the girls now regard this as their home. Their dad is now under contract with his latest girlfriend on a six-bedroom, five-bath stately Tudor on a very fancy street about a mile from us. The contrast between my house and that house could not be greater. And though I know we would all like more bathroom space, I have no doubt that this will continue to feel like my kids' home, however spacious and upscale his new digs are."

A home with closets and shelves free of unused junk from life phases past—those are goods that do not require real estate. They do not accumulate dust, or need to be rummaged through to find the Phillips screwdriver, or rearranged when new photo albums or kids' art projects need to be stored. There is no clutter to occupy your headspace. Obliterating clutter maximizes money, time, and energy, just like everything in your single life ought to.

It is powerful to surround yourself with new things that represent your new life. While I stayed in my home I had shared with my ex, I gradually cleaned all of his stuff out of each and every closet and cupboard, and discarded or replaced marital furnishings to make the home truly mine. This included framed vintage posters that were especially sentimental in my marriage, but now made me cringe. Even a butcher knife that, while handy, irked me because it reminded me of the argument we had after he bought it for me as a "gift" (we didn't need it, and his purchase violated our agreement about budgeting). This process, however, was indeed gradual, and although I wish I'd done it sooner, I look forward to being able to afford to replace an armoire in what is now *my* bedroom but was once crowded with evidence of my ex's overspending. After all, financial liquidity is key, and it is important to make these purchases as you can afford them, no matter how tempting it is to create a bonfire of his belongings in the driveway (cue Angela Bassett in *Waiting to Exhale*) and go on a shopping spree.

Estate Planning for Single Moms

THIS TOPIC IS AS PAINFUL as it is boring. No one ever wants to think about what will happen to their children should they die, but as the chances are that your kids rely primarily on you, their single mom, the stakes are especially high for you to create and maintain your estate documents.

The main reason to take care of these important documents is that your wishes will be granted in the event of your death, as well as expedite any transfer of money or custody. Otherwise, these decisions will be left to the court system, which can be a gruesomely slow, expensive, and painful process for your survivors. It doesn't matter how much money you have; estate planning is for all income levels. If you had a will with your kids' dad, or a spouse from whom you are now split, you need a new one, in your name only. Here is my quick and dirty estate planning guide for single moms.

Life Insurance

Life insurance for reasonably healthy people is surprisingly affordable. I recently bought a $1 million, 15-year term policy for $34 per month. This is what you need for life insurance:

- Term life insurance. If you are just starting your financial planning, stick with term. Universal, variable, and whole-life insurance policies double as savings vehicles, with mixed results.
- General rule is to buy ten times your annual income. You need enough to support your kids through college, and if your plan was to finance college in full, then include that in coverage calculations.
- Cover your kids through college, and no more. The fifteen-year policy I recently purchased replaced a thirty-year policy I'd bought when my daughter was born, eight years ago. If I die when my kids are off on their own, they don't need a windfall. They'll already inherit my unused retirement investments and home.

Disability Insurance

The US Social Security Administration estimates that 25 percent of today's twenty-year-olds will experience a disability sometime in their lives. For working parents, especially single parents, disability is a very real threat that can shatter your family. I have seen firsthand how a disability can devastate a family of any income bracket.

If you are an employee, your company likely offers disability insurance. You can also buy your own, especially if you are self-employed. Disability insurance is reasonably easy to find. I recently priced out the cost of $6,000 monthly insurance with rich features (it would kick in 90 days after disability, and includes partial disability, "own occupation" benefits, and other perks), for about $300 per month.

There is such a thing as having too much insurance—cancer insurance and pet insurance, for example—but disability insurance is an often-overlooked coverage that can really change your life for the better during a difficult time.

While all workers technically qualify for social security disability coverage, that is notoriously difficult to obtain, and with low payouts.

Legal Documents

- **Will.** This lets your wishes be known in terms of who will care for your kids in the event their other parent is not legally the default guardian, how they will be cared for, and what property will be inherited by whom, and it names an executor.
- **Living trust.** This legal tool allows you to put all of your financial assets into a trust, and maintain control over them while you are well and alive. Should you die or become disabled, the executor you name will gain control over your trust. This is important if you have minor children—*do not name your children as inheritors of your assets*, but rather a trusted executor who will make sure that your wishes are responsibly honored. A living trust is an important tool for avoiding probate court.
- **Nomination of guardian.** If your children's father is fit, custody in the event of your death defaults to him, regardless of who you nominate in this document. However, in the event that he passes away or is unable to care for your kids, this person would likely be named guardian. It is advised the guardian is a person other than the executor of your estate, to avoid conflict of interest.
- **Power of attorney.** This names the person who will legally manage your financial and legal affairs in the event you are unable to.
- **Advanced health care directive.** Similar to a power of attorney, this person will make medical decisions on your behalf in the event you are mentally unable to. This includes a do-not-resuscitate order and other wishes regarding your quality of life.
- **Beneficiary forms.** These designate who gets what money. Never name minor children as beneficiaries, as they legally cannot make financial decisions. Instead, by naming the trust as

the beneficiary of life insurance, retirement and savings accounts, and real estate and other investments, you ensure your children can have controlled access to your assets, as overseen by the executor you have named, who knows your wishes.

List of Accounts

If you were to kick off today, what kind of mess would your loved ones face, even if you had everything tidied up? Help them immensely by creating a list of all your bank, brokerage, insurance, and other accounts, including account numbers, websites, and login information.

Estate planning is not fun. I avoided it for a long time, because the thought of the process was so uncomfortable. I dreaded thinking through what would happen to my kids should I die. I dreaded asking people in my life to step into the role of executors of my estate. The process reminded me of how fragile life can be, and even more so without a committed romantic partner. It was all painful. But the dread and stress of not doing what I knew I should do was also painful. So I did it.

Creating a will and related documents does not have to be expensive. I've worked with online sources including LegalZoom and Rocket Lawyer, both of which offer a very affordable option for creating legally binding estate planning documents, including access to attorneys in your state who can offer advice on local laws for formalizing your end-of-life affairs. If your finances are complicated, or the process makes you especially anxious, a few thousand dollars with an attorney to oversee the process is a solid investment.

EXERCISE

Have you tackled every part of your estate plan?

- ❑ Life insurance
- ❑ Disability insurance
- ❑ Will
- ❑ Living trust
- ❑ Nomination of guardian
- ❑ Power of attorney
- ❑ Advanced health care directive
- ❑ Beneficiary forms
- ❑ List of accounts, with login information
- ❑ All signed, notarized

College Saving
for Single Moms

A COUPLE OF YEARS AGO, financial giant Allianz found that far more than other families, upper-middle-class single moms make a classic financial mistake: prioritizing college savings over retirement. The women in this survey were clearly smart about career and finances, earning on average of $78,800 per year and receiving 10 percent or less of their income from child support. Yet nearly half said that saving for their children's education is their greatest motivation for developing a long-term financial plan—above saving for retirement. Compare that with just 26 percent of other families who say the same.

However, these very smart single moms were very wrong. You must always prioritize your own financial well-being, including retirement, over paying for your children's college education. Here's why:

- Financial aid formulas generally do not count retirement funds, while 529 college savings accounts are heavily considered.
- Tax breaks for retirement investments are far more generous than those for college investments. Contributions to a 401(k), for example, are tax deductible, and often come with an em-

ployer match, while 529 contributions for college savings are, at best, sheltered from state taxes.

- There are no federal loans for retirement, while there are lots of ways to finance a college degree.
- Single moms, more so than married parents or single fathers, are more likely to be poor in their later years.

Today, 24 percent of adult children expect to help their aging parents, according to Fidelity Investments. And the likelihood of this dependency is heightened for the single moms in the Allianz survey, as 79 percent say they worry about running out of money in retirement.

Takeaway: Make sure you are on financial track, paying off consumer debt, on schedule for a comfortable retirement, and have a decent chunk of cash in the bank before helping your kids with their higher-education costs. If you feel guilty for being an unmarried mom, work through that with a therapist—not by ransoming your financial future!

Perhaps most important of all: Have honest talks with your kids about college and related costs, and start early. Let your children know your values about education, and financing, and help them think through the schools they will consider, majors and careers of interest, and related costs. Make it clear how much you expect to contribute, and what their responsibility will be. Make sure your children understand the real cost of loans and interest, and how borrowing money for school will affect their future lifestyle and choices. It is your responsibility as a parent to educate your children about personal finance overall—not just college costs—just as it is your responsibility to teach them about manners, nutritious eating, and safe sex.

One of the biggest mistakes parents make is to tell their children: "Get into the best university you can, and we'll figure out the finances later." That is like saying, "Win your volleyball match and I'll buy you any car in the world!" There needs to be a clear return on your education investment. If your student is passionate about social work, it does not make sense for him to leave school with two hundred thousand dollars in student debt. In that example, help your student strategize creative solutions, like attending a community college or local state school for a few years and then transferring to a reputable program to attain a degree. Also, technical degrees in various health care and engineering tracks are increasingly gaining popularity, thanks to the low cost of education against high earning potential. A certificate in coding may have an incredible return on a very minimal investment.

It can be easy for single moms to slip into a guilt-ridden tizzy when it comes to college planning for your kids. As with choosing an appropriate home and creating a monthly budget, make sensible decisions about college choice and financing. This is a great opportunity to relax into your own reality and set an incredible example for making responsible decisions, regardless of what your kids' classmates or your own Facebook friends are deciding. Also, it is important to remember: Your kids are adults once they turn eighteen. You can only inform their decisions, not control them. And you are no longer responsible for them financially.

Another note about choosing a college: I am cynical about name-brand universities. Unless you can afford one with zero financial challenge, or there is a clear connection between money spent at a school and the end results, reconsider. Why?

Brand of school does not determine professional success.
A noted study published by Alan Krueger, a Princeton professor who went on to be chief economist for the US Treasury, found that by the time they reached their thirties, top-performing high school students who were admitted to both Ivy League and middle-ranking states schools (like Penn vs. Penn State) earned about the same salaries, regardless of which school they attended.

In other words, it is more about the student than where the student goes to college.

The quality of top-ranked schools plummets while costs soar.
The American Council of Trustees and Alumni (ACTA) released its report on twenty-nine top liberal arts schools. Overall the verdict is that these name-brand institutions are guilty of grade inflation, flimsy educational standards, and wayward spending—especially on administrative and building costs, which grow faster than funds spent on teaching. Between the 2007 and 2012 school years, these institutions' sticker prices rose by as much as 17 percent, while many school presidents earn at least four hundred thousand dollars, and on average administration expenditures are more than one-third the amount spent on instruction.

No one is learning anything in college anyway.
Academically Adrift: Limited Learning on College Campuses, published by the University of Chicago Press, reports that 36 percent of college students do not demonstrate any significant improvement in learning during their college careers. It's no wonder—the National Survey of Student Engagement found that 47 percent of college seniors study fifteen or fewer hours per week. I'm not surprised. My main memories of college are five-dollar happy hour pitchers of Miller Lite at a scuzzy but awesome pub called Murphy's, my giant crush on the campus concert promoter, and vaguely learning about fair reporting in an investigative journalism class.

It's even worse at top schools.
Now just imagine if I had spent my college years getting drunk and chasing stoned hotties at a more expensive school. This would have been an even bigger waste of money. In the ACTA survey of those twenty-nine top-ranked liberal arts colleges (where on

average an education comes with a quarter-million-dollar price tag), just two require graduates to take an economics course, three require a US history course, and only five insist students take literature courses. The survey report emphasizes that these core classes have been replaced with courses with titles like "Food in the Middle East: History, Culture and Identity," and "Mad Men and Mad Women: An Examination of Masculinity and Femininity in Mid-20th-Century America."

Plus, all schools increasingly rely on adjunct professors, so your student will not be attending all courses guided by world-renowned experts. I recently went out with an adjunct art professor at an Ivy League school. He hadn't achieved much professional success, and said he usually had zero background in the courses he taught each semester, preparing for his lectures by reading a few books on the subject.

In other words: Elite schools teach a lot of fluff, and the value is in the name-brand diploma.

Technology is changing the economy—and an academic education is increasingly irrelevant.
One Harvard report predicts that a third of the 47 million new jobs expected to be created in the United States by 2018 will require only an associate's degree or certificate. This is hardly surprising considering the high number of degreed bartenders and baristas in our midst.

Elite networking is available to everyone.
People argue that elite educations are valuable for their networking opportunities. You know what else is valuable? LinkedIn, professional organizations, conferences, Burning Man, Teach For America, the international backpacking circuit, and strategically chosen happy hours—all of which are accessible to most everyone. Again, technology and the breakdown of old-fashioned so-

cial structures (for example, patriarchy!) have flattened the world. Smart, creative, driven people want to meet each other, regardless of where they were accepted to college at age seventeen. Personally, I have gotten more client leads from my kids' bus stop and Twitter than my college alumni association.

As a single mom, you already live outside traditional societal norms. Don't fall prey to following the herd when it comes to big decisions like college choices. Think through this decision critically, and with an eye toward what is truly right for you and your family. And remember: Your kid is indeed an adult at age eighteen. You are not morally responsible for paying for college, but you are morally obliged to do your best to equip him or her with the tools to make sound decisions.

College Financial Aid for Students with Divorced or Separated Parents

WHEN COLLEGE APPLICATIONS do come around for your teen, there are special financial aid considerations for students of parents who are not married. For the inside scoop on maximizing college financial aid for children of divorce, I turned to Mark Kantrowitz, publisher of Cappex, a website about college admissions and financial aid.

When a student's parents are divorced, which parent's income should be listed on the Free Application for Federal Student Aid (FAFSA)?
When a student's parents are divorced, only one parent is responsible for completing the FAFSA. This parent, called the custodial parent, is the one with whom the student lived the most during the twelve months preceding the date the FAFSA is filed. Generally, if the custodial parent is the parent with lower income, the student will qualify for more financial aid.

If custody is not legally distinguished, the custodial parent is based on whichever parent provided more financial support. So, to some extent the parents can control which parent completes the FAFSA. However, colleges can ask for a copy of the divorce decree and child custody agreement. So if the living arrangements don't match both of these documents, it's best if the parents get the court to modify the agreements.

What happens if the parents are separated but not legally divorced?
If the parents are divorced or separated but living together, they are treated as though they were married and the financial information of both parents is required on the FAFSA. If they are legally separated and living together, or informally separated and maintaining two separate residences, then only one parent must complete the FAFSA.

What happens when one or both parents remarry? How do the stepparents' incomes affect financial aid?
If the custodial parent has remarried, the income and assets of the stepparent must be reported. When choosing the custodial parent, the parents should take the finances of the stepparents into account.

Note that if the stepparent provides more than half support to his or her other children, these children get counted in household size, even if they don't live with the stepparent. In particular, if any of these children are in college, they get counted. Increasing the number in college can have a big impact on eligibility for need-based financial aid. So, while including the stepparent's income and assets on the FAFSA may decrease eligibility for need-based aid, including his or her other children in the "number in college" figure may increase eligibility for need-based aid.

Should custody always be switched to the lower-earning parent?
It should be genuine. College financial aid administrators have more experience sniffing out fraud than parents do gaming the system. It's best if the child's high school is in the same district as the custodial parent's home address in addition to having court documents supporting the change in custody. Otherwise, the col-

lege financial aid administrators will suspect that the change of custody is a sham. Also, any 529 accounts should be held in the custodial parent's name.

Can't parents just work it out between them in a friendly agreement so the lesser-earning custodial parent gets child support or alimony under the table, off the books?

Under the table is fraud. There may also be tax implications. It seems very rare that divorced parents have an amicable divorce and are willing to compromise for the benefit of the children. Children of divorced parents are much less likely to graduate, in part because they get caught in the middle.

Retirement Savings for Single Moms

ONE OF THE SADDEST MOMENTS during my divorce was when worrying about my monthly budget, I logged on to one of the many online retirement planning tools, took a deep breath, and prepared to contend with poverty in my late life. The second question after my (then very modest) income in the fear-mongering digital tool whose name is Will You Have Enough to Retire? was "Do you want to consider your spouse's finances?"

"Even this stupid digital brokerage calculator rubs my nose in the fact that I'm *divorced*?" I wailed. Cue sad divorce tears, and terrified-of-being-an-old-bag-lady tears.

I'd always been pretty good at saving, taking advantage of my employers' 401(k) plans, and saving in a Roth IRA and rollover plan after becoming self-employed. But while I was married, my ex's generous corporate retirement plans were a big focus of our joint planning, which, like so many women, meant I saved less in my own accounts (for all the married women out there: DON'T MAKE MY MISTAKE! Plan for your own retirement as if you were single!). In other words, I thought of any money in either of our accounts as "our money," and after I bought him out of our apartment and the legal standards for splitting joint accounts materialized, I was way, way behind on saving for my own retirement.

I've since been able to catch up, and feel confident I am on track for a comfortable retirement, something that far too few single moms prioritize, much less enjoy.

According to the Social Security Administration's Office of Retirement and Disability Policy, divorced women have dramatically lower incomes and higher poverty rates than other women. Around 20 percent of divorced women age sixty-five or older live in poverty, compared with 18 percent of never-married women and 15 percent of widows. Retirement-age women are 80 percent more likely than men to be impoverished.

The reasons? Women continue to earn less than men and therefore are less likely to save and invest, and they save less when they do. Also, women are more likely to take time off to care for children and other family members, and the less you work, the less you accumulate in Social Security benefits throughout your life. Further, married women cede financial power in relationships far more often than many realize. In fact, a recent Fidelity survey of married couples found that 21 percent of women admit to having only some or no input in the day-to-day financial decisions in their household, and just 19 percent of wives say they are the primary decision maker in their households when it comes to long-term investments, like retirement.

I'm not surprised to hear these figures. Earlier this year I attended a luncheon at a large wealth management firm in Manhattan. The event was aimed at women considering divorce, and the panelists were a divorce attorney, an accountant, and a wealth manager. After the speakers were introduced, they each shared the number one challenge faced by their female clients. The answer was universal: "They are clueless about their household finances." Most of the clients of these leading New York City divorce professionals were highly educated women, often with multiple degrees from top schools and high-powered careers of their own. So many of these very accomplished women had no idea about what accounts their husbands had, how much money was in any of them, their spouse's income, whether he received a bonus, whether her name was on the mortgage—or even if there was a mortgage on their home. The panelists' advice to these women? "Rummage through drawers and closets. You likely won't find a full statement, but if you find a single page, that is helpful. And if any accounts are based in Switzerland, that's a red flag."

What is going on in the world that our most accomplished women—and women overall—choose to hand over their power to their husbands? This is the behavior of a child. But if you note the likelihood of divorce in marriages in which women are the primary breadwinner, it is reasonable to deduce that women understand that not all heterosexual marriages can withstand financially empowered women. As a result, many women sabotage themselves by choosing to be financially ignorant, and they often under-earn. The financial consequences of this self-sabotaging extends beyond the length of the marriage and into retirement age, when women are disproportionately poorer than men. Never-married women are far poorer than married women, and divorced women are the poorest.

When it comes to saving, the onus on single moms to prioritize long-term investing, including retirement, is paramount. The likelihood of starting behind the eight ball is higher, while financial stakes are greater. After all, women are more likely to live longer than men, less likely to remarry after divorce, and have an increased chance of being the primary caregiver of children, both healthy and disabled. That means that you have a lot of near- and long-term responsibilities that can distract you from prioritizing your own financial well-being. Long-term saving and retirement investments are a critical part of this equation.

To figure out a retirement strategy, I recommend meeting with a professional financial adviser, even if it is for a single strategy session to set you on the right track. Assess how much you will need to save for retirement, how much you should put away each month, and how to invest it. A few key points to consider:

No one is going to save you from yourself. You have to make retirement savings a priority, and take full responsibility for your own financial future.

A man is not a financial plan. I know you think you know that, but a man is not going to save you. He's not. OK, he might, but you might not like that as much as you think you will, and then it might not work out anyway. Stick with: A man is not a financial plan.

Investing does not have to be complicated. There is a reason that financial investing seems intimidating: The bazillion-dollar financial services industry is designed to intimidate you into handing your money over to their experts to manage for you, at a steep fee. While I do suggest you seek out the expertise of a trusted adviser, investing in a low-fee target-date index or exchange-traded fund is a very reasonable move you can do yourself.

Save for retirement over saving for your kids' college. As previously discussed, this is an especially common and painful pitfall of single moms. Guilt has no place in financial planning. Your kids can find any number of ways to finance their degrees. There are no Pell grants or loans for retirement. And whatever you do, do not pay for your kids' weddings if your own retirement planning is not on track!

Find a retirement club or buddy. Online communities can be great sources of support as you work toward your financial goals, as are local investment clubs, or even a friend who is also serious about reaching a money goal, and who can serve as a goal buddy.

Communicate your financial philosophies and goals to your children. Not only are you fulfilling your parental responsibility by making sure your kids understand the very critical concepts of earning, saving, and giving, but by doing so, you also hold yourself accountable. When kids are as young as four, start them on allowances, and use it as an opportunity to teach them about personal finance, as well as share your own values around money, including saving. In my house, since my kids were four years old, they have received an allowance, which they must divide between Spend, Save, and Give jars. Each month they must give away a quarter of their income to a cause they believe in. I use this as an opportunity to share the causes I support with my income. They also save their money in bank accounts, and we talk about big things they are interested in buying in the future, including the importance of saving for college. I share with them how I save for vacations, and explain what retirement is. "It is important to me that I have enough money so that you don't have to worry about me when I get older. We all prioritize our money based on what is important to us." They are small, but they get it.

EXERCISE

Your Kickass Single Mom retirement checklist:

☐ Do you have an IRA or 401(k) you are currently contributing to regularly?
☐ Does your employer offer a contribution match? Please tell me you contribute at least enough to reap this benefit.
☐ Find a retirement calculator you like and trust, and spend some time there (stick with this one going forward). I like the ones at Fidelity.com, PersonalCapital.com, and Chase.com, but there are dozens out there.

❑ Find a financial adviser:
  ◆ Ask friends and family who are in a similar income bracket.
  ◆ Look for someone who is a Certified Financial Planner, or CFP. They're licensed and regulated, and are mandated to take classes on different aspects of financial planning.
  ◆ Seek fee-only advisers, who tend to be more objective in their advice.
  ◆ Meet with your adviser in person, and make sure you get a good vibe. This is someone you must trust and like.
❑ Whether with an adviser or on your own, devise a plan on how you will save for and invest in retirement. Stick to that plan. Revisit and revise once per year.

On Alimony and Child Support

You may have noticed that my monthly Kickass Single Mom Budget does not mention child support or alimony. There is a very good reason for that: Kickass Single Moms do not depend on either.

Alimony and child support were huge feminist wins when they were institutionalized and mandated. Before women had legal rights or legislated earning power, alimony and child support were sources of critical support not only for women but also for children, nearly all of whom were cared for primarily by their mothers, per traditional gender roles. That both were created and enforced was a great testament to the work of many feminist activists. Think about the 1960s and 1970s, when no-fault divorce, thankfully, became the norm in nearly every state, and both sexes were free to leave a marriage without arguing for a reason why. This was especially important for women, who we know are disproportionately subject to domestic violence and other abuse (marital rape didn't become illegal in all fifty states until 1993!).

While both men and women were free to leave a marriage, during those early decades and before, women simply had a fraction of the earning power you and I enjoy today, and they had far fewer legal rights. Factoids for your consideration and, perhaps, your daily gratitude exercise:

- Banks wouldn't allow a woman to open a credit card in her own name until 1974 (after which they have incessantly run ad campaigns promoting the inane stereotype that all women like to do is *shop, shop, shop*).
- A woman in the United States could be legally fired from her job because she was pregnant until 1978.
- Ladies, we didn't even have the right to vote until 1920—a full *fifty years* after "men of color" and freed slaves were awarded the right vote.

When courts awarded women alimony and child support, that made sense, was just, and protected people with few opportunities. However, times have changed. Women now have incredible opportunities to work, build careers, and earn. Women are breadwinners in 40 percent of households with children, are the majority of undergraduate students, and are increasingly equal earners and holders of powerful positions in business, academia, and government. "Lesser sex" is today a laughable term, and it is a very real truth for women today that we have the opportunity to build whatever lifestyle we want, and get just as accustomed to that lifestyle as we please!

Part of my stance against relying on funds from your kids' dad is practical. A small fraction of moms owed child support actually see it regularly, and alimony is increasingly being limited by court reform and judges' discretion. Also, both alimony and child support are contingent on another person's income—a person who very likely does not like you and is motivated to find ways not to pay. In other words, it is irresponsible financial planning to count on money that you may never see. The goal, after all, is financial independence.

But there are other, more devastating ramifications of agreeing to take your ex's money, including the co-parenting relationship you have with your kids' dad, which is deeply connected to whether or not he is involved.

First, let's tackle alimony.

Alimony reform is under way in just about every state in the country. In most states, lifetime alimony is now a thing of the past, and the sums and rules granted to payees grow stricter all the time. Policy makers and judges enforcing the law have seen for years how alimony stifles divorced couples' ability to effectively co-parent by creating tension between exes, and prevents the lesser-earning spouse (nearly always the wife) from moving forward with his or her life. Alimony, judges know, disincentivizes both the parties paying and receiving spouses from building their careers, and results in years of expensive and bitter appeals in court. In fact, alimony is the number one most appealed issue in divorce courts. If your lawyer is urging you to fight for—or over—alimony, consider his or her motives.

Morghan Richardson, a family lawyer in New York City, says that mothers are often stunned to hear divorce and child support judges order them to work full time—no matter how many or how little their children are. In the mommy wars, the increasing numbers of female judges (who themselves are often working moms, having clawed their way to the bench in a hostile, male-dominated field, while their children were in full-time day care) have their say. And they say stay-at-home moms need to return to work and start earning. Alimony and child support payments reflect this growing sentiment from judges of all genders, in states across the country. This trend is accelerating.

Even more than the realities of divorce court rulings, the real reason for eliminating alimony from your financial plan is that it holds you back in every part of your life. The subtitle of this book includes the promise of financial independence—and that is exactly what I want for you. There are few things in this life that are as delicious as assessing your home, your bank account, and the career and business you built, wrapping your arms around yourself, and saying: "I did this. I did all of this! And if I can do *this*, just look what *else* I can do in this world!"

You cannot live your full potential as a mother or person if you choose to be financially dependent on anyone else, much less a man with whom you are no longer romantically entangled.

Indeed, as you will see in this chapter, accepting alimony or child support results in women holding themselves back professionally, financially, and even romantically, and stymies their ability to truly thrive in this new phase of life. Also, money exchanged between co-parents nearly universally compromises co-parenting. I have never met anyone who has paid a nickel of alimony to an able-bodied ex and was not a little-tiny-bit-a-lot bitter about it.

I understand why.

Often, the argument for alimony includes the fact that the wife was a stay-at-home mother—or otherwise compromised her career—which had financial value in the family in the form of childcare costs and housework. She abandoned her career and earning potential, will likely never catch up to where she'd be had she stayed in the workforce, and therefore should be compensated for this contribution to the family and fueling her husband's career, the story goes. But we saw in an earlier chapter that that equation is now obsolete, as technology largely replaced housewife work, children don't benefit from countless hours with their parents, and women are now free to build careers and earn.

In the broad picture of gender equality, financial experts and family court judges agree: Every single woman must always have her own income and money in her own name, in part because of the great likelihood that she will become a single mom! We are in a very difficult moment in women's history, and unfortunately there is an entire generation of women who were pressured to abandon their careers in the name of being a "better," stay-at-home mother and wife, while also being presented awe-inspiring opportunities to build a career. All the while they faced an approximately 50 percent chance of divorce. The trifecta of feminist confusion!

Take as a precautionary tale Sheila, who was a very active member of my Facebook group, Millionaire Single Moms, for women of all income levels "who are committed to growing their careers, businesses and personal wealth, thinking big, and refusing to accept that exterior challenges define us or limit our potential." Sheila holds a master's degree in counseling and a coaching certificate, and before she had children and quit working, she had a solid career history.

Over several weeks in the Facebook group, Sheila added a series of increasingly fraught posts explaining that her oldest child was about to graduate high school and move to college, and her child support and alimony were about to be slashed significantly. She posted pictures of rooms in her home she planned to rent via Craigslist, and talked about unsuccessful efforts to attract coaching clients and other desperate attempts to make ends meet. What, she asked the group, could she do to earn money, ASAP?

It turns out that Sheila had been divorced for ten years. I called her to ask her more about her situation. She'd had so many opportunities to build a career during the years after her marriage ended—how did she find herself suddenly in such a pickle? She told me:

During our marriage I stayed home and sacrificed my career so my husband could build his business—and he became very successful. Then, he had an affair, left me for his mistress, and continued to earn even more. I felt that if I earned enough so he didn't have to pay me anymore, that would be letting him off the hook. He needs to be punished for what he did, and I should be compensated.

As I'm fond of saying: Living well is the best revenge. Sheila, however, in her attempt at revenge, had been living horribly for a decade—even if she received five thousand dollars per month from her ex-husband. Not only did she find herself in a financial crisis when that income phased out per court order set ten years prior, but she had not been living up to her full potential as a woman and mother all those years. Cushy support payments, ironically, held her back.

Another heartbreaking alimony story involves Teresa, a talented marketing executive and mom in her thirties, who won significant alimony and child support in her divorce from a Wall Street lawyer. A couple of years after her divorce, Teresa was offered a prestigious promotion and raise, but turned it down. Why? "If I accepted, I wouldn't qualify for alimony anymore." Regardless of whether her immediate net income would increase or decrease, this dependence on alimony—and therefor her ex—held Teresa back professionally both immediately and in the long term. This was a setback not only for her, but for women overall. How will the pay gap ever close if women choose to compromise themselves for the sake of payroll from ex-spouses? How could she ever grow as a professional and reach the income heights she is capable of if every decision was predicated on alimony? How could she explain this with any pride to her children?

I really feel for women in these situations. There are few messages out there to women who divorce higher-earning men, other than: *Get what you can; make the bastard pay; think about how much you sacrificed.* They often find themselves in very scary financial straits, the rug seemingly pulled out from under them and the financial agreement of their marriages (he earns, she cares for the kids), which they truly believed their husbands would uphold. Acting in anger is understandable, but playing victim in perpetuity is not a life strategy.

Women as a gender will never, ever gain equity in any realm until we stop forcing men to care for us financially for our entire lives. Instead, you owe it to yourself, your children, and future generations to take every step possible to be responsible for yourself in every way, including when it comes to earning and managing money. After all, as I walked down the aisle, I knew there was a very excellent chance of divorce. You did, too. We wear our seat belts and buy life insurance for far less risky propositions, and don bike helmets and cook meat to 160 degrees to be safe. Similarly, it is reasonable to expect everyone in a marriage to protect themselves financially in the likelihood of divorce. Often, to attend to small children, women step off their career paths, go part time, or turn down promotions because doing so makes life easier for the whole family. Then the marriage ends, and your career is so far behind his. It isn't fair, and it sucks so much.

You know what sucks even more? Dependence. So does trying to parent with someone who really, really resents that huge chunks of his paycheck go to a woman he truly hates.

In other words: If women want equal opportunity, you and I must assume equal responsibility.

Another argument in favor of spousal support is parity of lifestyle. I was on WCCO CBS radio in Minneapolis speaking about this with my friend, anchor Jordana Green, who receives alimony, and was arguing my anti–spousal support stance. "Isn't it unfair if you're used to living in a five-hundred-thousand-dollar house but have to move into an apartment when you divorce?" she asked.

My answer? "If you want a five-hundred-thousand-dollar house, pursue a career that affords you one." Entitlement has no place in an empowered woman's life.

Or as one alimony reform activist wrote in an e-mail: "Alimony law was created to 'keep the lesser-earning spouse in the lifestyle in which they are accustomed.' Using that logic, wealthy parents should be legally obligated to support their kids throughout their lives." I agree.

Why should it be your ex's responsibility to give you a lifestyle that you yourself cannot afford? If it is to compensate you for your stay-at-home years, that argument does not hold up, especially if your ex is a high earner, which renders you entitled to generous sums of maintenance. After all, the median market rate for childcare and housecleaning is around ten dollars per hour. Why should you be paid more just because your ex is successful? Were you somehow more valuable on the marriage market because you are pretty/smart/ from a nice family, and therefore priced as a higher-than-market-rate commodity? Of course not. You are a fallible human who happens to be divorced from a rich guy.

My hope for women facing these decisions: Set aside your fear of not making enough. Free yourself up to truly have an independent life. Yes, money may be tight for a while, and yes, you may have to downsize. But what you get in return is the unbelievable confidence and pride that comes with building a life that is truly on your own terms. You will be forced to face the very real fear of financial destitution, and you will push through that fear and into a life that you have made, and reach goals that you didn't know you had the courage to set or exceed. By doing so, you set an incredible example for your children and other women in your life, and create precedence for future generations of young people to always prioritize their own careers and financial autonomy, so that they will never face the limits of dependence.

Perhaps the biggest reason refusing alimony is great for women is that without it, both parties are allowed to move on with their lives.

Dependence on an ex only keeps you emotionally embroiled in a marriage that is now over. I have a friend who abandoned a thriving small business she'd built for fifteen years when she married a successful New York City tax attorney and had a baby. The marriage ended. He pays her a sum each month that keeps her in an Upper East Side two-bedroom, three-story townhouse, while she struggles to rebuild her business. Sometimes the check is late. Sometimes, she said, it is humiliating to remind him to pay. Sometimes, she finds she doesn't express concerns over his parenting for fear that the money won't arrive that month. "Tell your readers to never stop working," she told me recently. "There is nothing worse than being dependent on a man who you are trying to separate from."

On the other side of the alimony equation is Dana Lin. She was a stay-at-home mom for most of her marriage, and admits there was a measure of pride in not pursuing alimony or child support in her divorce, even though she could barely support herself—selling her wedding and heirloom jewelry to make ends meet, and not eating on some days when her children spent time with their dad.

Lin, the mother of two grade-school daughters at the time, also didn't want money complicating her relationship with her children's father. "I never wanted him to be able to say, 'I can't spend time with the kids because I have to work long hours to support you,'" says Lin, who at the time of the split worked part time as a school office manager for twenty dollars per hour. Today, she says, she has a very friendly relationship with her ex, who "is an amazing father now."

Professionally, the move was a boon: "I was very ambitious and had great earning potential," says Lin. "I didn't want anyone to say I couldn't make it without him." She pursued her dream of being a screenwriter, today working as a script doctor and ghostwriter. Also, with a partner, she launched ZenLife Services, which provides stress management training skills to law-enforcement employees. "Living lean taught me to be more disciplined," she says. "Sometimes if you have too much of a cushion you're not as aggressive in pursuing your dreams."

It is rare to find a divorced person who is happy to pay money to someone he believes is capable of supporting herself. Since your ex is angry about paying alimony (and child support), that anger will manifest in all sorts of ways in your relationship, which has now been reduced to co-parenting. It may not be fair, it may be court-sanctioned, but you are lesser co-parents because this money comes between you.

As I will elaborate more deeply in the co-parenting part of this book, decades of research finds that the more contentious a divorce or breakup is, the more contentious co-parenting is likely to be, and the less likely the father is to be involved with his kids. More conflict between parents means an astonishingly high chance that your ex will stop being involved with his children altogether. I realize that this is amoral, that he is your children's father and he has an obligation to parent them regardless of any conflict with you. However, the evidence is clear: The more you and your ex fight, the less likely your children will see him. Even if he is regularly involved, if there is money exchanged, it will likely heighten any tension, making co-parenting exponentially more difficult.

If you are facing divorce, and alimony is on the table, I urge you to turn it down for the sake of your own potential as a professional and as a person, and for the sake of your co-parenting relationship. Child support, which I elaborate on in the next section, is not very different, but there are nuances. If you do accept alimony, prepare to have plenty more headaches as well as attorney fees, because your ex is likely to take you back to court for a modification—again, alimony is cited as the number one reason for appeals in divorce court.

If you really, truly cannot get on your feet without some financial help, and you are easily entitled to it through a divorce settlement (without a court battle), agree to alimony for a limited time that will allow you to boost your career or find a new one. Two years should be plenty. By setting this limitation, you create a fire-under-the-ass deadline for yourself to work hard and make some real money. This also signals to your ex that you do not intend to exploit divorce law, or make his life hell just because you can, and that you fully intend to be financially independent of him sooner rather than later.

Another strategy to employ is to prioritize any payment you are legitimately owed to be paid in a lump sum, as opposed to monthly payments. Say, for example, that the formula in your state would entitle you to two thousand dollars in monthly alimony for ten years, or a total of $240,000. Instead of taking that in monthly payments, which will only remind your ex every four weeks how much he freaking hates you—a sentiment that will likely manifest itself in all sorts of passive or not-so-passive aggression—find a way to take that money as a onetime lump-sum payment. This may come in the form of cash, more equity in your home, or retirement account transfer. The gist is that one painful transfer minimizes ongoing tension that is fueled every time a fat sum is withdrawn from his account and deposited into yours, month after month after month. It is not uncommon for alimony payers to hide income, take lesser-paying jobs, or otherwise finagle ways of paying less. Do you really want to expend your energy on keeping an eye on his every move, and hauling him back to court if you smell foul play?

But What About Child Support? Isn't That Different?

Yes and no.

It is a very legitimate argument to make that child support is your kids' money, not yours, and you have an obligation to fight for it and accept it.

That is right, but sometimes you can be so right you are wrong.

To start, the average sum of child support single mothers receive is just over two hundred dollars per month, and less than half receive the full sum awarded by the courts. Even if the amount is higher and you do receive child support regularly, still think very carefully about accepting and pursuing this income.

The indisputable argument against any type of support is that it's irresponsible to build a life around income you have no control over. Your kids' dad could lose his job, die, become disabled, choose a lower-paying career, see his business tank, hide all of his income offshore, get busted for cooking meth in a trailer in the middle of the New Mexico desert and be sentenced to the can, or simply go MIA. You have no control over that, and if you depend on his income, you live in fear every single day that it will go away. That is a terrifying, exhausting way to live. Shift that toxic, fearful energy into your own income and career, which you do have control over, and watch your life change forever and for the better.

The Two Types of Child Support

Extras

Child support is typically broken into two segments: the support itself, which is a percentage of the non-primary parent's income, designed to pay for the daily life of the children; and "extras." Extras include childcare, health insurance and medical costs, and extracurricular activities like sports and music lessons. They are typically divided according to the parents' income. Usually, both these sums are added together and paid in one lump from the non-primary custodial parent (usually the dad) to the primary custodial parent (usually the mom).

Sounds perfectly reasonable, and it is. It makes complete sense that both parents should pay for childcare so they can both work, as well as medical expenses and extracurriculars that are obvious out-of-pocket costs of raising children.

Except in cases where there is an extreme disparity in income, wherein paying for a share of art camp would be a real hardship for one parent but a drop in the bucket for the other, find a low-conflict way to divvy up these extra expenses. However, if these expenses give off even a whiff of conflict between you and your kids' dad, find a way to manage it without having to discuss it each month. Be creative. One amicable co-parenting couple I know share a credit card, put all the kids' expenses on it, then divide it equally at the end of the month. Maybe the lesser-earning parent adds the kids to his or her work-subsidized medical insurance, and the higher earner pays out-of-pocket for day care. Perhaps the exact sums owed will be off by a bit, but in return you get a low-conflict way of managing a practical matter.

If in your case support is something you have to sort out through family court, that is OK. But keep in mind that kids' expenses change year after year, as do parents' financial situations. How much time and energy do you want to spend fighting in court every single year to get these calculations amended? Is it worth the time, energy, and stress of returning to appear before a judge? Wouldn't it be easier if *you just paid this all yourself?*

Child Support

The other, main part of child support, designed for the noncustodial parent to pay directly to the custodial parent to support the children's daily expenses, is another issue. Consider very carefully whether you want to pursue the *support* part of the equation.

As you will read later, I am a very strong proponent of shared parenting, with equal time with each parent being the goal for everyone. Exceptions include abuse, severe mental illness, addiction, and other situations where the children's safety is in question. Otherwise, there is no reason that all other separated families shouldn't aim for shared parenting and an approximately equal time split with the kids, and therefore equal responsibility. The current presumption is that the mother has the children the majority of the time, while the father gets occasional visits. This is outdated and damaging to children, their relationship with the noncustodial parent, and gender equality overall. After all, the current "Friday night special" visitation schedule, wherein the dad sees his kids every other weekend and for Wednesday evening dinners, then pays the mother child support, presumes that men are incompetent parents and women are incompetent earners, and shoehorns both parents into stereotyped gender roles.

If we want men to be involved fathers, teach our sons that dads are just as important as moms, and model for our daughters the type of good man she should choose as an eventual partner, we must do everything we can to allow men to step into their power as fathers. That means equal parenting time and shared decision making.

If you and I want equal opportunities for ourselves and our daughters in the workplace, then we have to step into our economic power and pursue careers and earning with abandon. That requires time away from our children, and dads are to be expected to care for their children at least half the time.

In cases of shared parenting, child support doesn't make sense. After all, both parents have roughly equal time with the kids, which results in equal food consumed, electricity bills paid, and random activities like movies, gifts for birthday parties, and museum visits. Both parents have to maintain homes big enough for the kids, so real estate expenses are a moot point. And both parents have equal free time to build careers, as well as enjoy their free time without paying out-of-pocket for babysitters. Why should one parent pay the other in these cases?

What happens when one parent pays the other for support, just like in alimony, is that every single dime spent comes into question. If you argue that your kids are entitled to support because you can't pay the rent otherwise, then your ex will raise an eyebrow—and likely a fit—if he shows up to see the kids and you have a new sofa, or you always have your nails professionally manicured, or he hears about frequent trips to Chuck E. Cheese's with your boyfriend. If you want your daughter to join a hockey league and you ask their dad to pay his share, he may balk if he already feels he pays too much support.

But the cost of depending on child support is bigger than this. If you take and depend on that income, you are less likely to launch the business of your dreams, act on your urge to go for a big promotion, or go back to school to pursue a new career. After all, you know that the more you earn, the less he will have to pay in both support and extras. While you may tell yourself that money is going into a savings account for the kids, it is very difficult to mentally shut it out of your monthly budget, especially if it is a significant sum. The more you depend on income from your ex, the more power you give him over you, and the less ownership you take for your own success.

Like alimony, child support income can disappear at any moment. You can't control if your ex gets fired, starts a new family (therefore his payments will likely be reduced by the court), or decides to quit paying because you annoy him. You can choose to hunt him down or visit and revisit family court, and you may have to make the very difficult choice as to whether to pursue incarcerating your kids' dad if he falls behind—which will not help your bottom line because he can't earn or pay child support from jail.

Candace e-mailed me, desperate:

> My ex is barely involved, but does pay child support, as it is deducted from his paycheck. I recently learned that he has a new baby, and he has filed for a reduction in payment, which means my check will be lowered by $300. I am furious! Can this happen? What can I do to fight it? Without that money I cannot afford childcare, will have to pause my degree program (again), and stop trying for the promotion I've been working toward.

My advice? Stop focusing on the pittance of three hundred dollars per month, and focus on what you can control: building your dream career, earning big, taking care of your kids, and being a fantastic role model for them (and anyone else who is paying attention!). Do not, under any circumstances, drop out of your program, and gun like bloody hell for that promotion. Stop giving your power to anyone else, much less someone who clearly cares little for you or his own children.

Failure to pay child support is a moral issue, a financial quandary for all parties, and a giant time and energy suck for moms. This is often a case of being so right you are wrong: You may indeed be very legally entitled to tens of thousands of dollars in unpaid child support, and morally men should step up and care for their children— financially and otherwise. Fighting for this money may indeed be about providing for your children, holding a man responsible for his kids, and showing your children that you are fighting for them.

But there comes a point of diminishing returns. That sense of justice and obligation can quickly turn to revenge and rage. It takes a lot of time, a whole lot of energy, and a boatload of anger to go through the legal hoops to collect that child support—all with a very good chance that you may never see it at all.

If you are facing years of family court battle, or live in a state that ties the amount visitation time to sums of money they pay in support (the more child support paid equals less visitation time, and vice versa), reconsider.

Imagine: What if you never spent an iota of energy on child support again? What if you came to complete peace with the idea that you will never see a nickel from your kids' dad? You are no longer compelled to think about that money, confront him about it, have arguments in your head with him about how he's not pulling his weight, or spend hours complaining to your friends and family about what a dog he is.

How would it feel to just *let it go*? What would you do with all that newly freed time and energy?

What if you took half that outpouring of toxic time and energy and funneled it into a side gig? What if you invested in evening courses that would lead to a promotion at work, or a real estate license, or a coaching certificate? What if you took that energy and joined a mastermind group of brilliant women who would pull you up and elevate your life in untold ways? Or simply committed to spending one evening, guilt- and rage-free, at a networking event in your dream industry, hobnobbing with other people who are thriving and not angry about small sums of money owed them?

Gayle, a pharmaceutical executive and mom of two, initially resented that her ex didn't pay his share of expenses or any child support. Ultimately, she is grateful. "I've let it go," she says. "It was really scary to let go of what seemed like an entitlement. But I became super motivated at work." She earned huge raises, and within two years earned the annual employee appreciation award out of five thousand people in her organization. "That felt pretty damn good. But even more important is that I found comfort in succeeding in my career during a time when I felt like I was losing everything. It centered me. Made me a better mother. I own my destiny. I'm motivated by my own ability to 'provide and conquer.' And in the end I'll have raised two kickass daughters who will be fine to take care of themselves, with or without a partner."

Now, take a moment and think about what it might be like to co-parent with a man with whom you have no financial entanglements. What if money never came between you and your kids' dad, and in the absence of that tension, he was more likely to see them when he said he would, and communicate more openly and freely with you? What if by letting go of that money—no matter how much he actually owes it to you and his kids—you ensured your kids gained a truly involved father, and you gained a really great co-parent?

If you currently depend on those biweekly or monthly payments, ask yourself: *How does that hold me back professionally, financially, and personally?* Do you find that you take measures to make sure your own income does not exceed a certain sum so that your child support payments are reduced or eliminated? What is the cost of that maneuvering to your career potential? Earning potential? Potential as a woman and mother?

If you find you are in a contentious relationship with your kids' dad in which it is a battle to collect child support, and you are adamant about seeing it through, here is what you do:

1. File all necessary papers with family court and ask the sum be deducted from his paycheck.
2. Move on with your life. Let it go. Let the courts do what they will (and they may not do much at all), accept that it is out of your hands, and refocus all your reclaimed energy on earning, saving, investing, and enjoying your kids and life.

If you currently receive child support, and it comes regularly and without major conflict, take steps to minimize it in your financial planning. That way, its significance is lessened in your plans and goals for your own success, and it will not set you back in the event those funds fail to materialize one month.

Set it aside in an account you do not depend on, say, a college savings fund for your children, or a savings account for an expensive sleepaway camp that is outside regular budgeting.

If you get support but it creates conflict or even tension between you and your kids' dad, brainstorm with him a creative way to take direct payment from him to you out of the equation. Automatic deductions from his paycheck or bank account are the easiest way. Or, set up a bank account that the two of you have access to, out of which extras like after-school activities, your son's orthodontia, and college investments are withdrawn. Alternatively, agree he will make specific purchases equivalent to the sum he owes his kids each month in child support payments. One study published in the *Journal of Marriage and Family* found that low-income noncustodial fathers were more likely to contribute financially if it went directly to their kids in the form of baby supplies, clothes, or even payments directly to the children's moms, rather than through the child support enforcement system. Why? By personally buying things the kids needed and used, they felt more appreciated and involved.

In my family, there is no financial requirement between my kids' dad and me. My income is higher, and it is only fair that I take on more financial responsibility, though he takes it upon himself to buy the kids' clothes, which he happens to really enjoy and has great taste in kids' apparel. I am thrilled about this arrangement, since I hate shopping and care little about fashion. Should our financial situations change (because, let's get real—life has taught us these things can change on a dime!), that equation may reverse.

Again, do what works.

While contention over support payments can drive a wedge between co-parents, money can also be the tie that binds.

On one hand, there is the story of Christine in Kansas, whose boyfriend of seven years moved to his hometown of London, UK, shortly after she gave birth to their son. Her kid's dad visited every year for the month of their child's birthday, and they planned for more frequent visits as the boy got older. On one recent trip, Christine and her ex agreed that he would pay for all of the day-care costs, since he didn't make any other financial contribution and nearly all of the parenting fell to Christine. He paid for three months, then stopped. "He said, 'Why should I pay when I don't get to spend time with him?'" When Christine pushed back with the argument that paying is only fair in light of the fact that all of the expense, time, and work falls on her shoulders, her son's dad responded: "But you get the enjoyment of raising him."

It is easy to let your blood pressure spike upon hearing such a statement, but pause for a moment and listen to what he is saying: Sometimes men connect parenting time with financial contribution. That challenges my moral compass, and I hope it does yours, too, but ultimately that is something you and I cannot change. If money comes between you and your ex, how can you more effectively make him feel involved with his kids, and therefore more financially responsible to them—and vice versa?

Consider Carla. Her boyfriend left when she was pregnant with their son, and moved in with another woman. He wanted nothing to do with the baby, and fought paying any support. Eventually, Carla took him to court, and was easily awarded payments.

> He never saw our son until child support ordered him to start paying, when he was 10 months old. He said, "You think I'd pay for him and not see him?" Like our son was a car: If he were making payments on a car, he'd make sure to drive it. I like to think that he is a good dad, but money is the only thing that motivates him to be involved.

It is hard to argue that Carla shouldn't take that child support if it motivates her kids' dad to be involved, no matter how twisted the logic may be. As in many parts of co-parenting—or any relationship, for that matter—sometimes you just do what works for the greater good, and take moralizing out of the equation.

EXERCISE

Take a very hard look at your child support and alimony situation. How is it working out? Does money come between you and your ex? If neither of you paid the other, would you be better co-parents? Do you seek or accept alimony? If either of these sources of income disappeared tomorrow, what would you do to replace—or exceed—that income? If you had your dream career, what would it be? Why aren't you pursuing that career? Would you be more motivated to pursue it if you were terrified of being broke, without a backup source of income? See what I'm getting at?

Good Guys Like Women Who Are Financially Independent

WOMEN WHO ARE financially independent of their exes are very attractive to men—especially successful ones. After all, rich men are very familiar with women who pursue them primarily for their financial assets.

Men receive so many toxic messages about dating and gold diggers, baby mamas, and other mooching women. There are indeed plenty of women in the world seeking men to take care of them financially. As I will say throughout the chapters on dating: Men are people, too! Men, like other humans, crave love and acceptance for who they are—and any whiff that you are after their paycheck sends them running. This is especially true, I've found, for men who are older than, say, their early thirties and have been through a divorce or other big breakup. Pretty much everyone hates paying child support, and anyone paying alimony believes the other party is a lazy, entitled, conniving mooch. This is not my judgment. This is what men believe about their exes if they support them financially.

Early in my dating, I fell for a successful media executive and dad of two little kids; he had extremely progressive, feminist politics. His ex had far more education than he did, and had been a stay-at-home mom for less than two years. My boyfriend had to pay her thousands of dollars each month in alimony, in addition to the mandated child support and extras, even though they shared custody and visitation time approximately fifty-fifty. They had been married less than five years, during which time they both had successful careers, though he out-earned her by more than a hundred thousand dollars. Over several months of dates (that we took turns paying for), he and I spent a lot of time talking about business, money, and divorce. "I am trying really, really hard to understand the morality of paying her all this money," he said over bites of Korean barbecue. "I want to do the right thing, and take care of my kids. But it just isn't fair." He was pissed, and understandably so.

Men like that then hit the dating market, and they are looking for women who are not like their exes. And if their ex-wives get a lot of their hard-earned money, these men are looking to date women who do not live off of their kids' fathers.

Charlie is a single dad friend of mine who owns a successful small business and pays his ex a lot of child support and alimony, which he of course resents (and ladies: He's cute and a great, 50-percent-time dad. E-mail me with your bio if interested). "I prefer dating women who are financially independent. Even the thought of paying more alimony and child support down the line for yet another ex (even if you want to believe the second time is the charm!) just brings the previous relationship into the new one, and complicates things."

Or, consider the thoughts of David, a tech executive I went out with a few times:

It would be hard to get excited about a grown-ass woman who gets alimony. Support wouldn't bother me; I know most dads don't show up and it's almost always necessary, but because of my history I'd be very sensitive to injustice in either case. I'm in a situation where my girls live with me more often than my ex, I'm far more active at school and after-school events, and pay for extracurricular expenses, yet I pay her more than full support for my income range. That sets a shit example for my girls, and any woman who seemed to be like that would be a real turnoff for me.

When You Pay Child Support
or Alimony

INCREASINGLY, it is women who pay child support and alimony, and their vitriol about the matter is often far more acute than when payer and payee fall along traditional gender lines.

Karen was the mom of a five-year-old when she filed for divorce after filing charges against her ex for domestic violence. She was then ordered to pay $275 per month in alimony to her ex, who fought for and won 50 percent custody, though he very rarely sees their daughter. "Paying alimony every month to an abusive, narcissistic man was one of the greatest challenges of my life—especially when things were very, very difficult financially, like forty-dollars-in-the-bank-account-and-seven-days-till-payday difficult," the Colorado mom told me. The resentment only added to her anger about problems in the marriage, including her now-ex's failure to work full time and spendthrift ways.

Talia was the breadwinner in her marriage, while her husband pursued a writing career, unsuccessfully. Today she pays him fifty-six thousand dollars per year, a requirement that forces her to stay in her high-powered corporate sales job, which requires she travel three nights per week—a schedule both she and her ex agree is far from ideal for their young kids, as her ex lives in a different city. She told me: "I'm working very hard on acceptance. I'm still resentful of having to pay him when I was such a supportive wife, never forcing him to work, letting him figure out his way through life. I spent years paying for everything while he went to graduate school, played around with a small business, spent thousands of dollars on writing coaches, and then took unpaid freelance work."

Talia says some eight years before the end of the marriage, she gave up on her ex's career, especially when it was clear his lack of work ethic was to blame. "When he did work, he'd go in late, come home early, and brag about spending all day on Reddit. Certainly I know it sounds like I allowed myself to be taken advantage of, and there is likely some truth to that. However, I never want to be the one who forces another to give up on their dreams. But before we knew it, I was light years ahead career-wise, emotionally, socially. Now that we are split it is like I let go of this heavy weight that kept dragging me down."

One of the most painful parts of alimony payments is the vitriolic comments both she and her ex face. "My family and friends are outraged that I have to pay, and pay so much. To my face, people in my life call him a freeloader, make comments about his manhood, and even his lack of fatherly duties since he technically does not pay child support since he is not employed. My father said it is my fault that I have to pay because I didn't force my ex to be a real man when we were married. My sister and mother think I should have forced it in court (even though what I negotiated through mediation is far less than a judge would have ordered), and my friends make comments about how he should just man up and not accept my money."

Talia contends with these comments by noting to the mudslingers that were gender roles reversed, they would likely not question alimony payments. She also reminds herself that the financial inequality in her marriage was, at least initially, born out of her love and support for her then-husband and his professional dreams. While she is looking for a job with a more flexible schedule, Talia says she does enjoy her career and the lifestyle it affords her family, and she's hopeful that her ex's shame about accepting alimony will be the impetus for building the career of his dreams.

Karen, on the other hand, has held back on her urge to pursue her lucrative former career as a nonprofit executive, for fear her ex will once again take her to court for alimony. "I know the more I earn, the more I will pay him, but I am still trying to clean up the financial pieces, and still just skirting by. It's difficult to imagine adding one more financial obligation on top of everything else, especially to pay someone who chooses not to work, or be an involved dad." She does recognize how that stifles her potential professionally, emotionally, and financially: "But, if I was earning more, I could pay off much more of my debt, much more quickly and not have to worry about that as much, leaving me more income." She's just not there yet emotionally, and therefore held back financially.

If you are a single mom who must pay alimony or child support, it is very important that you never, ever hold yourself back professionally or financially to spite your ex with lower payments, or illegally hide income (because committing a crime is stressful, as is jail time, no matter how flattering orange may be on you!), or stall your career goals in order to be required to pay him less. You do any of these things, you only give your ex your power. You live a smaller life rooted in anger, the world misses out on your talents, and you set a lesser example for your children. In the short term, money may be tight as you support two households, but in the long term, focusing on the big picture of growing your career and income will pay dividends in every single facet of your life, including your relationship with your ex.

If you pay your ex, here are some tools to help you manage resentment:

- Prioritize coming to peace with the situation. Tell yourself: "Within one year I will have accepted that I must pay him, and have adjusted my mind-set, budget, and career goals to make this work for me." Then, write down action steps for how you will do this. Earning more may mean you pay him more, but you will also earn more! This will mean not only more money but also that you will achieve career goals, take on more interesting and high-profile projects, interact with more successful and high-profile colleagues, and fulfill your potential, living within your power and not mired in resentment.

- Stop talking about it. Women paying alimony or even child support to men is a controversial and compelling topic, and your friends, family, nosy neighbors, and prying colleagues will be enthralled. They will have all kinds of nasty things to say about your ex, and many of them will be very sexist—if not completely satisfying to hear in the face of your own anger. While it's understandably satiating for a time, shut this cycle of complaining and validation down ASAP. Move on.

- Minimize interaction. At the very least, automate any payments via bank transfer so that you do not have to physically write and hand him a check or manually send him the monthly sum. Offer to pay future support in a lump sum via equity in a home, investment accounts, or a single cash payment. One single resentful payment is ultimately less painful and incites less hostility between co-parents than payments made bimonthly. In her mediated divorce, Sasha, a music executive, and her ex, a sculptor, calculated how much she will owe him in alimony and child support payments for the next ten years, when their three kids are scheduled to graduate college. That sum totaled her approximate equity in the home they shared, which she relinquished in lieu of paying painful monthly payments. "Sometimes I get really angry about it, especially since my family gave us the down payment for that house," she says. "Even though I have to start over in my retirement savings and currently live in a small apartment, I am so happy to be out of that marriage."

- Ask your ex to fund the kids' college savings plans. Part of Talia's agreement with her ex is that she pays him 28 percent of her annual bonus. He agreed this payment goes into their two children's 529 college savings plan.

- Accept that this is the price you had to pay to get out of a bad relationship. Whether the split was your idea or his, it matters not in the eyes of the court. What does matter is that it wasn't working for you as a couple, and now you are free to pursue a life and relationship that does work. Good things often come at a price. In your case, this is a financial price. As one divorce attorney told me: "I often have men come into my office, having saved wads of cash for years in a box in the back of the closet in order to be able to finance a divorce. It's like saving for a boat or retirement home on the beach." These men understood specifically the price they had to pay for the divorce they wanted.

- If you truly cannot afford your current lifestyle while making these payments, downgrade your lifestyle. Yes, it may seem unfair, but accept that this is your situation, at least temporarily, and embrace it. Focus on the fact that a smaller house is easier to clean, has a smaller impact on the environment, and teaches your children about materialism and your values. Replace resort vacations with road trips to spend time with family and friends, and appreciate how these relationships are deepened because of it.

- Remember that alimony and child support were a huge, wonderful feminist coup. How would you feel about a situation like yours if the gender roles were reversed? While alimony is ripe for reform, our current laws were designed to protect women and children who really had few other financial options. As the system slowly evolves to reflect current opportunities for both genders, there is a middle, gap generation that must pay the price, just as in any revolution. You are a revolutionary for this cause.

Andi told me: "I was resentful at first. I was the one who paid for our wedding, and the down payment on our house, and paid off his truck and so on . . . and it would have been extra easy to play the victim/pity card. However, I recognize that the laws that are in effect now that make me pay are the exact same laws that would protect me and help ensure I could carve out an existence for myself and my son if I had given up my career for our family and had been a stay-at-home-mom or if I had been less successful in my career. So I shut up and pay and am honestly thankful that I have the ability to support my son. Period."

- To be part of the solution for other families, find the advocates for alimony reform in your state and get involved.
- Peel away the layers of resentment, which are rooted in what happened during the relationship. Jessica recognizes that her ex had little motivation to build his writing career because she never demanded he be financially responsible to the family, including taking over childcare duties when he was between jobs. Resentment toward others is nearly always rooted in resentment for ourselves, and the role you played in cocreating the situation. If you are bitter about paying your ex, explore why and how the situation came to be, and own any part you played in it. Did you enable your ex's lack of motivation? Did you cocreate a situation in which you felt more powerful because you earned the money or had the higher-profile career? Did you dream of saving your low-earning spouse from a flailing business, martyr-style? These are all common and very normal scenarios. Aim to understand the root of what happened. Forgive yourself. And aim to forgive him, too.
- Just decide to let it go. Said Caitlin: "We have a fifty-fifty custody arrangement but I pay child support due to our income disparity. We also split extracurricular costs, nanny costs, medical costs, and other expenses based on income share. Since I cover a larger portion of these expenses, in addition to support,

I feel like I get completely screwed in this arrangement. But I agreed to it and it's not worth it to me to fight about at this point. Money was always a big issue with us when we were married, so it's no surprise that it continues to be in divorce."

- If you truly believe you are paying too much, weigh carefully the costs of revisiting the issue legally, and do your best to approach this as a practical process and not an emotional one. Ask yourself: *Am I seeking reduced payments because I believe legally it is the right thing to do? Or am I really trying to punish him for being such a dickhead?*

- If it is a matter of returning to family court to amend child support payments because your ex's income has increased or yours has decreased, or one of your kids has aged out of your agreement, make hasty work of the process, and calculate the time, energy, likely conflict with your ex, and other negatives before launching a campaign for revisions. Likewise, if you are seeking to reduce alimony, consider the likely large legal fees and related time and stress in your future against the likelihood that payments will be reduced. In other words, apply the time + money + energy equation with a level head.

- Never tie time with your children to payments. In some states, child support payments are calculated based on how much time the kids spend with each parent. That system is rife with issues, including that paying parents often fight for more time with their kids in order to owe less in support, but then fail to see their kids as ordered by the court agreement. The result is disappointed kids, the frustrated other parent, and a clogged family court. This system reduces kids to collateral. Do not be part of the problem.

- Hard as it is, do not threaten to stop paying your ex. As you co-parent, there will be lots of reasons to fight. You may never completely rid yourself of resentment about paying him, and that is very human. But try your very, very hardest not to threaten him with nonpayment of support. There are likely serious legal ramifications if you do. And there are definitely negative consequences for your relationship. In other words: Try your damnedest not to threaten.

- Refocus your rage into fuel for earning more. In most states, child support and alimony payments are capped—but when it comes to how much you can earn, the sky is the limit. I have seen so many fabulous cases of people who after becoming single moms harnessed financial stress to gloriously successful professional lives. Make this your story. After all, you likely have little control over how much you have to pay. But you have 100 percent control over how much you can earn.

- Remember: Everything is temporary. You could lose your job or ability to earn, and the financial tables could turn at any time. Kids age out of child support, and your ex could become far more successful than you'd thought he was capable of. Acceptance tempered with hope and kindness are your BFFs. This is a call for grace.

Rachel for a time received child support from her ex, but when she started earning more and he lost his job, she was obliged by the courts to pay him support. She chose to pay him more than required, even though the years when he paid were riddled with skipped payments and snide comments about how his obligation was too much.

I pay more than what the state has mandated, and wrote it as such in my modified custody order. I also buy more things on top of that because that is my child, and I want her to have a certain quality of life while she is with her dad. I can say without a doubt that going through this modification has set aside a lot of the resentment between my daughter's dad and me. He finally understands how expensive it is to raise a child, and that child support doesn't go far. I have no issues about it at all and I am very happy to give more when I can. I think my ex also appreciates what it was like for me when I was struggling financially. Now that we traded places we have a much better and very flexible co-parenting relationship. And my daughter is so much happier because there is less hostility between us.

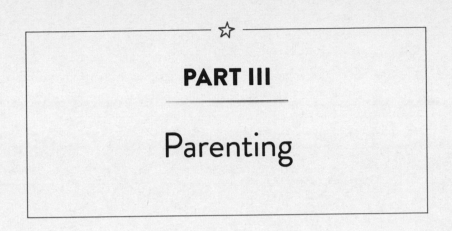

PART III

Parenting

Parenting and the Single Mom

JUST LIKE WORKING MOM GUILT holds women back from living their full potential as professionals, mothers, and women, single mom guilt holds unpartnered parents back in countless ways. The most common message to parents of all family types is that divorce is horrible for children, and all social ills are rooted in the recent surge in single motherhood, most especially *unwed mothers* (eek! Unmarried women having sex *and babies*!). If you are inclined to unconsciously buy into this thinking (and therefore hold yourself back unnecessarily), do not under any circumstances google "Ann Coulter + single mothers." Also, remove from your mind President Reagan's admonishment of the "welfare queen" (whom no one was ever able to find, and who in fact was a propaganda construct), or George W. Bush's $1.5 billion failed Healthy Marriage Initiative, aimed at curbing all the supposed misfortune rooted in the upward trend of unmarried moms.

Instead, a growing body of research finds that children who grow up in single parent households are not sentenced to lives of poverty, crime, or addiction simply by way of their parents' marital status. In fact, by many metrics, the majority of kids who grow up with single mothers fare just as well as their peers raised in traditional, nuclear, two-parent families. For example, in one study of 1,700 children by Cornell University researchers, found that single mothers' education levels and abilities as parents had far more influence on their children's academic abilities than their relationship statuses or even incomes—and this was true for all races.

In fact, lots of research comes to the same surprising conclusion: It matters little the family structure that a child grows up in, though it matters a lot the dynamics of that family. For example, there is no evidence that divorce is universally bad for kids. Children whose parents have a high-conflict marriage fare better after their parents break up, and the vast majority of children of divorce do just fine within a few years of the split. One nationally representative study of all kinds of family types found that it didn't matter if the children were adopted or if the parents were married, single, or remarried. What does matter, found the study, published in the *Journal of Marriage and Family*, was whether the home was ruled mostly by harmony or by acrimony, and whether the children experienced a warm, secure environment or a cold and neglectful one. Research also found that children raised by single mothers tended to have closer relationships with extended family like cousins, aunts, uncles, and grandparents, and other adults in their lives. This, I will argue, is something most Americans could use more of.

In other words, family is indeed what you make it, and you can create that warm, secure, and loving home life that is the springboard for a healthy child, regardless of what your family looks like. Just as you have countless opportunities to build a career and earn, you also have the freedom to build a family that you are proud of, to raise wise, hardworking, loving, and kind children. You can and will build not only a home life in which you and your children thrive, but a larger web of loved ones and community members who rise up and support you—and whom you also support in return.

That said, I won't sugarcoat this: There is plenty of very legitimate research that finds that children raised by single mothers are more prone to not-great outcomes, including teen pregnancy, dropping out of school, and incarceration. However, studies also point out that correlation does not automatically equal causation. In the most stark contrasts between kids raised by single mothers and those raised in two-parent households, when controlled for poverty, maternal depression, and lack of support, outcomes are more or less the same.

Another factor in the outcome for kids: All children fare better when both parents are actively involved and co-parent amicably. In this part, I will elaborate on how to promote a relationship between your children and their father, and how to fill in the gaps when he is not involved—and understand that an absentee father is not a life sentence for a lousy existence for your son or daughter.

Many studies found that poverty associated with single motherhood is the common thread in families that fare worse than two-parent households—not the solo parenting in and of itself. It's not rocket science why. With just one income and no second parent to help with childcare, single parents have to work more to pay for the basics, and have higher childcare costs and fewer dollars for music and sports lessons, SAT prep tests, healthy food, or real estate in safe neighborhoods. Plus, poverty, or any financial hardship, is tied to depression, anxiety, and generally being a stressed-out mom with less patience for her kids and more arguments with the adults in her life.

I know this firsthand. Over the years, when money has been tight, I find myself yelling at my kids more, and feeling especially resentful toward their dad for various perceived slights. *If he helped out more, I could work more and earn more and wouldn't be so freaking overwhelmed!* I scream in my mind. Then, lord help him, if he asks to pick up the kids thirty minutes late I'm far more inclined to rip him a new one if I'm worried about paying the mortgage than if I just scored a fat new contract and am lounging around in the new pair of overpriced sweatpants I just bought with the spoils. Money doesn't make single moms happy, but it makes you less unhappy, and this is just one of the many reasons that the money section is positioned at the start of this book.

One of the most cited studies about single mothers is the harm caused to children by the instability of boyfriends moving in and out of their home and lives. Leading researcher on single mother families Sarah S. McLanahan, of Princeton University, found that children raised by single mothers (who tend to be younger and poorer than married moms) are more likely to struggle academically because these single moms have less stable relationships with their children's fathers, and men overall, with new boyfriends and their children moving in and out of the family home. It is fatherlessness and poverty—not divorce or separated families per se—that put kids at risk. McLanahan writes in several posts on the *Children and Family Blog* (one of my favorite sources of research on all things family):

> We found that divorce and separation play a limited role in shaping children's cognitive abilities, such as language and mathematical skills, which are tested in conventional school examinations. Maternal education and poverty are much more important in this area. In contrast, family instability plays a much bigger role than mothers' education or poverty in the development of "social-emotional" skills. For example, family instability has twice as much influence as poverty does on whether children develop aggressive behavior. It is on par with poverty in causing childhood anxiety and shyness.

In another posts, she writes:

> There are considerable costs of such changes. For example, in a household whose children have several fathers, some men may be reluctant to pay child support. A father may feel that, because another man's child lives there, he cannot control how his own financial contribution is spent. Likewise, mothers may hinder access to children fathered by ex-partners. So, whereas fathers in intact parental relationships are spending much more time than in the past with their children, they are often spending much less time, or perhaps

none at all, when separated from the mother. In short, in unstable households, there are disincentives for parents to operate in a way that maximises the use of their time and money in favour of the children.

This research is important, and I urge you to heed it. But do not let it scare you into celibacy, or shame you into sneaking or lying about your romantic life, or keep you up late worrying that decisions that led to this point have sentenced your children to a crappy life.

Far from it.

This research highlights mothers' relationship instability, which is within your control. The research is not about financially independent, unmarried moms who date different people without committing to them. The risks associated with partner instability have little to do with men who do not live in your house, who are not automatically designated boyfriends and do not move in with their children or spur other major life changes that come with serious, committed relationships. The risk of negative outcomes for your kids, we can assume, plummets if you have a healthy attitude about romance, and are financially stable enough that you are not compulsively tempted to cohabit out of financial destitution rather than healthy commitment to a shared future with a person you love.

Consider Sinead, a single mom going through a tough time after her divorce from her longtime husband. While her career as an insurance agent was stable, paying the bills for her two preschool kids was tough. In addition to the normal heartbreak, loneliness, and stress of her divorce, her parents' disapproval of the breakup weighed heavily on her. "My folks have been together since they were fifteen years old, and all my life I saw them as the ideal: completely committed to each other and their family, enjoying all the same hobbies and friends. It was a hard act to live up to—as evidenced by my divorce!—but especially so since what they have is so special. And they haven't been especially approving of my breakup."

Shortly after her husband moved out, Sinead started dating a man she'd met through work, even though she knew he struggled with alcoholism, and had been arrested for domestic violence during his marriage to his twin daughters' mother. Both were stressed about money and overwhelmed with caring for their kids, so the couple quickly moved in together, and attempted to blend their families while sharing expenses. Needless to say, things quickly imploded. The boyfriend's drinking escalated, and the related fights were worse than those during Sinead's marriage. Three years later, her boyfriend moved out. Sinead has landed on her feet financially, but both she and her children are now in therapy, dealing with post-traumatic stress due to the situation. "I was so scared to be alone, and so sure that the best thing for all of us was to find what my parents have. I figured that if I had someone at all, and had some help with bills, it would be better than no one. I realize now that is so messed up. I wish I'd just calmed down and settled into being a single mom for a while, dated and tested the waters. I'm not sure I'll ever get married again, or even live with a man, though I look forward to dating again when I'm ready."

Sinead's story illustrates what research finds: Cohabiting adults, especially those in a stepparent scenario, are less stable than both a married biological parent household *and* a single mother–led home. Likewise, divorce rates, especially those when children are involved, are far higher in second and third marriages than in first marriages.

You may not be able to control right this moment whether you have a supportive, loving romantic partner, or a seamless co-parenting relationship. But you do have a lot of control over how much you earn, spend, budget, and save, and how that affects your quality of life, in direct and indirect ways. Financial power is just one part of a huge parenting equation over which, as a solo mom, you have enormous power. Who lives in your home is another important thing you have power over.

☆

The Argument for Equally
Shared Parenting

As I WRITE ABOUT CO-PARENTING, I preface the topic with
this:

I do not take any sort of abuse lightly, ever, and know that actual
abuse is under-reported, and under-prosecuted. That said, I also
know—as any family attorney, judge, and researchers in the field
knows—that false abuse claims abound in custody and visitation dis-
putes.

The biggest, most heartbreaking surprise of writing so extensively
about separated families over the past few years has been learning
about how many children grow up without their fathers. According
to the most recent survey from Pew Research, just 22 percent of fathers who live separately from their children see their kids more than
once per week, and 27 percent never see their kids. I admit that
shocked me, and I am very guilty of living in an East Coast progressive bubble where many separated families more or less mimic the
Gwyneth Paltrow Conscious Uncoupling model.

Absentee fathers are not specific to any race, geography, or income. In fact, contrary to many assumptions, African American fa-

thers of separated (and married) families spend more time with their kids than any other race.

If you ask the mothers of these children about their kids' fathers' involvement, the response tends to be a heartbreaking description of men who choose not to see their kids, move away from where the children live and visit them infrequently, fail to contribute financially, and often remarry and start new families elsewhere. Incarceration is a huge part of the absentee father issue in this country, which is only exacerbated by child support mandates that often keep fathers in a perpetual cycle of payment arrears and imprisonment, which stifles their employment opportunities, leading to more arrears, more prison sentences, and less contact with their children.

It is easy to dismiss a whole generation of men as crappy fathers and men. But the situation is much more complex than that, and also removes from all responsibility you and me: the mothers of the children we share with these fathers.

While media headlines and politicians for decades have screeched about deadbeat dads and fatherlessness, there is a large and important movement to connect fathers with their children by changing both the courts system as well as attitudes about men's ability to parent.

"The presumption in the media and in our culture is that fathers are dolts like Homer Simpson, putting the diaper on with a staple gun, and mothers are clearly the better parent," says Terry Brennan, cofounder of Leading Women for Shared Parenting, the organization spearheading changes in state laws to presume that in the event of divorce or separation parental custody will be shared, and visitation time shared as equally as possible, with a minimum of 40 percent time with each parent. "Instead, there are vast sums of research that find that fathers are just as important to the well-being as mothers, and just as capable of bonding with their children. While there are some fathers who don't want to be involved, the majority of dads genuinely want to be an active part of their children's lives—and should be."

There are forty-three academic papers that support shared parenting, concluding that at least 35 percent of time with each parent is required for a child to truly bond with them. It is the simple quantity of hours at each parent's home and the ability to relax, develop routines and rituals, and share in the mundane rhythms of life that bond a parent and child. The flip side of this organic, close bond is the compulsion of often well-meaning fathers who default to the Disney Dad (also called Uncle Dad) routine that can be easy to slip into when time together is so short, as it is in the current presumption of every other weekend and Wednesday dinners that has dominated family court settlements for decades.

But there are other, critical reasons that shared parenting should be the standard in every separated family, barring abuse. Study after study find that children fare better when their parents' split and subsequent communication is low conflict, and conflict between parents is dramatically reduced in equal and shared parenting arrangements. Perhaps most important, fathers are far more likely to remain involved and active with their children when the conflict is low, and courts, culture, and their co-parents expect and promote active involvement. By some measures, in cases where "standard" visitation is awarded—every other weekend—fathers become depressed and uninvolved, and within three years, one study found, 40 percent of children in an unequal visitation arrangement had lost complete touch with their noncustodial parents, which are nearly always the fathers.

One book on this subject, *The Equal Parent Presumption* (an important but boring tome written for policy makers, lawyers, and mental health professionals), promotes an "Equal-Parental-Responsibility Presumption," arguing that the current mainstream model, which grants one parent primary residential custody, is based on an idea that the other parent has "access" or "visitation" to his children. It is a powerful mind-set shift away from being arbitrarily *granted minimal visits* with your kids to automatically being *held responsible* for your children.

Today, twenty states are considering shared-parenting legislation, and Utah and Arizona have successfully adopted laws that default to maximize residential time with both parents, without forcing the deciding judge to explain why. In both states, the outcomes have been positive, and other states are paying attention and making changes. Whether you like the idea or not, there is a good chance the judge will force you to share more equitably time with your kids' father, regardless of whether you are already.

This can be a very difficult thing to accept, and I suffered bitterly at the hands of my parenting arrangement.

When I was going through my divorce, there were very real medical considerations, owing to my ex-husband's brain injury. He acted completely different from before the accident, and I was traumatized by the situation, and by the thought of a man who was so different caring for "my" kids overnight, which he fought for.

At the time, my rationale was this:

The kids are tiny, he is unpredictable, I am the mother, one is a nursing newborn, and because I don't have a brain injury, and because I am the mother, I am by default entitled to a bigger vote in this matter. And my vote is to have the kids nearly always with me, with short visits with their father until his behavior changes.

Also, what I didn't share with the (superfreaking expensive) lawyers was my own broken heart, which bled with these thoughts: *I love being a mom so much and I cannot bear for one moment to be without my kids. I am the mother! They are supposed to be with me! The baby is nursing, for crying out loud! They will be traumatized by a separation from me that they cannot understand. And I cannot bear to think of being away from them for days at a time!*

I literally got out a calculator at one point, and counted the sum of time the proposed schedule would allot me versus my ex, praying the percentage would tip grossly in favor of my identity as a primary parent that I so wanted—and felt entitled to.

My attorney told me what to expect from a judge: *Tough shit.*

Because my ex had never hurt the kids or otherwise put them to any harm, because he wanted so much to have shared parenting, he was presumed to be a competent parent and therefore should have the kids a reasonable amount of time, including overnight visits.

Fast-forward a few years and our biggest point of contention is my push to transition to a parenting arrangement that is closer to fifty-fifty. In the ensuing years, my kids' dad has indeed fought to recover and is truly an involved and very safe parent. I actually now want less time with my kids, for a variety of reasons, including that I believe that morally he should have equal time with the kids, and has equal responsibility to care for them half the time, as well as that I want both my son and daughter to see men being equal parents.

I share my own story to share with you: I get it. I get what it is like to feel like you are losing your kids. I get that you think he is not as good a parent, and the kids are better off spending time with you. I understand that you had a very clear idea about what family life should look like, and this new arrangement of the kids half the time here and half the time there is an aberration by comparison. I get all of it. Those feelings are real, and valid.

But courts may challenge you, and that can be a bitter pill to swallow. Not to mention a confusing one.

On one hand, the world is changing very quickly in a positive way that promotes and supports fatherhood, which is good for everyone. But the world and our culture continue to tell you and me that as mothers, we know what is best for our kids, are the better parents, and should of course have a bigger say in how the kids are raised, and they should spend the majority of time at our house. We also get the message that as mothers, we should crave being with our kids all the time (you know, as that fulfilled full-time stay-at-home mom), and we are lesser mothers for relinquishing parenting time to the other parent.

I understand that, and yet I still sometimes feel a twinge of the golden uterus complex that suggests, wrongly, that *mother knows best*.

However, I am here to tell you: We have to let that go, for the sake of our kids, and for ourselves, too. You and I and everyone else who has a say in matters of families have an obligation to allow fathers a fair and equal chance to exercise their rights to parent, so that some of these painful kinks will be ironed out for our sons and daughters and future generations. After all, our culture that tells couples that moms are competent and dads are bumbling fools informs how men behave inside marriages. Many moms report that their now-exes blossomed into fatherhood after divorce or a breakup, partly because they were forced to, without a second adult always in the house as backup, but also because the mother is not there to micromanage and dictate childcare. In other words:

Give the guy a chance and he will likely surprise you.

Take it from Kelly. One of the biggest points of contention in her marriage was that she felt that her husband, James, didn't do his share around the house or with the kids. He also didn't contribute enough financially, a point that drove much of their decision to split parenting time fifty-fifty, since they live in a state where support is tied to visitation. "He was so broke, he couldn't afford to pay attention, much less child support," Kelly joked, wryly. "I don't think he really wanted to have the kids half the time, but he couldn't afford it any other way." Much to everyone's delight, the new demands of full-on parenting every second week pushed James into his fathering potential. He flourished in his role as an equal father, becoming very involved in their son's and daughter's homework, practicing sports with them after school, and planning camping trips and other meaningful activities that he would have passively relegated to his wife when they were married. "At first he didn't like it, but ultimately being a single dad made him a better father, and everyone benefited from it," Kelly told me.

James and Kelly's once contentious relationship mellowed into one of mutual respect and warm cooperation for their children, and their weekly handoffs were amicable. James and their son and daughter were not the only winners in this story. Kelly also benefited big time.

Yes, she has the satisfaction of knowing her children have a wonderful father, she has a true co-parent whom she can count on to discuss things like their son's recent challenges at school, paying for college, and the occasional schedule juggle when one kid gets sick. If her ex were bitter about being only "allowed visitation" certain days, or angry about paying child support he felt he couldn't afford, those sorts of parental support would be far less likely.

Plus, there is the matter of time.

As any single mom without a great co-parenting relationship will tell you, it is the lack of free or flexible time that is the biggest strain in life. Kelly came to love her weeks off from parenting. In those newly free hours she started a real estate brokerage on the side, enjoyed dating, took vacations with girlfriends, and spent time at the gym. "Just coming home after work, ordering Mexican food, and watching stupid movies on Netflix is a great luxury many of my married moms are jealous of."

On my blog, a divorced friend shared in a hotly debated post called "My dream for my daughter is to be a single mom," in which she talked about the joys of shared parenting:

> My dream for my daughter is that she be in a loving relationship, and have a good ex-husband who really does a great job with the kids, 50 percent of the time.
>
> People forget the joys of divorce—sharing your kids without guilt and having alone/me time.
>
> I am a better mom as a divorced mom than a full-time mom who was stressed and distracted. Even though I love my child, having time away from her has allowed me to have and live a more complete life—and be a better mom when I am with her.
>
> Thanks to the fact my daughter is with her dad half the time, I have been able to nurture a lucrative career that I am very passionate about and proud of. There is so much less "mommy guilt" when I have to attend evening work events or travel, because it rarely means working around my child. I just go.

I also have time to exercise, enjoy vacations that are relaxing and involve lots of book reading, and I have had time to nurture a relationship with my new husband, with fewer of the stresses of blended families.

Plus, by the end of my kid-free week, I am recharged and ready to be a mom. If you have your kids all the time, they can sometimes suck your energy, leaving you little opportunity to recoup. My married friends can never compete with my Saturday or Sunday afternoon events and activities for my daughter and her friends. I'm the mom who throws the sushi parties, and spends afternoons with my daughter and her friends making cupcakes. I give my daughter some wonderful experiences because I miss her and want our time together to be special and memorable. And because I work full time, I have the financial resources to take her on trips and other special activities.

My sister is a married, working mom with two kids and she can barely get away to go to the gym. She feels guilty when leaving her kids with a nanny or babysitter because they are in day care all day. If her husband takes the kids, then she spends time alone without him. They lose their connection as a couple and become workhorses sacrificing for their children—the very reason so many marriages end in divorce.

From a purely financial standpoint, it is far easier to take courses, earn an advanced degree, attend networking events or conferences, or work late if many days during the month you don't have to rush home to relieve a nanny or pick kids up from after-school care. But the most immediate reason why you must promote equal, shared parenting with your kids' dad is that it promotes a close, involved relationship between both parents and your shared kids, and reduces the chances that dads will disengage from their kids' lives. Equally shared parenting is the best insurance that your kids will successfully transition to the rest of their lives.

How to Parent Without a Father

I N THE UNITED STATES, the majority of fathers who live separately from their children are not actively involved. The issue of fatherlessness in the United States, as well as worldwide, is incredibly large, complex, and devastating. The fallout from fathers not being frequently and closely involved with their children is tragic—for those children who do not get to know their dads and, often, their paternal extended families; and for the mothers who are then fully responsible for caring for their children without a co-parent or regular breaks. It is important, too, to recognize that fatherlessness is also devastating for the fathers, who do not have the pride of fulfilling their parenting duties, or the joy that is singular to knowing and raising a child.

If your children's father is alive but not part of your lives, there may not be anything you can do to change that, and I recognize in you a heartbreak for both your children and yourself. You worry about your children's self-doubt in the absence of a dad, whether the scary statistics about fatherless children will manifest in your kids. You may find yourself full of resentment at the abandonment, the fact that the enormous task of raising a child has been dumped on you, and you alone. You may be enraged by his seemingly flippant freedom to choose whether to parent, while you had no choice at all. Meanwhile, you are left holding the proverbial bag, charged with figuring out how to explain to your child why his father does not see him, call him, or send gifts.

You might feel an incredible amount of shame and guilt about the fact your child does not have an involved father. Maybe you are angry at yourself because you worry you chose the wrong man, or that your actions drove him away. You are heartbroken, too, that your children do not have the father you'd want for them, and that your life may be harder—and therefore you feel you have less to give your kids—because of it. You stress that one day your children will blame you for their dad's absence, and that will irrevocably upset *your* relationship with them.

If your child's dad is not involved, or marginally involved, there are a few guiding principles for discussing your child's questions.

- Be honest. Don't say he died if he didn't. Never say, "He's working far away." Your child deserves the truth, even if it is painful for both of you to address.
- Be kind, and keep your feelings out of it. "Being a parent is really hard for some people, and your dad wasn't ready to be a parent yet."
- As you will do in your relationship with your child's father, as well as in your own heart, keep the door open to future improved relationships. At the same time, be very careful not to nurture false hope in your child. It's a tough balance, but an important one. Note the "yet" in the preceding sample script.
- Answer all their questions. Avoid saying things like "I'll tell you when you're older," or "We don't talk about that in our family." These create the notion of secrets, and secrets foster shame, self-hatred, and lack of trust.
- Focus often on the fact that yours is a whole family. In everyday conversation say, "In our family . . ." or "We believe . . ." or "Our traditions are . . ."

- Highlight the fact that there are all kinds of families, and every family is whole. Even if it feels silly, as you go through your day, or are watching movies or TV, point out gay families, interracial families, kids being raised by grandparents, multigenerational households, friends who live together, foster and adoptive families, how some groups of friends create families, and on and on. Then, name the people in your family—blood relatives, friends, your neighborhood network. Do this enough and nuclear, married, straight families start to seem like the weirdos!

- That said, do not dismiss or minimize pain that a child experiences by his father being absent from his life. It might be really, really hard to hear, but listen. It sucks to feel like he's the only kid at school whose dad isn't around. It hurts like hell when his birthday comes around and his father doesn't call. He worries he did something wrong, or he's unlovable, or deeply flawed—no matter how great you and his life are. My father was mostly not part of my life after age eight, and there was no space for me to talk about it. Growing up with my mom, I heard no positive stories about my father, and there was no room for any of us to ask questions, or to share hurt feelings about the matter. The few times I remember asking about my dad, I was just reminded of how good our life was, which only made me feel stupid and selfish for feeling so horrible for not having an involved father. I think my mom felt really bad about the situation, and didn't know how to deal with her own feelings, much less her kids'. Fast-forward to today, after plenty of therapy and other ways of processing my daddy issues, I now find myself answering my children's questions about why they don't know their paternal grandfather. While your son or daughter is not your bartender, talking with your child openly can be a wonderful way to heal your own heart, too.

- Do not always wait for your child to ask. For many reasons, your child may not bring up the fact that her father isn't part of her life. It is up to you to talk about it very early, even earlier than you may think reasonable. One day my daughter came home from preschool and said, "Today Sofia talked about how both our parents are divorced." She was three! Even as a toddler your child sees her friends with two parents. Movies, TV shows, and books are powerful messages, consisting almost always of a mother and father. It is your responsibility to address this, even if she doesn't initiate the discussion.

- Remember, life is long. The questions will continue throughout your life, and each conversation at each age will lend new perspective and healing for both you and your child, as well as your relationship with each other. Your kid's understanding and judgment of his other parent will evolve and change over time, even throughout his lifetime.

☆

For Single Mothers by Choice, "Who Is My Dad?"

I F YOU CHOSE to have a child without the participation of the father, there are special considerations other single moms don't face. It can be difficult for very young children to understand the concept of "choice mom"—whether your son or daughter came to be via sperm bank, agreement with a friend, adoption, fostering, or a relationship with someone who will not be part of your child's life.

There are no hard and fast rules for talking about paternity with your kid in this situation. Some guiding principles include many of the rules for communicating with kids whose fathers choose not to be involved—and your situation could very well fall in a gray zone between those two scenarios.

- Be honest, yet age appropriate. For very young children who ask why they don't have a daddy like other kids at preschool, you may say, "I asked a special man to give his seed so that you and I could create a special family. Our family also includes Grandpa, Uncle Ian, all of our pets, and our friends the Phans." For older children, a frank explanation of how they came to be is in order.

- Keep talking, keep answering their questions, and take responsibility initiating the conversation.
- Share what information you know about the father. Kids want to know what he looks like, his hobbies, where he lives, age, job, and other details. This helps your child understand herself, and who she is as a person.
- Share your own feelings about the situation, but don't dwell on them in your interactions with your child—your job is to inform and support your child. "I know it can be confusing and sad to try and understand why your dad and I decided that I would raise you. I was really sad about it for a long time, too. But some people realize they are not ready to be parents, and I respect your dad for knowing that about himself."
- Be frank and realistic about the chance of them meeting. Depending on the legalities surrounding your situation, let your child know if and when he can have access to his father's information. Let him know that it will be up to him whether he seeks out meeting, and that the man may not be interested. Let him know that you will support his decision, and it will not affect your relationship with him.

Co-Parent Like a Pro

ONE THING NO ONE TELLS YOU when you become a single mom: You have to maintain a relationship with your kids' dad. Think about it. You can eliminate pretty much anyone else in the world from your life. You can move away from and stop speaking to your family, break up with your friends, and leave you're a-hole coworkers in the dust when you take a new job.

But your ex will be part of your life, no matter what. Even if he passes away, you still have to manage his legacy by addressing him to your children. If he is incarcerated or is not involved, you still have to answer your children's questions about his whereabouts, history, your relationship together, and his personality traits.

More likely, you have to see him regularly, and negotiate matters as small as who will pick up your daughter after volleyball practice, or whose turn it is to have the kids on Thanksgiving. The two of you have to figure out big issues, like how to navigate a serious medical issue of one of your children, finance the kids' college, or designate a guardian in the event both of you die.

In other words, he is up in your grill all the time, and you are up in his, and the stakes for making this work are extremely high.

The number one reason that parents fail to be involved with their children is high conflict with the other parent. Robert Emery, PhD, author of the excellent *The Truth About Children and Divorce*, conducted his own study of couples in highly contentious relationships headed for high-conflict, lawyered-up divorces. With a literal flip of a coin, couples were directed either to continue on their path to court, wherein their lawyers would argue (and bill the crap out of them) and a judge would decide the fate of their family, or to go to mediation, which is a proven low-conflict, low-cost way for couples to negotiate a fair divorce with the help of a neutral third party, typically an attorney. Again, all of these couples were initially headed to court in a high-conflict divorce.

The results were astounding. Twelve years after the study, a full 26 percent of nonresidential parents who went through mediation saw their children once per week or more, while of those who went through a contentious court divorce, just 9 percent saw their children once per week or more.

The takeaway: Nonresidential parents, who by far are fathers, were three times more likely to check out of their kids' lives if they had a high-conflict relationship with the children's mother.

This book is designed for mothers in all stages of single parenthood, and you may be far beyond negotiating the initial split with your kids' dad. But that doesn't mean you can't take steps to improve your relationship with him and, by proxy, likely improve his relationship with your children.

There are many beautiful stories about separated parents co-parenting like true teams, respecting each other's strengths and challenges as parents and people, supporting one another, and sending a singular message of love, support, and security to the children. These parents get, intuitively, what research finds: Children fare best when both of their parents are actively involved in their lives and conflict is low (remember, kids in high-conflict marriages are the only ones who fare *better* after their parents divorce, though most kids fare well a couple of years out).

But the better your relationship is with your kids' dad and any other family members, the better it is for all parties involved—especially the children. In other words: Everything you failed to learn in marriage counseling you have to learn now. The sooner you get on board with this, the better.

Take it from me. In the months after my own breakup, my ex and I would get into shameful screaming matches in front of the kids. "They're so little; they won't remember," I'd tell myself. Helena was one, then two, then three, when one day her dad came to the door to pick her up and she sensed a brawl about to erupt. She parked her tiny toddler body between us, extended her arms, and erected her chubby little hands like a traffic cop. "You can't say ANYTHING!" she charged. "Only thing you can say is, 'How was your day?'"

With a couple of embarrassing exceptions (like an hourlong very loud and spicy discussion in the lobby of my large apartment building, where I know pretty much everyone—but, hey! At least it wasn't in front of the kids!), our disagreements have since been either vehemently hashed out via text or civilly discussed in person.

It took more than five years, but I am proud to say that today my ex and I can enjoy family dinners, discuss discipline challenges, and have even mentioned vacationing together in the future. A big part of this was our shift away from me seeing myself as the primary parent and both of us embracing equal roles in our kids' lives.

There are many ways you can do this, but in Valerie's case, she actively reached out to her ex and explicitly supported him in being a better father. It worked:

> The best advice after my divorce was from a counselor. I was complaining about the burden of having my kids most of the time because my ex (going through a period of self-loathing, pity, and guilt) was not taking the time to be with them.
>
> She told me that my kids needed me to be 100 percent of the mom I could be to them, but being 150 percent of the mom they needed

would not compensate for their dad being anything less than 100 percent of the dad they needed. I would be better off investing that extra 50 percent helping him be a better dad.

Something clicked in me and really shifted my perspective. It began with a discussion I had with their dad: "Our kids need more time with you. Our kids need you more involved in the day-to-day of their lives. Our kids need you to be 100 percent of the dad you can be. How can I help you?"

And I kept asking. Finally, one day he asked me to help him move furniture into his apartment so he could make it more of a home for them. I packed up some toys and clothes (and even dishes and cups the kids liked using) and took them to his apartment. I encouraged him to coach our son's baseball team and I helped with its administration. I encouraged him to take one of the kids to dinner to spend time one-on-one with them while I kept the other two. He became more confident as a parent. Once I started to give, he started to give.

That was more than five years ago. Our co-parenting relationship is balanced and in a very good place. It has been for a long time now—sometimes I forget it wasn't always.

One of the most important things you can do to support your kids' father's parenting is just that: Allow him to parent. Presuming he has not been legally proven to be an unfit parent, you must operate from the premise that he is capable of keeping the kids alive and is allowed to make all decisions when they are in his care. If you eventually have a great co-parenting relationship, you may find ways to cooperate on special diets, bedtimes, and discipline. Otherwise, he is allowed to be whatever kind of father he likes during his visits. This includes feeding them fast food, letting them stay up late, and allowing them to spend the night at his sister's house *even though you hate her so much about that thing that happened at your wedding.*

Do not call or text him or the kids frequently during their visits. Except for unusually long visits—which could be more than three or four days for very young children, or more than several weeks for older kids—do not call, FaceTime, text, or otherwise ask to engage with the kids. You must allow their dad to get into his own groove of parenting without your interference, and your kids should be allowed to get into the groove of life at their dad's house. I understand that you may miss them and worry they are having experiences that you will not share. I appreciate that this can be sad. But this is part of separated family life, and the sooner you embrace the wonderful benefit of having an actively involved, loving dad and fill your kid-free time in a meaningful way, the sooner these absences will stop being sad, and all parties involved can relax and flourish in the rhythms of your life. Plus, your children will sense if your calls stem from your own broken heart, and feel a need to care for you. That is not children's job.

I had an a-ha moment about these calls the first summer my kids went with their dad to Greece to visit family. They were to be gone for three weeks, and intellectually, I knew they would be well cared for by loving grandparents and aunts and uncles, not to mention their father. I realize now in hindsight I suffered some post-traumatic stress from the horrible accident that my ex had suffered, which also took place in Greece. I asked him, and he agreed, to touch base with me every day, and to let me talk to the kids every few days, while they were gone. After a week of this constant contact, I realized that it was no good for any of us—I imagined that the constant communication took away from my kids' dad's ability to relax, my kids were interrupted in the fun they were having with their cousins, and I wasn't fully enjoying my own time traveling in Scandinavia, where I was at the time. Enough! Since then, now when the kids are away with the other parent for more than a few days, we touch base once or twice during that separation, and everyone has a fabulous vacation with plenty to share upon our reunion.

If you struggle to get your kids' father actively involved, it may take a lot of time and trial and error. Identify the things that are important to him in parenting and as a person. Does he appreciate being able to provide financially? Find ways for him to take the kids shopping for school clothes. Does he enjoy encouraging their sports? Ask him to be responsible for taking the kids to practice, or to choose the league or make other athletics decisions.

I started paying more attention and found that the things that were important to my ex would never have occurred to me. One example is that he wants to feel included in things he has legal rights to be involved with per a co-custody agreement, including even routine medical and education decisions. When I noticed our daughter's teeth were a little wonky, I begrudgingly asked neighborhood parents for an orthodontist recommendation, signed up for expensive monthly appointments, and paid for her retainer. This, to, me, was just another pricey, time-consuming parenting chore. To my children's dad, it was a decision he wanted to be involved with, to feel included. He spoke up, hurt, that he had been excluded. He was right, and I was wrong, and I started to include him in more such decisions. I since have made it a point to ask for his input when the kids needed after-school care, or to switch pediatricians when our insurance no longer covered the one we'd had. It doesn't matter that he pretty much always defers to my suggestion, or that I am the one coordinating the decision and paying for it. The more involved he feels, the more involved he is, and the better our relationship is—everyone benefits. For example, one of my priorities is keeping the kids on a schedule, and ensuring that they get enough sleep. Once we started communicating more, and being more empathetic to each other's priorities in the best interest of the kids, their dad became more conscientious about getting the kids to me on our agreed-upon time, and bringing them early when they need extra sleep.

It may take time to figure out what works, as in Valerie's family. After all, most dads still have a minority time with their kids, and may have been marginally involved when you lived together. He can change, and things can get better. But he needs space and support to find his parenting rhythm. Nagging and fighting with him over the minutiae, such as the type of laundry detergent he uses on the kids' sheets, only makes him want to be involved less.

In our case, my ex has stepped into fatherhood in a way that may not have happened had he relied on me as the in-house mom who often felt so taken for granted. He has also stepped into fatherhood in a way that he may not have if I had continued to insist on how things went down at his house, or otherwise behaved as if I'm the primary, better, wiser parent—instead of one of two parents tackling the chore of parenting and loving the same two tiny people.

In the past year we've shared some very warm times—like joking about NPR shows while watching our kids' soccer game, and cohosting a nail salon birthday party for our daughter and bowling birthday expedition for our son. I very much appreciate that he dominates when it comes to getting the kids to complete homework, and entertaining a mess of eight-year-old girls at a birthday party. When he drops the kids at my place in the evenings, he supports me by saying things like, "Don't forget to take your shoes off," and "Listen to what your mom just said: Go put your pajamas on." I make a point of saying nice things about him to the kids, especially in front of him, and he does the same. A few months ago he texted me some cute pics of our son, Lucas, at a café, wearing a sweet smile and a hot-chocolate mustache. "We make good-looking kids," I texted back. "Yeah, we do," he replied.

One thing I have made a big point of that has helped both my kids and me is to make a point of sharing stories about their dad and me from before we broke up. Part of this is to inform my kids about their origins, and to show them that they came from a loving relationship between two people who love them very much. Sharing these stories also helps me remember good times, and keeps those times alive as family lore. An example of our oral history experience started when our daughter began asking about how her dad and I met. After the part about how he was a TV cameraman and I was a newspaper reporter, and we met covering a news story about a forest fire in Arizona, I told them about our early dates.

Their dad would pick me up to go out in his fifteen-year-old Honda Accord hatchback, which had been baking in the Southwest sun so long that all the dark blue paint had peeled off the hood. "It was July in Phoenix, and it was *sooo* hot, but the air conditioner barely worked, and felt like this"—I open my mouth as *wiiiide* as it can go and I huff out long, steaming breaths; the kids are giggling like piglets now—"and the seat belt buckle alarm broke, so even when we were strapped in, it would go, *beep, beep, beep, beep, beep, beep,* during the whole date." They are going absolutely bananas by this point. "I didn't care that your dad had a hooptie, and he didn't care I'd arrive at the fancy restaurant all sweaty and stinky, because we were falling in love." Every once in a while Helena and Lucas bring it up, and ask to tell the story with me. My assignment is to wheeze out the hot air while, at the same time, they chime in with the beeps—a trio of raconteurs, keeping alive our shared history.

I've come to accept that my ex is an old friend now, someone I love and who is in my life in a way that I could never have predicted when I married him twelve years ago, but that is no less significant. I admit that it still is not easy between us, but we both try very hard, and I think we both recognize that the other is a good person and a good parent, as evidenced by how awesome our kids are turning out. I give him a lot of credit for that.

Your Relationship with Your Ex's New Girlfriend

THERE IS NOTHING I love more than a happy blended-family story. Maybe you find a great man or woman who becomes your romantic partner, and you, your kids, your significant other and his or her children, as well as your extended circle of friends and family benefit. Love begets love and it can be a really beautiful thing. This really does happen, and it can happen to you. Your kids' other parent may be the one who finds the partner, and this can be a beautiful thing for your whole family, including you.

When Cass learned that six months after she and her ex-husband split, his mistress-slash-girlfriend was pregnant and they were getting married, she was furious. But it has been the best thing for her family. "He is still an asshole, but she is a gem, and a great mom and stepmom to our son," Cass says. Since the girlfriend stays home full time with her new baby, she also made herself available for after-school care for Cass's son—the girlfriend's stepson. "This has been a huge benefit to my career, since it frees me up so much to work longer hours without worrying about paying for extra childcare—or arguing with my ex over sharing the cost. Plus, she and I get along so well that it really facilitates a co-parenting relationship between all of us."

It can be incredibly difficult to put aside your hurt feelings for your children's father in light of his new relationship, but I urge you to work very hard to forge a partnership of at least a civil nature with your children's new stepparent (whether they marry or not). This is someone who will be spending a lot of time with your children and will have a lot of influence on the kind of co-parenting relationship you share with your children's father. Your relationship with the new woman can be either a fantastic partnership (as in Cass's case), or a giant thorn in your ass.

Even in the best stepparent relationships, there will be struggles. Some general guidelines for managing your relationship with your ex's new girlfriend:

- You don't have to be BFFs with her. Keep it polite and civil at first. Take it upon yourself to initiate conversation; be warm and welcoming.
- Give her the benefit of the doubt. She is in a difficult situation, too, and probably unsure of how to forge a relationship with you and the kids. Take the high road, forgive quickly, and take a leadership role in forging a relationship.
- If you hear about things happening that you don't agree with or are worried about, address these directly with your kids' dad. You two are the co-parents; she is not (at least at first).
- At some point if their relationship becomes serious, the three of you may choose to sit down and discuss parenting issues together.
- Things that should not happen: They don't call her Mom, she doesn't make major decisions about the kids, and of course they are safe and generally happy around her.

When You Should Meet the New Girlfriend (and Your Ex Meet Your New Boo)

THIS IS A NEW THING that people bicker over in divorce agreements: when each parent is to meet the other's new girlfriend or boyfriend.

This is unlikely to be upheld in court, and it is ridiculous.

The logic is based on the notion that your children should not be exposed to your romantic peccadilloes, and must be protected from bonding with partners who will only flit in and out of your life. The most common rule is that the kids are not allowed to meet a new partner less than six months after the relationship has started, and only after the other parent meets said partner.

Logistically, this is full of pitfalls. Who determines when the relationship started? What if the new partner is a childhood friend? What if you dated casually for years, but have only been committed for weeks? What if you have been monogamous and committed for five years, but your boyfriend lives out of the country and your kids interact with him a few days per year—do the same rules apply?

And, most important, what good can come of the other (jealous/angry/suspicious/threatened) parent "vetting" the new love interest?

If you don't like this new girlfriend's attitude/shoes/grammar—so what? There is not one thing you can do about it except throw a fit and speak poorly to your child about her dad's new friend. And if your ex doesn't care for the demeanor/small talk/profession of your new boyfriend, what's next? You have to break up? Not introduce the kids as planned? Do the men duke it out in an arm-wrestling match? Insane.

This provision is just one way that mothers try to control their exes, and jealous ex-husbands try to control their former wives, and it's a notion that is encouraged by divorce lawyers who know how contentious this topic can be.

If you are in the process of negotiating your custody agreement, skip this altogether. In the event that it is written into your agreement already, approach it with your ex. Say, "I've been thinking about that provision, and I think we should ignore it. I trust your judgment to bring decent people around our kids. After all, the more people who love them, the better. Good luck out there!"

Now, if you are the one interested in doing the introducing, I urge you to uphold the original agreement, including waiting those six months (will that really kill you?) and then introducing your new beau to your ex. Do this in the spirit of being honest and transparent for the sake of a trusting co-parenting relationship.

EXERCISE

If you are facing meeting a new partner of your co-parent, or your co-parent is meeting your new significant other, write down:

- What is your goal for your relationship with the new girlfriend? What is your goal for your kids' relationship with her and, as it relates, their dad?
- What are your fears about this meeting? What are your fears about the relationship?

- How realistic are these fears?
- Are these fears rooted in old issues—whether from your relationship with your kids' dad, childhood, or other past situations?
- What three things can you do to get off on the right foot with the new woman—or remedy a tense situation?

Finding Your Parenting Style

ONE OF THE THINGS I'm most grateful for from my single-mom journey is having the opportunity to explore what type of mother I really am. Raising children with a devoted partner with whom you jibe is an amazing experience, but so is parenting without compromising on every single little thing with another adult. I really appreciate the rituals and rhythms of my life with my kids, from our morning routines to bedtime, when we snuggle in my bed and read a chapter book, then the kids take turns doing somersaults across my body while laughing hysterically. I am free to more or less discipline how I like, and unlike when I was married, every single interaction with my children is not negotiated. The house is as tidy as I decide it will be, there are no adults arguing over how often towels should be laundered, and I am a happier woman and mom for it. I believe my ex is a better parent for the absence of these tensions, too, and the kids benefit in countless ways.

In recent years there has been a lot written about parenting research and trends, and what is and is not working for families. Just as science finds that children, moms, and the economy thrive when mothers pursue professional success (and I revel in this science), current presumptions about parenting style are also being thwarted. As a single mom, you are in a unique position to embrace these trends in ways that traditionally married moms may not be. After all, you don't have to negotiate with your children's father (as much), and you likely find yourself and your family in a period of transition ripe for a new approach to balanced family life.

One of the most important, glorious wrenches in the presumptions about parenting is the Free-Range Kids movement. Free-Range Kids, per the website, is devoted to:

> *Fighting the belief that our children are in constant danger from creeps, kidnapping, germs, grades, flashers, frustration, failure, baby snatchers, bugs, bullies, men, sleepovers and/or the perils of a non-organic grape.*

Tee hee! I'm a personal friend and professional fangirl of Lenore Skenazy, the founder of the Free-Range Kids movement and author of the book by the same name. Skenazy's work as a longtime journalist informs her admonishment that kids need to play, need independence, and require time away from their parents to thrive. Children are actually not at significant risk of fatal accidents, abduction, or other fear-inducing incidents perpetuated by the media and law enforcement. In fact, our world is much safer for children today than it was in the 1960s and 1970s, which we often imagine as a snuggly, safe utopia.

This ties closely to the stay-at-home mom myth that perpetuates the notion that children require many hours of high-intensity parenting all through childhood and beyond. This simply is not a fact—research found that for most of childhood, it matters not how many hours parents spend with their kids. In fact, over-parenting, a.k.a. helicoptering, creates anxious, incompetent young adults who struggle to make decisions and thrive on their own, much less move out of their parents' basements.

In the abstract, I completely support the Free-Range Kids movement, and believe that kids benefit when they have independence, responsibility, and the freedom to have experiences and challenges away from their mommies. It makes perfect intellectual sense.

But to a busy single mom, the movement also makes complete practical sense.

Helicopter parenting is an economic issue, and it is a parenting issue. If I am hovering over my kids at the perfectly safe playground all afternoon after school, those are hours that I am not working. I could hire someone to micromanage my children's after-school and weekend playtime, but then those hours wouldn't be free at all—I'd literally pay for them, and my kids would still be micro-observed and not free, either.

Because I personally do not enjoy the playground, I become resentful that I am not working, working out, watching HBO shows, having dinner with my friends, or doing other activities I enjoy, and I become a resentful mom. The more stuff you resent, the lesser parent you are. You know that. But, like most moms, you do a whole bunch of stuff that doesn't make sense because you feel guilty for not conforming to pressures to be the omnipresent mom.

Plus, playing freely is good for kids. One recent study by Canadian researchers found that kids who played unsupervised got more exercise; a study of six-year-olds found that children of "Free-Range Parents" who had more unstructured playtime were better at reaching goals and self-directing than kids who were told what to do all the time by their "Tiger Moms" (yes, the researchers used those terms!).

I hereby free you from that always-hovering Tiger Mom model, and urge you to let your kids walk to the bus stop by themselves, play outdoors without supervision, run errands for you in the neighborhood, and otherwise be a kid. This is good for the children and great for you as a mom, and it makes for a happier, healthier family dynamic. What's more, it is likely keeping our children safe.

Michelle Thomas, a psychologist, childhood sexual abuse survivor, and author of *Scared Selfless: My Journey from Abuse and Madness to Surviving and Thriving*, wrote in the *New York Times* about why she allows her nine-year-old to roam their town freely, and points out that child abusers are 90 percent of the time adults who the child knows, and who have been trusted to keep the kid "safe." Furthermore:

> Research on children's play suggests that when we don't allow our children to engage in so-called risky situations when they must face challenges and make decisions on their own, we rob them of the opportunity to develop self-confidence and risk management skills. In other words, we turn them into easy targets for the predators we are trying to protect them from.

Over-coddling kids in the name of safety is just one part of the story. Just look at our attitudes about chores. In a recent survey of more than a thousand US adults, 82 percent reported having regular chores growing up, but only 28 percent said that they require their own children to help out around the house. Recently, a Michigan single mom posted on Facebook a series of photos of her six-year-old son doing normal chores—laundry, making a sandwich, loading the dishwasher—in a feminist show of gender-neutral activities. The post went bananas, landing her a complimentary interview on *Inside Edition*, and also spurring a slew of critics calling the parenting "child abuse."

I'm not sure which is more insane: that doing chores for any child is news, or that chores are considered criminal.

Needless to say, I am firmly in the *kids should do chores every day* camp. I believe that all children should do chores, but in a single-parent household, that requirement is heightened. The point is *not* that with fewer adults in the house, your kids must step up and fill the chore divide left by a would-be husband. The point is that despite any inklings of guilt that your kids don't have a "perfect" family, it is not your job to overcompensate and spoil them. You are also not doing them a favor if you let them off the hook for doing their chores because you want to enjoy your shortened time with them. Just like you cannot afford to make financial decisions as a single mom, you cannot afford to make parenting decisions as a single mom!

Much to the contrary. Instead, the message to your children is: "We are a family, and in every family, each member must contribute. I contribute by working to earn money, which pays for our house, food, electricity, vacations, and car. I do the shopping and shovel the snow. You have a set of chores as part of this family, and you are expected to do them every day, just as I go to work and make sure we have food every day."

One common challenge for single moms is how tricky it can be to spend one-on-one time with your kids. Before I share my trick for this, let me emphasize that it is important to teach your kids to play by themselves. All this guilt that encourages moms to feel bad for stealing precious parenting time from children by way of work, or single parenthood, or personal time, pushes parents to spend *too much time* with their kids. As the aforementioned studies found, kids who are always scheduled can't figure out how to do stuff by themselves!

Plus, face it: You don't want to entertain your kids all the time. That is annoying, and steals from your productivity and enjoyment of motherhood, not to mention *life*.

So force kids to play by themselves. At my house I say: "When we get home from this movie, everyone is going to have alone time." That, of course, includes me! Everyone can do what they want, except be on electronics, and the idea is that each member of the family entertains him- or herself. The kids typically read, play Legos alone or together, cook, color, lie on their beds and stare at the ceiling, tease the cat, or jump rope. If you have a house and a yard, send them outside!

This is important when it comes to my trick about one-on-one time. I borrowed this from parenting expert Amy McCready, author of *The Me, Me, Me Epidemic*: Implement what I call "mommy time" each day.

Amy calls it "heart and soul time," which my kids would recognize as completely not my style, but the point is to make it your own.

This can be literally just ten minutes each day devoted solely to one-on-one time with your child. The kid decides what it will be, and everyone puts away their electronics. Your other kids have to go play alone. At my house, this can include my daughter choosing to wake up early to cook breakfast with me; my son likes to build luxury Lego boats. We sometimes play checkers, read books, watch *Bob's Burgers* or Melissa Clark's cooking segments on NYTimes.com. Trust me on this: Ten minutes each day is *magical*. Your kid gets so much out of that time, feels so connected and cared for and special, and you will, too. Sometimes we get out of the habit of mommy time, and things at my house get out of whack. Within a day of reinstating these special one-on-one segments, our whole lives run smoother.

EXERCISE

Create a family manifesto for your household. Write down all the things that are important to you as a mother, and what defines your family. This should include your values, such as being kind to others, expressing gratitude daily, and prioritizing relationships and experiences over things. Also include activities that make your family special. Perhaps you all play music or spend as much time as you can traveling. Your family can be defined, in part, by your faith, financial responsibility, cracking up a whole lot, giving back to your favorite charity, having lots of parties, and group activities like biking, rock climbing, or going to the beach.

Ask for your kids' input (if they are older than two), and engage them in creating a poster board of your family. Think of it as a family crest, but cooler. Post it in the kitchen or somewhere you will see it every day. Redo it at least once per year.

PART IV

Dating

W HEN IT COMES TO DATING, single moms are all over the place. Reactions to hitting the dating pool are wildly extreme: Moms either are adamant they find a husband ASAP, sneak around dating and having sex in shame, or shut down completely in regard to sex and romance.

It's no wonder why.

There are so few healthy messages in the media or the world when it comes to fun, positive, and meaningful (whatever that means to you!) romantic relationships for women who have children. On one hand, over the past forty years of the sexual revolution, feminists have done a decent job changing the world's viewpoint to see that women are entitled to live sexual lives of their choosing, without indignity or judgment. After all, most of us are perfectly comfortable with Lena Dunham and her *Girls*, and Carrie Bradshaw and *her* girls, enjoying various sexual experiences with abandon. Society has largely stopped freaking out about gay relationships, and most of the moms I know actively educate their kids about not only the safety precautions but also the pleasures of sex.

All of these people (and characters) are allowed to enjoy sexual freedom of their own design. Yet when it comes to unmarried moms, society tells us simultaneously that we must (a) find a husband, lickety-split; and (b) abstain from dating and sex, which contaminate our children with dangerously whorish messages while also stealing precious parenting time from our kids, who already suffer pitifully in their broken homes. And God forbid your children meet someone you're dating and it doesn't work out forever-and-ever-after, because they will be scarred for life.

Consider, for example, the single moms in *The Karate Kid* and *E.T.*—sympathetic characters who showed zero sign of romantic lives or libidos. Or the other extreme: slutty, negligent single mom Carla in *Bad Moms* ("I walk down the street and it is just dicks, dicks, dicks. Raining dicks!"). Then there is Helen Hunt in *As Good as It Gets*, who martyrs a romantic life for her sickly kid, so much so that she ultimately believes she is worthy of nothing but a rude, grumpy, ugly old dude.

Sally Field's character in *Mrs. Doubtfire* could be considered the exception, since she does date a dashing Brit for his charms alone, though the undercurrent is that—because in the end, traditional marriage is, after all, the ideal—Field does need the man who lives in her house full time, even if he is her dubiously cross-dressed ex. It's interesting to note that this was a popular 1980s plot device: Think Angela and Tony on TV's *Who's the Boss?* High-powered yet ditzy Angela never really is single, since she's in a sexually tense pseudo marriage with her macho-yet-sweet housekeeper, Tony. Then there is Julia Roberts's depiction of single mom of three Erin Brockovich, with her bum cheeks peeking out of her Daisy Dukes and her tits bouncing out of her tank top, wielding her sexuality unabashedly for professional gain. Again, note that Brockovich selfishly neglects her devoted, hot, Harley-riding, kid-wrangling, husband-esque boyfriend at home, suggesting both that single moms are floozies and that moms can't kick polluting corporate ass without househusbands they take for granted.

In sum: If you don't know which way to turn in dating as a single mom, *it is no freaking wonder*!

Initially, coming out of my own marriage and without much introspection, I assumed a hunt for a serious partnership that would lead to marriage. That, after all, was really the only model that I had. Casual hookups had not been my main mode of dating in my twenties, so that didn't strike me as a natural course. After some heartbreak, open-mindedness, and giving myself permission to explore without shame or guilt my own, unique sexuality, I can tell you this: I love to date. I have found love, serious relationships, plenty of casual sex, nice, one-off chaste dates with attractive and interesting people, a few atrocious encounters with total dingleberries, relationships that lasted several months, and periods when I dated not at all. All of these experiences were valuable, most of them highly enjoyable— even the dingleberries led to fantastic stories! I also would love to find a fabulous, committed relationship with a brilliant, sexy man who adores me and my kids, though cohabiting feels like a really bad idea for me, and commingling finances is the dumbest thing I can think of—but never say never. I had my heart broken a few times, and it wasn't always pretty, but it was way better than when I was in my twenties. I'm older now. I know the universe is abundant with love. There is always more.

If I were to rely on pop-culture references, I would assume that all this dating and sex renders me a sad, lonely, horny broad who is a horrible example for my children. But in reality, I frequently meet women who are, like me, single moms who have kickass careers and their own money, are devoted, fun moms who spend plenty of time with their children, and fully enjoy romantic lives of their own making. Some unmarried moms regularly enjoy hot, guilt-free sex on evenings their kids are home with a sitter or with their dad. Other moms have committed relationships with people who do not live in their home, and that is exactly how they want it. Still others are like me: I mix it up, depending on what zone I'm in, or my mood, or what present company offers, and I do so without one single bit of shame or remorse. In fact, dating during this phase of my life has been one of my greatest pleasures, an opportunity to explore myself, my sexuality and body, and other people (and their bodies), and connect with men in a way that was impossible for me the last time I was unmarried.

But what about your kids? Shouldn't you hide your dating exploits from them? Shield them from the emotional trauma that a romantically active mom inflicts on them?

The answer depends on your values about dating and sex. What do you want to model for your children when it comes to relationships? If you believe that dating is inherently unscrupulous, and enjoyable sex is reserved for certain people (like men, married women, or Samantha Jones), do you uphold that copulation should be restricted to marriage alone, and then only for the strict purpose of procreation? Well, then I can't help you.

But if you believe that romance and a healthy sex life are a normal, positive part of adulthood, then read on. If this is you, I urge you to openly model this for your kids by going out on dates and not hiding what you are doing from them. After all, your kids will date sooner or later, and like most young adults today, they will likely cycle through many romantic partners before committing (if they do at all—marriage rates are at a historic low, but that is for another book). If you are like me, you want your kids to enjoy meeting and dating people, to explore emotional intimacy, to find love, companionship, and safe and really fantastic sex. If you want those things for your children, why don't you deserve them, too? Furthermore, if you want that for your children, you must model healthy, happy dating yourself. If mothers with successful professional lives are proven to be the strongest indicator of whether their daughters grow up to be the same, the same logic applies to romance and relationships.

Not only do you, as a single mother, deserve to date. You should date. You must date. Being celibate—or maintaining a false facade of chaste celibacy—only perpetuates the sexist Madonna-whore complex that society holds about mothers, and sends so many negative messages to your children.

If your children believe that you do not—and will not anytime soon—have any romantic life at all, you convey:

- Good mothers are never sexual people deserving of love or pleasure. (Translation: *Love, pleasure, and sex are bad.*)
- Your love, child, is enough for me. (Translation: *I depend on you; you owe it to me to fulfill me. Also, I lack healthy boundaries with my children.*)
- I am sacrificing the joy any romance or relationship would bring me, for your sake. (Translation: *You steal my joy, and I hate you for it.*)
- I'm done with dating. I will never have a romantic partner. (Translation: *I will always be dependent on you.* Also: *I hate men.* Also: *Once a love ends, there is no more.*)

Regarding that last hopeless message that eunuch mothers send to their children, consider my friend Sasha.

As she faced her divorce, this mom of two's own childhood loomed large as her point of reference. After all, Sasha's parents split when she was in preschool, and she was raised almost exclusively by her mother, who was a great role model in that she rose from a store clerk to a corporate executive during Sasha's childhood. It's no surprise my friend has also become incredibly professionally successful herself.

But Sasha never saw her mom date. At all.

Contending with her own single status, she was terrified—assumed, even—that she also faced perpetual loneliness. Why wouldn't she? That was her model: You divorce, then you're alone forever.

However, this new phase of life opened a new chapter in my

friend's relationship with her mother, as these things tend to do. And it turns out that her understanding of her mom's personal life was inaccurate.

"Oh! I always had an active sex life," her mom confessed when Sasha asked. "I just kept that separate from my relationship with you."

My friend was stunned. This not only TNT'd her impression of her mom, but upturned her expectations for her own sexual and romantic life—which suddenly became so much brighter.

I love this story because it serves as such great evidence for why we should all be open about our dating lives with our children. I've said it once but it needs to be said a zillion times more:

There is nothing shameful about a mother dating. You are an adult woman with romantic, emotional, social, and sexual needs. Embracing this fact is great for you, and great for your kids.

Those needs do not conflict with your kids' needs of you, or your relationship with your family. In fact, happily dating is the healthiest thing you can model for your children, both now and in shaping their points of reference in adulthood. Being sexually fulfilled gives you the energy to parent to your greatest potential. Plus, a healthy romantic life—whatever that means for you—frees your children from their own sense that they must fill that void, now and in the future, which is prone to happen in single-parent families.

For me growing up, my own mother was more or less always single, though there were bouts when she'd get excited about dating. When she was newly divorced, she lost some weight, slipped into some size 2 Gloria Vanderbilt jeans, and often went country line dancing, or on what she called "paper dates"—pre–online dating connections through the local newspaper classified ads. My brothers and I were thrilled that the cool neighborhood teenager girl would babysit, and I'd swoon as I'd watch my mom, in all her 1980s glory, set her short, permed blond hair in curlers, and don some chunky gold earrings, Estée Lauder pearl lipstick, and a spritz of Norell perfume. Then, some handsome man would ring the doorbell and he often brought flowers (this was for a first date, people. Can we time-travel to the '80s, please?). My brothers and I would practice shaking hands and greeting the adult, and my pretty mom was giddy. Sometimes the guys would turn into boyfriends, they'd stay over and sometimes their kids would come along, and we'd go to the movies or to a restaurant. It was just a couple of normal adults hanging out and dating. Like adults do.

When I started dating as a single mom, I was equally candid with my kids—even if guys don't travel to my apartment for the honor of chaperoning my fair hand to the local gastropub for microbrews and overpriced fish and chips. The reason for this is just more practicality and evolving customs than morality, as I usually date when my kids are with their dad for the weekend (and only one man I went out with, recently out of a very long marriage that probably started in the '80s, picked me up for a first date, and brought me a pop-business book and box of Godiva chocolates). However, my kids often hear me chatting about dating with my friends, and when they come home from their dad's house, after they tell me about what they had for dinner or what movie they saw, I tell them about a new or recent guy, and answer all their questions as maturely and candidly as is appropriate.

If I fudged the truth ("Oh, I went for a ridiculously expensive dinner with an . . . um . . . er . . . friend . . . who paid from a fat wad of cash, talked about himself all night, and drank way too much bourbon."), they would understand the lie. On some unconscious level, everyone knows a lie when it is handed to them, and kids are no exception. In fact, I think children, with their nubile and unfettered instincts, are exquisite at detecting lies. My children don't hear about my sex life, and yours shouldn't either. Kids also don't need to hear anything that would suggest how their lives might change—for example, any man becoming a semblance of a permanent fixture in their lives—until that is absolutely certain.

And this is where so many single moms get it wrong. The world puts so much pressure on you to marry, or at least quickly form a committed partnership. And there are so few models of happy relationships that are not rooted in a traditional marriage. Finding love and lasting companionship may indeed be exactly what you long for, and that is a great goal. If that is what you ultimately want, I urge you to believe that you can and will find it, and then seek it out eventually.

I understand the urge to commit to a partner immediately. Reasons include that you're human and lonely! Sharing a life and home with a person you care for is so inviting, and it's your normal. Maybe you are very used to married life, the financial comfort, daily rhythms, and the social acceptance that comes with cohabitation. Maybe you simply cannot stand all the family and societal pressures to have a man in your life.

But if you are coming out of a marriage or other serious relationship: Slow your roll. I know that the standard-issue advice is to abstain from dating for one year after a big breakup. I dismiss this. There is zero harm in enjoying the company of a nice person who flirts with you and makes you feel like the beautiful woman you are. After all, what magical healing happens after exactly 365 days? Your heart does not automatically mend; prior poor judgment does not immediately improve; your taste in men is not suddenly awesome. These things happen in their own time, sooner, later, or . . . let's get real, for some people, never.

Some of you out there simply cannot be single. The world shakes a judging, critical finger at you, warning you to be celibate postdivorce, when all you want to do is couple up, ASAP. Lots of people cannot stand to be without at least someone to text, or sleep with occasionally, and no amount of ink on this page is going to turn around your inability to stay single. If that is you, I'm not going to add to the chorus of voices screaming at you to not date. However, heed this advice, please:

Don't make any commitments at all. None. Not living together, or God forbid, marriage or making a baby. Just slow your roll. There is no rush. Seriously, just chill.

After a divorce or other big trauma, you are a mess. Every vertical of your life unravels. Your energy is twisted out of whack, your attention on just making it through the day. Instead of focusing on making a new, "perfect" family, give yourself the gift of time. Time to understand who you were inside your relationship. Time to think about what you may want in this new phase. Time to be kind to yourself.

Another reason to pause on big relationship moves: It's not just about you. If you are new to single motherhood, a whole lot of people in your life went through a lot of stuff. Your kids, of course. Your family and close friends, as well as your ex's family and friends were part of your breakup. Their relationships with you, your children, and your ex also changed. They are grieving and healing, too. When a family changes in a big way, everyone in that family's orbit goes through trauma, large or small. You may have behaved in ways that made those you love most question your judgment, or lose some trust. These things can be repaired after a long time. But those people may need a break from your romantic life. They may not be ready for more drama, no matter how great this new guy really, truly is. Introducing him to everyone needs to wait a bit.

But perhaps even most important: If you skip the alone-time part of single motherhood (which you are free to revisit at any point), you miss out on a fantastic opportunity at a new life experience, namely *being single*. I like to think about divorce and single motherhood as simply another life experience. I have been single, I have been married. I had the experience of divorce, of being a married mother, and of being a single mother. I have dated as a single woman, and I have dated as a middle-aged mom of toddlers. Each experience was worthwhile, as is being alone and without a man while also being a mother. Says Erin:

I needed to figure out how to be me. I found I was sillier with my children without my perceived judgment from my ex-husband. I learned to do things on my own, or who I needed to call when I couldn't do things on my own (like troubleshooting why my toilet was leaking into my dining room!). I learned how to enjoy the company of my friends and connect deeper with them, especially the ones who were going through other life-changing things. I learned how to take stock of my emotional needs better and do something about it if I wasn't in a good place—make a phone call, make plans, exercise, bake. I've joined a book club, gone on vacation by myself.

Lana told me:

Spending time being single, I started noticing how I felt about everything. Tiny examples, like I was using highlighters and realized I prefer orange or blue, or that I learned that I love comic books—especially with female protagonists like Captain Marvel and Ms. Marvel! I also learned to truly understand who I am, what I value, and what I'm looking for in a relationship. I had never taken the time to think about it. I was getting to know myself, and I prioritize making time for what I knew I loved, like learning about new music.

Says Vicky:

Taking time off after my divorce allowed me to assess my new situation as a single parent, and figure out why I dated the kinds of people I dated in the past. I also found myself again. I had lost so much of who I was in my last relationship I needed to remind myself of why I didn't suck. I got back into my passions of belly dancing, martial arts, and swimming. Now I'm writing again. And I've accepted the most important romantic relationship I'll ever have is with myself first and foremost. Which is why my OkCupid profile says I'm in an open relationship!

Shondra told me:

I finally took 100 percent responsibility for my life and my actions. It had been so easy to blame my ex for his difficult behaviors, I had been letting myself off the hook. Then, when I was on my own, it turned out I had a lot of work to do on myself, too. I took stock, spent my therapy sessions discussing me instead of him (oh, if he could only have benefited from the hours I spent talking to therapists about him!), and found out I needed to pull my financial act together. Today I am out of debt, bought my own home, am building my business. I also got sober and I'm far more focused on my inner life, attending ten-day silent meditation retreats, support groups, and journaling daily. Now I am intentionally single and loving it because I love the person I'm with, myself.

My friend Alaina Shearer, who blogged at *Ms. SingleMama*, was a solo mom for the first five years of her son Benjamin's life, enjoying dating (and writing about) many men, and empowering other single moms to embrace the freedom to be without a husband, partner, or the constraints of what society tells you a "good mother" does with her life and body. After a broken engagement, and settling into months of weekends enjoying Lifetime movies on TV with her dog by her side, Alaina forced herself to get back on OkCupid after a happy hiatus. "On one hand, I was truly content being single. My life was so full with my son, friends, and my business. But I wanted love, and I wanted true partnership—not to mention that a woman has needs!" She quickly met and fell deeply in love with a hot single dad, Seth Gray, whom she has since married and had a baby with, and who has adopted Benjamin. With his support, Alaina has built her Columbus, Ohio, digital marketing agency, Cement Marketing, into a seven-figure business within a few years. "It has been such a great and unique love story because we were both single parents who had found our own independence and happiness after divorce. If you're truly fulfilled on your own, you have a much healthier lens when you meet someone new, and know whether they drain your energy or enhance your life."

While I challenge you really assess your values around introducing your kids to men you date (and not assume the cultural edict that dating hurts your children), do exercise sensitivity. While you may embrace your options in relationships and are comfortable pushing the limits of our culture's ideas about what is an acceptable partnership for an unmarried mom, your kids' notions about romance may be rooted in the marriage that made them, or the serious, long-term boyfriend their mom was with since they were very young, who just moved out. They watch Disney movies and are surrounded by a singular message about relationships: You meet someone you like, then you marry him (or her). You may have very different, progressive ideas about dating, and that is fantastic. But your kids may need extra coaching and attention from you to help them understand what healthy dating is, and what they can expect from you, and the people in your life.

Imagine your kid's BFF is his pet guinea pig. Morning, noon, and night your son and his pet frolic and play and cuddle. Then, one day, you visit Peru and your child is unexpectedly served a roasted guinea pig. That is a perfectly fine and humane meal in that country, but your child's heart breaks because he has never, ever even entertained the notion that anyone would eat an animal that, in his experience, is a beloved member of his family.

In other words: You will be dating and exploring relationships outside marriage—even if you eventually find a traditional partnership—because that is the very nature of dating. But your kids need to learn about this normalcy through you and your positive example.

So, why not? Why not just chill out for a bit and luxuriate in what kind of mom you are now that you don't have to co-parent full time? Invest in a really fantastic vibrator, and maybe check out some porn or erotica. Take up Latin dancing, or political activism, dig into your biggest, wildest career dreams and income goals, and lean into what those goals feel like as a single, independent woman who is committed to living her own, best life.

Even if ultimately you attract and commit to a fantastic partner, you will never have regrets about your alone time, though you may regret immediately and desperately trying to fill your life with another husband. Simply commit to a different and new experience, and try it on for size. Give it a shot. Thank me later.

☆

A Sexually Satisfied Mom
Is a Happier Mom

S cience says: Sex is good for you. And "you," FYI, includes moms.

Research proves that frequent sex boosts your immune system, lowers blood pressure, and improves stress and sleep. And the more sex you have, science found, the better the sex is that you *do* have.

I had always had a pretty healthy libido and sex life, including during most of my marriage. But something happened after I divorced—a time that happened to coincide with becoming a mother. I was thirty-three when my marriage ended, and it was a little more than a year later that I went on a couple of tepid dates, and about eighteen months that I got into a serious relationship. It took some weeks to be ready to jump into bed, but when I did, there was no turning back, even when the relationship ended. That was more than five years ago, and I am so grateful for this time of dating, but also for the sex.

I hear from women with similar stories of finding incredible sex during this time of your life. "No one tells you how fantastic the sex is after divorce!" they squeal. "I never knew my body could do all these things, or feel this way!"

There are a lot of reasons why sex is often so incredible for single moms.

For many women, it is because they're coming out of a sexless relationship or a period of not dating or getting laid. So it is a simple equation of getting a piece of something really, really delicious that you had forgotten you'd even enjoyed in the first place.

If you are coming out of a big relationship, like a marriage, the end was probably really horrible. For at least a time, you *fucking hated that fucking asshole*, and were filled with so much rage for someone you once adored, loved, and craved. Even the most civilized divorces are so incredibly stressful, and your energy and focus was on other people and processes: Your kids, finances, where you would live and work, which family members were supportive and which disappointed you.

A lover turns that all around. Now you suddenly have a relationship that is all about receiving and giving pleasure, for pleasure's sake alone. It does not involve obligations to care for children, or to pay bills or argue over whether you should pay someone to power-wash the driveway. This is just about being cared for, touched, and adored. *It is intoxicating.*

Plus, if you are like me, all that hard-knock life that you just lived through made you a better person. And better people just don't give a shit about things like cellulite, perfectly minty breath, or perky tits. You also don't care so much about whether your partner's back is furry, or his gut paunchy, or his head dome-y. Maybe you're not quite there yet on any of these fronts, and that is OK. I address this later on.

For many moms, including me, motherhood freed me to connect with my sexuality in incredible ways. After all, having a baby is all about bodies—my body swelling and birthing and nursing another human body. I found a sensuality in those years being pregnant and breastfeeding for the sake of another person. I found acceptance, too. Along with the beauty and power of childbirth is pain, and excreting body fluids in front of others, and paying very close attention to what my body felt, as well as being in tune with another person's body—

sensibilities that were then ignited in new and different ways when I connected with men.

Also, I stopped giving such a shit about things that used to stand between me and very powerful sex. Kids—and getting them into the world—involve people pooping and peeing on and near you. You likely pooped and peed in front of other people. And there was lots of unabashed nudity—all in the name of arguably the most gorgeous thing in the world (which you can argue is either a baby or sex).

Earlier in my life, I was a little self-conscious about my small banana boobs with their flat nipples—my college roommate would tease me about my "bologna nips." But those banana-bologna boobs nursed two gorgeous babies who immediately flourished into deliciously fat, healthy little monkeys I could not be more delighted to take some credit for, thanks to my awesome breasts. Suddenly, I loved my banana-bologna boobs!

All these experiences of motherhood and sexuality flourished in a new appreciation for the universality of womanhood. Early in my single mother years, I would spend lots of time with my baby and toddler at the playground near my home in Queens, New York, which has been noted for being the most diverse place in the world. I noticed that nearly every mom at the park was from a different part of the world—a mom in a hijab going down the slide with a toddler on her lap; the Armani-clad Italian mom whose husband works at the United Nations chatting on her phone; the Mexican woman selling Italian ices while her baby sleeps in a stroller nearby; the Caribbean women chatting and laughing on the bench. While there often was not a common language we could share, there was a common understanding. When a mom frantically looked in her purse for a tissue, another mom silently handed her snotty-nosed kid a wipe. When someone fell from the monkey bars, any number of moms would rush to pick him up. A smile and a nod to an otherwise stranger ensured that stranger and mom would watch your kid while you took your other child to the bathroom.

Motherhood connected me not only to my child and to my own body, but to mothers and women everywhere. As many women say, becoming a mom made me love and appreciate my own mother and grandmother in new ways, and all mothers and grandmothers throughout the world, and throughout time. Every single one of these playground mothers' love for their children transcends time and geography. If we shared the same feelings for our children, then we all shared the same experiences with our bodies. The pain and shame and fluids and smells are universal and bound not in time. As are the pleasures.

In that universality of motherhood I found my own freedom to pursue love and sex and romance as I choose.

By pushing your own boundaries about what feels good in romance, you ultimately challenge others' boundaries. Like it or not, you are a revolutionary in the war on single moms.

One of the most delightful relationships I've enjoyed during this phase of my journey is an involvement with a single dad I met while in Copenhagen one summer. We visited each other in our respective cities a few times, including a summer sailing trip on his boat around some Nordic islands. That relationship was a real turning point for me, as there was never any commitment or talk of the future or family entanglements—only the enjoyment of each other's company when it transpired. The space that arrangement gave my feelings to bloom is an experience that I am so grateful for, and something that I would never have experienced if I'd not had time outside a committed, monogamous, traditional relationship. But not everyone in my life got it.

The first visit from the Dane was in New York over a weekend when my good friend was hosting a barbecue. He joined my kids and me at the event, where he mingled with many of my longtime friends.

The next week I bumped into one of my friends, a long-married stay-at-home mom whom I am very fond of, who said, "I chatted with Jens at the party; he's really great."

"Yes, he really is," I agreed.

"If things go well, maybe you and the kids can move to Europe," she suggested.

"Oh, no. He's not my boyfriend," I corrected her, brightly. "He's my lover."

Her mouth was agape. Her eyes searched mine. The words did not compute. I believe her brain melted.

"Have to run to a meeting! See you later!" I smiled, and bolted.

When you live within your own truest self—whether by pursuing a healthy lifestyle that gives you energy and sets a great example for your children, or by devoting your focus to a joyful career that you are proud of—you are a better mother. The key is to come to whatever activity in your life from a place of pride and confidence, as opposed to shame or desperation; if you do this, you simply can't go wrong. Of course, the trick is to know in your gut if it is fear, shame, or some desperate hope that is driving your decisions, and this is especially true in dating.

So, try it out for size. I don't need to lecture you about appropriate sharing with your kids. Your children do not want to know, nor should they know, the details of your sex life. But they are entitled to know that their mom is an adult woman who has romantic needs.

So, tell your kids you are going on a date. Let them meet the man you are seeing—even if you are not sure where the relationship is headed. The more you embrace your sexuality, the healthier it is, and the easier it will be to share with your kids in a way that doesn't make anyone squirm.

Why Dating as a Single Mom Is So Much Better Than Before

THE LAST TIME I WAS SINGLE, in my twenties, I was very eager to get married and have children. I distinctly remember at age twenty-four chatting about dudes and life with my good girlfriend Kirsten at the newspaper where we both worked:

ME: Well, you have to have babies by the time you're thirty [my mom said this to me once. I took it as truth].

KIRSTEN: Right, and you want to date someone for a while, and then live with them a couple years before getting married.

ME: Yeah. Then wait at least a little bit before having kids.

(We looked at each other, eyes wide): *That means we gotta get on this!*

Within a year, I'd met my husband-to-be, a year later we moved in together, two years later we married, and I had my first child at age thirty-one. I'd consider that more or less a win for sticking to schedule—one I am very glad I adhered to, as biology is no joke. After fourteen years in New York, a city teeming with childless women aging out of their childbearing years and desperately trying to find a partner to start a family with, I am so unbelievably glad that

I listened to my mom, partly because all the men these women are dating can smell that desperation from a mile away—and run like the wind.

The most wonderful part about dating as a single mom is that that kind of pressure simply does not exist for most of us. As I write this I am forty, my body is falling apart as forty-year-old bodies tend to do, and the baby shop, I have decided, is officially closed for business. Which is great for my dating life.

After all, in this phase of my journey, I have my babies, I have my own money, and so all I am really looking for is cool guys to spend time with (double points if they are brilliant, nerdy, hilarious, kind, great with kids, aggressive in bed, and have broad shoulders). I'm looking for a man who is interested in me as a person and woman, and not just my stunning, rock-hard body and enormous breasts (these last details are lies, read on), and, I've been delighted to find, men appreciate this. In other words: If you choose to be with a man for who he is, and not how he might save you from yourself or fill some unmet need in you—whether financial, a healthy set of testicles, because you are terrified of being single, or that he offers free babysitting and not a whole lot more—the other party picks up on that. If a man feels you like him for who he really is, any attention you bestow upon him is intoxicating to him. After all, which is the better compliment: "I adore your intelligence and wit, and you have such a big heart and are a wonderful mother," or "You look so freaking hot in that dress I want to fuck you right now"?

Yes, there is a time and place for everything, and during your single mom dating journey, I really, really hope lots of men find you freaking hot in whatever you're wearing, and that you have so much hot sex. You get my point.

But more than having checked off some major life to-dos, there are many wonderful things that come with age that make dating so much more delicious than the last time you dated.

For one, you are so much a better person than you were before you had kids. Motherhood, if you are like me, makes you a softer, more patient person—qualities that are not only attractive to romantic partners, but are so important for healthy relationships. Before I had children, I was prickly—quick with the barbs and criticisms, caustic in the persona I used in dating and relationships. I liked very, very much to be right, and was rarely afraid to argue for the sake of arguing. It doesn't take a psychology degree to understand (now, in hindsight, of course!): I was terrified of getting close to people, mortified at the thought of getting hurt.

When my daughter was born, I was stunned—*stunned*—by how much I loved her. I was mostly full time at home with her then, and I would sit for *hours and hours*, rocking her in the glider, staring in awe at how beautiful she was. I was completely amazed by how much love I was experiencing. My thoughts began to turn to how much love I had missed out on until then and I wondered how much more I might encounter in the future.

I'd thought I understood love. I'd loved many people—my family, friends, men, including my husband. But children busted up my heart, and when it put itself back together it was so much bigger, so much more available. My priorities shifted. I stopped being so obsessed with a tidy house (because, let's get real). I cared less about getting my way in petty arguments. I learned to appreciate early on how my children's personalities were so evident upon the first moments of meeting, giving me new appreciation for the fact that humans' ways are far more hardwired than I'd previously realized. This gave me a sense of acceptance of others and myself. Forgiveness came easier. I found I stopped trying so hard to control other people, and when I did, relationships were easier, frustrations and disappointments fewer.

Then, just as you probably have in your single mom journey, I went through a lot of heartbreak. Divorce. Trauma. I made so many mistakes during that time, and was so devastated by the loss all around me. But I survived it, and as with many horrible stories in life, I came out the other side, and I chose to be better. Stronger and happier. I learned to pick my battles, carefully. I took full control over how I spend my energy (not on laundry, toxic people, or work projects I don't enjoy), and generally relaxed into a better, more grounded, happier person than I'd ever been. These are all changes that make dating so much more fun, and less stressful, than if I were still in my twenties, working through so many of my issues (at least the ones I haven't resolved yet). Plus, a truly happy person without an aching agenda (like marriage and babies before age thirty!) is always attractive to others.

And, if you are like me and have leaned into your professional goals with confidence, that is an incredible asset in attracting successful men. If you have a career you are proud of and that fulfills you, are financially comfortable, and are perfectly capable of paying your own bills and buying your own dinner, men pick up on that confidence, especially the really great ones who appreciate great women. After all, at this stage of life, anyone who is dating—man or woman—has been through some challenges and heartbreaks in his or her life, and also longs to connect with someone who can appreciate both his or her vulnerabilities and strengths.

What if I really want to find a partner to have more children with?

This is a totally realistic and common desire. There are many, many men out there who want to have a baby with you—some are dads who want more, like you do, and others are childless and hear their biological clocks ticking. I have met several men in their forties, fifties, and older who believe they are too old to have children of their own, but regret not becoming fathers, and would love to be part of a family with kids at home.

If you want to grow your family, spend some time meditating on the nut of that desire, and the many ways it can be fulfilled. Does your desire for more kids stem from some unresolved issues around your previous relationship? In other words, have you come to terms with the fact that your plan A for a family did not work out, and can you work to resolve that wound? Just as all single moms must accept that their current family is a perfect, whole family, you must accept that your current kid count is also perfect. Consider how your quest may be affecting your children. I think of an old friend, Sarah, who is the oldest of a family of eight. "I always worried that I wasn't good enough, and that is why my mom kept having more kids, to satisfy what she saw lacking in me."

Then, truly open yourself up to other ways of satisfying your goal of having more children. For example, if it is important to you that your current child have a sibling, could that be satisfied with step-brothers or sisters? Is it a requisite for your desired baby to be conceived with a husband, or could you have, adopt, or foster a child on your own? Given the likelihood of divorce in second and even third marriages, how comfortable are you with having two (or more) ex-husbands and co-parents?

And finally, accept the real possibility that you may not have more children in your immediate family. At some point, you must grieve that that dream is not coming true, and that is OK.

Emma, I'm struggling financially and professionally. Am I doomed to be single or only attract losers?

Nope, not at all. There is a huge difference between being perpetually down and out and being in transition. If you are starting a new career or business, digging out of financial debt, or otherwise rebuilding or renovating a life you are excited, passionate, and positive about, that is sexy as hell to other wonderful people. I have struggled financially on and off in my single mom journey, had ups and downs in my business—I would be a weird and boring unicorn if that were not true. Any reasonable person you date will have had these same challenges. And if he is someone who is also positive and passionate, he will see in you that spark that it takes to succeed. And he'll love the shit out of you for it.

--- ☆ ---

If You're Stuck and Not Dating

THERE IS NO MAGICAL TIME it takes to start dating again as a single mom. Everyone has their own timetable, and I urge you to lean into what makes you comfortable. However, there comes a point at which what you may tell yourself and others about why you aren't dating is an excuse masking fear, and not simply a time of healing.

There is no denying that you must have a romantic life. Maybe this means the pursuit of a husband (though, let's think about this for a moment. If traditional marriage is so great, why is everyone divorced? Why are 57 percent of millennial moms unmarried, and why do 44 percent of young adults say that marriage is obsolete?), some hot sex, or dates to simply explore who you are and what you may be open to in this phase of life. After listening to my giddy exploits, a dear friend who has been married for fifteen years to a man she met when she was nineteen shook her head wearily and said, "I am so glad I'm not dating. It was miserable last time around!" Well, sunshine, that was fifteen years ago. Life has changed, and you have, too. This part of your life is a gorgeous blank slate that you can fill and play with, explore and improvise on to your heart's delight. There are so many horror stories out there, but you cannot afford to listen to one, mainly because most of the people who are dating are miserable themselves. Dating isn't working for them. They are not your role models.

If you have been completely inactive in dating and sex for more than one year, you likely are telling yourself stories that simply are not true. I get it—we all do this in many parts of life. For years, people told me I should be on TV or the radio—suggestions I secretly loved, and aspired to. However, I told myself (and anyone who would listen) that I could never work in front of the camera because I'm not pretty or thin enough, and my Midwestern accent has no place on the airwaves. Really, I was just scared of going for my secret dream and being rejected, or being ridiculed for my appearance or voice, or otherwise failing. I got over it, and accepted what others around me saw and what I craved, and now I'm in the media all the time, and I love it.

If you are not dating, I know for certain that on a very visceral, human, and female level you would *love* to go out with a nice, good-looking, kind man. Someone who is interested in hearing about your life, what you're interested in, what your kids are like, and the funny things they say. Someone to pick up the bill and hold your hand on the street and make you feel like a woman. You want to be held in bed, and made love to in that special way you crave, and to wake up and have breakfast with him in your panties, and then to do it again next weekend. These are normal, human female desires, and you deserve to have them fulfilled.

If you're not enjoying dating, you are likely telling yourself lies about why you don't get out there. Common self-fibs include:

There are no good guys out there at this stage of the game.

If I had a nickel for every time I heard this, I wouldn't have to write books for a living. The women who say this are usually the same ones who say: "Well, if he is so great, why is he still single/divorced?" Did you hear what you just said? If a person is not married, he or she is permanently flawed. Do you really believe that? Of course not. You are single, and you are lovable and datable. You're wonderful! You also deserve that great single guy, of which there are equal numbers of men and women. If you are under the impression that most guys suck, check yourself. You are raising children; man hating has no place in any family. Man hating also has no place in dating. Love yourself. Love all people. Good men will be attracted to you.

Good guys don't want to date a woman with kids.

People will tell you that, and you have to shut that out. Ever since the dawn of humanity, men have dated, made sweet love to, fallen head over heels for, and committed to women who are mothers. Some of them have kids themselves, and prefer women in a similar situation. Others are men who hit their forties or fifties and regret not becoming fathers themselves, and are thrilled to be part of a unit with children. Still others are men in any number of situations who will meet you, think you're fantastic, and want to spend time with you because you are awesome. It's not complicated. The less you are looking for a man to fill some role you perceive as otherwise unmet—paying bills, fathering, or filling a pitiful hole in your life and heart—the more he will feel appreciated for who he is, and not just what he can give you.

No man will want to have sex with this gross mom bod!

If you happened to look me up online, there are a bunch of pictures of me where I look reasonably attractive, but I'm clearly no supermodel— or even a natural beauty. Those are me on an excellent day, most of them were taken by professional photographers after a professional hair-and-makeup person did a number on me, and then they were photoshopped. Others are snapshots taken with a nice filter on my phone, on a good day, at a good angle, in good light.

The reality is that I am 5'6", weigh around 155 pounds, am a size 6 or 8, and have small boobs, and my thighs have never, ever, ever in my life (a) not had cellulite on them, or (b) not rubbed together. Before kids, my tummy was always flat and firm. Now it is gooey and prone to muffin tops. I have a C-section scar, and in the first few years of dating, my breasts would not stop lactating, even though I hadn't nursed for years. I almost never have my nails done, and I get my hair cut and colored three times per year. Most of my clothes come from H&M or the Gap, and all of my cosmetics from the drugstore (I wrote an article on whether premium cosmetics are worth the price. Research says: NOT AT ALL! You're welcome!).

For a couple of months I went out with a handsome fifty-two-year-old Hollywood screenwriter whose Instagram was populated with supercheesy pics of him swinging kettlebells with a (slutty-hot) personal trainer, and at clubs on outings with random (slutty-hot) twenty-six-year-olds. At least once per date with me, he would take a step back and assess my body from head to toe. Aside from that nonsense, I am here to tell you that men just don't give a shit. They are just not that picky. Sure, some guys are really, really into Barbie bodies, and maybe they are gym rats or athletes and their partners' physiques are paramount in dating. That is fine. There are also millions of middle-aged men who just don't look as great as they did twenty years ago. They are worried that their T-shirt shows off their man-boobs, or what you will think about their arms when you're making out with them and squeeze their biceps.

Also, *a lot* of men deal with impotence. A lot more than the last time you dated. In fact, this is a huge, new problem that I want to write a whole book about. So while you are worried what your tummy might look like when you're riding him, he is terrified his dick won't work. His fear is worse.

In other words, ignore social media images, tabloids, and Hollywood messages about what you have to look like to find romance and love. Just ignore it *all*! One of my absolute most favorite things I've read in the past few years is an essay on xoJane.com called "I'm Fat, Forty and Single and I'm Having No Problems Getting Laid All the Time." The author, who weighs three hundred pounds and is a size 28, writes about going through a divorce and committing to a fabu lous sex life, which she greatly enjoyed with many people. These included numerous traditionally attractive and successful men, all of whom could not get enough of her or her body, in a wonderful, nonfetishist way. She writes:

> Probably my favorite guys are those who find me really, really physically attractive and have no problem owning that desire. Guys who love my softness. Guys who massage my belly, who grab handfuls of my ass, who bury themselves between my breasts. Guys who can't get enough of every last inch of me. To them, I am a revelation—an ample woman with no body shame who says sure, let's have sex with the lights on.
>
> One such friend tells me that he long ago stopped approaching women he was attracted to in bars. He is a quite conventionally attractive man, with an extremely muscular build, and his preference is for women of my size or even larger. The most common reaction he would receive was one of anger from women who were so conditioned to believe in their own unattractiveness that they automatically assumed he was making fun of them.

I don't have time to date. I need to focus on my career and kids, and dating is a selfish distraction from my family.

One two-hour date per week (plus some fun texting in between) will energize you, put a bounce in your step, and give you good hair days all week long. Your career, kids, and Netflix habit can afford that time. By recognizing your femininity and honoring your very real romantic needs, you no longer spend toxic energy denying those needs. The dividends on igniting your dating life know no bounds.

EXERCISE

Write down why you don't date. Write down every single thing that comes to mind. Even if it sounds ridiculous as you write it, even if you see the error of your ways as it materializes on the page, just get those thoughts down.

Next, unpack each excuse. Is it really true? Where did that story come from? Then, write a new story, a new truth that will guide you going forward. The new truth might be:

- *I am a sexy woman deserving of romance, love, and sex, and lots of men find me attractive.*
- *Dating is a priority, and I have plenty of time for it.*
- *Good moms date, and I am excited to be a positive relationship role model for my kids.*

A Date, Defined

ONE OF THE BIGGEST, most common mistakes that people of all ages make: They don't know how to date.

First, what a date is *not*:

A date is not prospecting for a future husband. Especially if you are new again to dating, you need to realize that to find a husband on a date is impossible because you have no idea yet what you are looking for.

A date is not a free dinner, or any other way for men to lavish their money on you.

A date is not a giant deal. When you first start dating again, a date can feel like the biggest freaking deal in the world. The idea of making a romantic connection, the promise of that heady attraction, the possibility of sex and love . . . it is electrifying, and don't let anyone tell you different. For the first few dates I went on postdivorce, I bought a new dress each time. I stressed about whether black or brown eyeliner was the correct choice, and on several occasions, I arrived so early that I had to walk around the block multiple times so as not to appear to be the nervous nerd who shows up thirty minutes ahead of schedule and gets trashed on margaritas by my lonesome at the bar before the date has actually even started. That was cute, but not sustainable. Nor was the numbing anxiety of waiting for his text afterward, recruiting friends to help decipher every word, and the emotional pummeling that ensued after each one failed to materialize into the relationship of my dreams. Ain't nobody got time for all that! Plus, it puts so much pressure and nervous energy into the occasion that the whole thing gets off to a weird start. It will take time and practice not to be a nervous nerd (even though that is OK).

Here is what a date *is*:

A date is a meeting of two adults of compatible sexualities who have committed to spend time together in an enjoyable activity while exploring the possibility of continued romantic involvement.

Yes, you can kiss. You can sleep with him. Go dancing or play Ping-Pong. You decide the details.

But the essence is: Get together. Have a nice time. Get to know the other person. Decide if you want to see him again. *That is all*. I realize my definition is rather sterile, but it needs to be to make the point clear. Dating should be fun, playful, creative. It is of your own making, and the more positive energy and open-mindedness you bring to the situation, the more fun and promising the experience will be.

Where Can I Meet Good Men?

JUST OVER A YEAR after my separation, my good friend Betsy said, "I think you need to get out there again. Let's set you up on a date!" The thought terrified me, but also the very notion opened something in me that had been shut down for a very long time. It was as if she had reminded me of a dessert that had been my very favorite when I was five years old, one I had not thought about for thirty years, but the mention of which made me salivate and feel as greedy and giddy as it had all those years ago. I agreed.

I recently found an e-mail I sent to another friend:

> So Betsy and Kris are setting me up on a date. I am horrified. You might have to come over and help me figure out what to wear (and give me a Valium).
>
> I'm so nervous but also really excited. The prospect of a human male being nice to me and thinking about having sex with me seems like a new and wondrous prospect. Like a virgin! Touched for the very first time!

It was really the perfect first postdivorce, I'm-a-single-mom-and-I-have-no-idea-what-that-means-in-dating date. Joe was a good friend of Betsy and Kris. He was ten years older, which gave me confidence I had some sort of leverage in the dynamic, and he was smart, nice, interesting, and dorky. We enjoyed some beer, got to know each other over a couple of hours, shook hands on the street afterward, and that was that. (Never mind that a couple of years later my friend told me Joe, who had been a struggling tech entrepreneur, had sold his start-up and was now worth $15 million. I'm here to tell you: Money can't buy chemistry.)

I went out on a couple of other blind dates with equally nice, attractive, ill-suited men. It really was the perfect foray into getting my feet wet, feeling confident and attractive, and learning that dating is different-not-different from the last time around. Then, about eighteen months after my marriage ended, I decided that I wanted a *relationship*. It was a summer night, my kids were with their dad, and even if I'd had plans, the thunderstorm was so brutal that everyone was locked indoors. So, to make myself feel less lonely and miserable, I watched *Moonstruck* on Netflix. I cried and cried, and opened an account on Match.com.

The first person I met there turned into a serious relationship for a year. Since then, I have dated so many people, most of whom I've met online; others I've met through work, or parties, or on the subway. There is no right or wrong place to meet men. I think it is OK to date work colleagues, fellow church members, neighbors, or your kids' friends' hot single dads. Remember, this single mother business is by design renegade. Why would you follow some corporate HR expert's advice?

If you're new to dating again as a single mom (or, like many women I've met, you married someone you met early in life, and never really dated at all. This is a fantastic opportunity to explore this ritual for the first time!), online dating is a great place to start. I'm loyal to OkCupid because in New York City, where I live, I find it has the best selection of people, and the technology is fantastic. However, online dating is highly specific to your location, and while

OkCupid in New York City has served up great dates with all kinds of men, including those who are relationship- or marriage-minded, the site has a reputation for casual hookups in other cities. So, ask around to your other single friends about which sites they like, and why, and try out a few.

A few words to the wise when creating your profiles:

- Pics. They're important and they need to be recent and accurate. The very last thing you want is to show up on a date with a guy with whom you've enjoyed fantastic text chemistry, only to have him see in real life that you are heavier, or older, or shorter than you portrayed online. Of course all of our pics are the best versions of ourselves, but honesty is paramount.
- Yes, include in the bio that you have kids. You don't have to share a lot of details, but that is important, and a deal breaker for some people (which is totally OK! You have lots of deal breakers, too!).
- Be positive, unique, and real. There is a lot of noise out there on the Internet. Share a few details that express who you really are, let your wit and warmth shine, and cut through the clamor. Ask a friend to help highlight your very best qualities.
- It's great to reach out to men first. In online dating, guys are used to being rejected. It is simply the name of the game. When you contact him, mention something specific about his profile, or a funny or cute picture he posted. Just a line or two shows you were paying attention and are different from other women.
- Meet quickly after connecting. I appreciate that you are busy, and you may feel nervous about getting together with a stranger. But you really need to cut to the chase. By insisting on texting or phone talking for weeks and weeks you will only delay the most critical part of dating: face-to-face chemistry. Plus, if you wait too long, stalking him online, reading and rereading his every message, your idea about who this guy is will be exagger-

ated and twisted beyond human recognition. So, within the week of sharing a few promising texts, arrange to meet for a coffee or drink and see what is what.

- Remember: Just because a guy shows interest doesn't mean you have to go out with him! Recently, on Millionaire Single Moms, a woman posted about an online encounter with a man who said his kids lived across the country. She politely asked why and he got testy with her, and eventually stopped communicating. It is a deal breaker for this woman if a man has children but is not intimately involved with them, and so she makes sure not to waste her time on men who don't fit that requirement. Many of the other moms vehemently argued that she was too harsh and should have met him. That is insane. You have no obligation to meet anyone, especially if they violate something that is really important to you! That suggestion is an example of a poverty mentality in dating: the notion that there are so few men out there that you must jump on the first decent-seeming person who happens along. Hogwash.

- Don't be so freaking picky. Have a short list of deal breakers. Then, outside of those line items, if a man seems like a reasonably good person and you find him attractive and interesting, meet for that drink already.

- On sites that ask you to check what kind of relationship you're seeking (committed, short-term, long-term, casual sex), either check none, or check several. This is less about what you express to potential mates and more about what you express to yourself. Each date, remember, is not a trial marriage. Each date is its own precious microcosm. It is really fantastic if you know you want to find love and commitment. I do, too! But along your route to that goal, you may go on a date with a really fun guy whom you know you don't care to see again, but who is just fantastic company and in whose presence you have one of the best nights of your life, whether shooting pool, walking on the waterfront, or enjoying a hot night in the hammock on his balcony. Or, you may find people you love for a time, or enjoy dating for a while, and then become platonic friends. Checking only "Seeking commitment" limits you not only in the people who will respond, but in the experiences you are open to considering.

More Thoughts on Meeting Men

ASK YOUR FRIENDS FOR SETUPS: "I'm thinking of dating again. Do you know anyone nice you think I might want to meet?" Cast your net wide, and outside your comfort zone. I'm not talking about compromising your standards, but keep an open mind. Even though I nearly always date white-collar urban intellectuals who share my politics, I was surprised by how much I enjoyed dating Sal, a Sicilian American auto-body shop owner from a working-class part of Brooklyn, who kept a bench press in his living room, admonished me about my unpolished nails, and offered to buy me a Cadillac if I gave him a baby. Our affair was one part really hot sex, one part mutual anthropological research (Me: "These women you date, what are they like? Where do they work?" Him: "My last girlfriend was a cocktail waitress who was a 42DD." Me: "Oh, so she had a boob—" Him: "Doesn't matter. Doesn't matter.").

Also, something that is likely new since the last time you were single: Younger men are incredibly plentiful and interested. While not what I'm typically attracted to, I have dated a few guys who were five or ten years my junior, and lots of women absolutely adore younger, hot men who are bananas for older women. In researching this topic, for a while I queried the young Columbia Law School students and engineers who look like they should be dating cute twenty-four-year-old PR account executives, but instead ping me on OkCupid. I asked a cute and witty twenty-six-year-old architect: "You're young, hot, smart, and successful. Why are you hitting up old moms?"

His answer:

Younger men have always had crushes on older women: teachers, neighbors, their mom's friends. But until the Internet, there were few opportunities to connect to these women. Also, an older, more experienced woman can teach a younger lover something in bed. Also: If a young man can please an older, more experienced woman, that proves his studliness. Unlike women my age or younger, older women don't play games, know what they want, and are less inclined to be needy or pressuring for commitment.

One of my all-time favorite old-mom, younger-man stories was Greta, who told me:

I live in a college town and have no trouble meeting gorgeous younger men to have great sex with. Now, I'm 42, my vagina has pushed two babies out, I'm 20 lbs. overweight, my tits disappear when I lay on my back. But one of my guys is on the college football team, and absolutely perfect. Younger men appreciate a woman who is comfortable with her sexuality, someone who appreciates their libido and bodies. One of my guys is usually broke because now that he's graduating from college, his parents cut him off financially. So when I need my house cleaned, or some handyman work, I call him, and get the work done for half the market rate. If there is still time before my kids come home, we have a roll in the hay, and I consider that a great investment of time and money.

Outsourcing and getting laid like a proper kickass single mom if I ever met one.

Dating and Your Kids

ONE OF THE BIG, negative, unreasonable messages that single moms get about dating is that it is a peril to their kids. The reality: It's not, except when it is. Let's break this down into the common warnings:

If your kids meet a man you're involved with and it doesn't work out forever and ever, it will be yet another devastating heartbreak for your kids that you can prevent, and should. Wait at least six months before introducing your kids to any man you're seeing.

There is research that finds that children raised in single-parent households where the mother changes live-in partners frequently fare worse than in homes where there is stability—whether the parents were married, the mom cohabited with the kids' dad or another partner long-term, or was single the whole time. The takeaway is *not* that the moms had different boyfriends that hurt the kids, but rather whether the home unit was stable. Dating different people does not inherently disrupt your kids' lives—or your life for that matter! It is possible to model a healthy romantic life for your kids without your children being scarred for life.

After all, every single year my kids move from one grade to the next, leaving behind a teacher they usually loved a whole lot—

someone who was a big deal in their lives, who they saw every single day. Then, they graduate to the next class, or the next school, and rarely or never see that teacher again. The kids are sad, but they don't die, and there certainly is no social shame for mothers sending their children to school, where their hearts are scheduled to be broken and abandoned.

The difference between teachers and mom's boyfriends? No one expects that the teachers will be part of their students' lives forever (though sometimes that happens). But our culture is married (no pun intended!) to the idea that romantic relationships for mothers must include full-frontal, full-time commitment, and taking on the role of father to any children in the house. The same analogy I used about school teachers can be applied to friends and neighbors, some of whom will inevitably move or drift away from your family, or grandparents and pets who will die. Love and loss are part of life. We must encourage our children to live boldly, and to recover from heartbreak bravely. Romantic love is no different, whether it is their own relationships or those of their mom. Normalizing dating and what should be expected of it lessens the blow to the kids if and when one of your relationships ends.

One of the silliest stories I heard was from a mom who started dating a sweet and hot dad she met at the playground after they'd known each other for more than a year, including playdates at the respective families' homes. After they got involved romantically, the woman put the kibosh on any more playdates until the romance had progressed to the magical six months that many single parents adhere to for such an introduction. The boyfriend was incredulous. "That is crazy—I've been hanging out with your kids for more than a year!" he protested. She would not relent. He called it off, saying he felt she used the rule as a way to protect herself from getting emotionally involved and push him away. I agree.

Of course, the onus is on you to think outside the pressure to create a church-and-state divide of your romantic and parental lives, to find your own path, deviate from some Disney model of soul mate ever after, and embrace the fact that moms are people, too. This can be really, really hard. Romance and dating are confusing, often soul crushing, and you may not be sure what you want from one minute to the next in regard to a person you are involved with, or about the meta-view of life and love.

Which is why I urge you to pay no mind to the silly shaming of single moms with regard to dating and just slow your freaking roll.

Part of this is lightening up about when your kids meet anyone you're seeing. Remember my memories about my mom dating? I urge you to replicate that as it suits your life. Tell your kids, no matter how small or old, "I'm going on a date. This is the guy I'm seeing this evening; we're going to the theater and I'll be home by eleven." Answer their questions. Maybe he comes in and says hi for a few minutes. Maybe later, he comes by on a Saturday afternoon and watches the game with the rest of you, just like your brother or male friend might. Dating is just a normal, healthy part of adult life. Some mothers date their husbands, who are also the fathers of their children. Other mothers date in other ways.

Also consider how allowing men into the fold of your family can be seen as a practical consideration, too. After all, if you have any idea that this relationship might be serious, you want to see how he is around your kids. Furthermore, you want to spend more time with him, which is hard to do if you're constantly sneaking around when your kids are away at camp or sleeping over at their friend's house. You also want him to see you in your element. You're a great mom, loving and patient, fun and spontaneous. Let him see that side of you and fall in love with that most wonderful mother that you are. He needs to try you out before committing, too.

All this said, there are many very good reasons to keep a man separate from your family life for a while or to forgo integrating him into your family indefinitely, including:

1. You recently broke up with someone else. Even though you may be ready to move on, you're not sure your kids are.

2. You find it impossible not to jump to marriage or serious relationship thinking with every man you get involved with. Some people can't do anything but date very seriously. If this is you, wait to intro the kids.

3. You're afraid your new guy will be really awesome with the kids. Which will make you totally love him way, way more. Maybe you're not ready for that kind of emotional intensity. It scares you. That's cool. Take it slow.

4. You're afraid he might not be so great with your kids. That doesn't mean that you shouldn't date him—it means that he might not be part of your family life. Sometimes you just need a lover or someone to take you out to dinner now and again. Not all relationships are the giant, *Brady Bunch*, 24-7 kind. Maybe you'll want that sort of partnership in another phase of your journey.

5. You want to prolong the courtship. Face it: If he's spending every Wednesday enjoying meat loaf and mashed potatoes with you and the kids, those are Wednesdays he's not taking you out for wild-boar-and-cremini-mushroom confit with truffle-laced heirloom purple potato mash at that cute place downtown. Family life is wonderful. But that shit's not glamorous.

6. You're afraid your family life will make him run. Truth? It might. Especially if he doesn't love you (yet). It might be hard to imagine that a man who did not sire your kids might actually like your children, and also want to fuck you. But it happens all the time. Maybe you want to feel more secure in the relationship before you bring him home to the circus that is your life. Take your time!

7. You don't want to signal to him it's serious (yet). You may not feel that introducing a guy to your kids indicates that he's your

forever boo. But he may see it that way—which is understandable because most people in our culture would, too. If you're playing it cool and not ready to jump in with your heart and soul, but worry he will think you're eager and commitment-ready if you invite him to join your clan for Disney on Ice, it's fine to wait.

8. You want him all to yourself. This is not selfish. See number 4 or 5. Not every relationship is meant for marriage or family, or even boyfriend-girlfriend business. Having a lover who is separate from your daily life can be a fabulous arrangement. If that suits you, embrace it.

Ultimately, like any other part of Kickass Single Mom life, assess this part of your journey with an open, enlightened mind, not one loaded by ancient, sexist ideas or your own tunnel vision. You will make mistakes, and you will get hurt. But that is where the good stuff is. When you give yourself freedom to explore, to define your own journey and morals, you magically open yourself to the wonders and fun of romance. Godspeed!

---☆---

A Few Hard Rules About
Men and Kids

I HOPE YOU APPRECIATE that I am liberating you to do a whole
bunch of fun stuff that everyone else tells you not to do. Yes, I am
a social libertarian, but there are some rules that you must adhere to:

Rule 1: You are not allowed to sneak men in.
Even if the kids are asleep and they are the world's soundest sleep-
ers, you can't do that.

A few years ago I dated for a minute a cute single dad. On a
rare weeknight date in my neighborhood, after a shared pitcher of
sangria, one thing led to the proverbial other and we wondered
where we might convene. After all, his kids were home with a
babysitter, and my kids were home with a babysitter. I won't lie: I
was tempted to invite him up to my place, settle the tab with the
sitter, and pray to sweet baby Jesus that the kids didn't awake in
the middle of our adult time.

But I don't do that, and you shouldn't either. Why? Sneaking
is lying. Maintaining privacy is different from lying. If you have
to sneak him in it is because you feel guilty about it. Kids pick up
on that. They will know—unconsciously or overtly—that some-

thing is wrong when you walk around with a guilty conscience and morning-after bounce to your step.

Don't even try to have him stay over without discussing it at all, get up in the morning, and pretend like there is nothing weird going on. I come from a long line of Midwestern Protestants who wrote the book on serving up casserole while pretending every-thing is fine when *everything is totally fucking wrong* and I'm here to tell you: Your kids are not morons. Don't insult them, and don't disrespect their instincts that sound alarm bells when you say *that guy wearing Mommy's bathrobe got tired while we were watching a movie and slept on the couch.*

Yes, you pay the bills and make the rules, but it is their home, too, and kids deserve to feel safe in their own house. Dark-of-night visitors bring into your home their own vibe—good or bad—and other people pick up on that. It's there in the house whether or not they outright bust you or pick up on that weird energy. Keep it on the up and up.

And of course, you might get outright busted. And that would be so, so bad. Not just weird and embarrassing, but really, really bad. Like Naomi, who snuck in her beau when her eight-year-old son was being watched by a neighbor outside; the boy stumbled in to see his mom getting it doggy-style on the family room couch with a man he'd never met. That is a true story and I want you to read it again.

The upside of the downside of limited places to fool around is that it can be really hot. I repeat: It can be really hot. Like, for example, that chilly September night when the single dad and I made our way into an alley behind an apartment building and he chivalrously laid his navy peacoat on the pavement next to recy-cling bins and we had a go at it in the late-summer rain.

Rule 2: Talk to your kids about your dating and about sex, but don't talk to them about your sex life.
I'm a big advocate of early, frank, and frequent sex education, in-

cluding biology, safety, respect, and the importance of enjoyment. But when it comes to sharing the details of your sex life, feel free to gossip with your friends all you want, but do not share that in any way, or even nearby, with your kids. I defer to what my wonderful seventh-grade sex ed teacher, Ms. Anderson, said when she started the course: "You can ask me any question at all. There are only two reasons I won't answer: One, if I don't know the answer, or two, if it is a personal question." That was 1988, before Google took away parents' luxury of saying number one.

Rule 3: Condoms.
One in six people in the United States has genital herpes. There are other things, too. Just be smart.

Rule 4: Don't talk with your kids about the ups and downs of your relationship.
Eventually, you will get into a relationship, and your kids will likely know that person. Even if you play it super cool, your kids will hear people asking you when you're getting married. This revolutionizing moms and dating business is a family affair, for better or worse, and your children may feel anxious about the new person leaving their lives, or whether he will move in, and what that might mean for their relationship with you, or their dad. Relationships are often messy, with their ups and downs, and those later in life are prone to even more turmoil. Just as a married parent shouldn't announce divorce to their kids every time there's tumult in the marriage, do keep a layer of protection between your children and the drama of your relationship, until you know for sure it is ending or that you are fully committing.

Rule 5: Be gentle with yourself.
You're not going to get it right all the time. Your kids are going to hear you talk about the ups and downs of your relationship. Your

dreams of marriage may slip into your conversations with your kids about dating. They might very well hear you having sex with your boyfriend, because that happens when adults live in the same house with children. Be kind, and be forgiving of yourself. This single mother business is old, but it is also new. In many ways, you are charting new territory, and helping write the rule books for a new generation of parents.

How to Introduce
Your Boyfriend to Your Kids

So, HOW EXACTLY do you introduce a man you're seeing to your kids?

My guiding story was what my good friend Kari told me about meeting her now-stepmom. This was a big deal to Kari, whose parents divorced when she was in middle school; her mom, whom she adored, was in and out of her life owing to severe mental illness. Two years after the split, her dad became involved with Sharon. "I remember feeling really nervous about the first time we were going to meet," says Kari, who was a sophomore in high school at the time. "When I came into the house on the day I was to meet her, Sharon was cooking in the kitchen. My dad was really relaxed, introduced us casually, and she was just totally cool, offered me some food and we all sat down and ate." Kari and her stepmom have grown to be very close over the years, and Kari remembers that first meeting fondly.

The key here was that the adults were cool and confident, and the kid followed.

But what about when the guy sleeps over for the first time?

This is the conversation that ensued when one of my boyfriends started sleeping over. My kids were four and six at the time, and had met him a few times when he came over for dinner.

I first mentioned to my son, who was four, "He's going to sleep over at our house Thursday."

When his sister, six, came home, Luke eagerly rushed up to her: "Helena! Helena! Guess WHAT! Mommy's boyfriend is going to SLEEP at our HOUSE!"

HELENA: "Where is he going to sleep?"

ME: "My bed."

HELENA: "Where are you going to sleep?"

ME: "In my bed with him."

HELENA: "I think you wiggle too much at night. Maybe he should sleep on the couch."

LUCAS: "I know! I know! He can sleep in MY BED!"

ME: "Where are you going to sleep?"

LUCAS: "With you."

ME: "I'm going to sleep with him in my bed because he's my boyfriend and I want to snuggle with him."

LUCAS: "What about OUR morning snuggles?"

ME: "We will still do that—there are plenty of mommy snuggles to go around."

The day of the Great Sleepover, I picked Helena up at the bus stop and she giddily skipped along the sidewalk holding my hand.

HELENA: "My mommy's boyfriend is going to sleep at my house! My mommy's boyfriend is going to sleep at my house! I told everyone at school—even my teachers! My mommy's boyfriend is going to sleep at my house!"

The rest of the evening was pork chops and roasted cauliflower and cupcakes my boyfriend brought for the kids. He cleaned the kitchen (even the stove top, which I religiously leave for the house-cleaner) while I got the kids into the bath and jammies. I read Helena one of those English Roses books by Madonna and he read Lucas a book about airplanes. There were kisses all around, followed by yelling to get back into bed, and it couldn't have been more normal or cozy.

And it was, at its core, a normal and cozy Thursday evening with the kids. I put on my long-sleeved pajamas, washed my face, and slipped into bed next to him, my head resting in the crook of his arm and then on his chest. We turned off the light and talked about what, I don't remember. I wish I had a funny story about stifled howls of passion or a knocking headboard that awoke the kids, and while there were some steamy adult snuggles under the predawn covers, we crawled out of bed to make coffee and muffins and listen to NPR as I admonished the kids to hurry up and get dressed already. And then the day had begun.

Several months later my boyfriend and I broke up. I explained, simply, to my kids that he and I decided to end the relationship, and that is often what happens—not only with romantic relationships, but also with friendships, that school friends move away, and people die. It can be very sad, but there are always new friends to make and new boyfriends or girlfriends we can meet.

A Special Note About Dating for Widowed Single Moms

THE DATING CHALLENGES for mothers whose partners died are unique, but not insurmountable. This is advice from my friend Candalyn Winder, a Utah educator and mom of a four-year-old daughter. Candalyn's husband died of cancer when her daughter was two. Today she heads a local chapter of Soaring Spirits International, a support group for people who have lost their partner. Her advice:

> Grief is enduring. It never goes entirely away. A lot of guys have been turned off when they hear that I still love and miss my husband. Even though my grief is completely healthy, they just don't like that. It takes a secure guy to not be threatened by it. I keep an urn with my husband's ashes in plain view in my home along with pictures of my husband, daughter, and myself. I don't want to erase him from our daughter's life.
>
> I've had a lot of guys assume that as a widow I have "too much baggage" and check out immediately without exploring what my baggage is really like. Also, while not unique to single parenting, there is obviously zero co-parenting or time off unless you have family or

childcare to step in. Even when I can arrange care, no one is fully invested in my kid the way her dad was. That's all on me.

I am really up front about being widowed in dating conversations. When a guy asks about my custody situation I drop that since I'm widowed, there is no joint custody. I lose 50 percent of the guys right then, but I figure it's an easy filtering mechanism! But I also share right away that I'm lucky to have a great support system, and I can always get care if I want to get out for a date.

Another challenge is the group of men who want to dive into all the gory details of my story, and there are some rubberneckers. So while I'm up front and direct about my situation, I choose not to share a lot of details in the first few dates. I do this partly to protect my privacy, partly to avoid becoming cemented in their head as "the widowed chick." I'm really open about my situation in general, but in dating I don't have any interest in sharing feelings until the man has earned some emotional intimacy.

Some widows have life insurance settlements. While I do not, nearly everyone assumes I'm rich and settled for life. I've had dozens of guys ask me how many hundreds of thousands of dollars I have in the bank. I also know through my network of widows that many, many women were conned into losing life insurance settlements by men who preyed on their situation specifically. That problem is so prevalent that my local widow's group keeps a running list of men who are known to prey on widows. For this reason, when meeting men, I like to find a way in the first couple of dates to drop in that there was no settlement, but that I've always been the breadwinner so I do just fine. That scares off the con artists, but makes it clear I'm not looking for a meal ticket, either. For women who do have sizable settlements, I would guard that information diligently, and even minimize the sum, as much as I hate to deceive people.

Another challenge of dating as a widowed mom: It complicates the stepparent role. Dad is on a pedestal to some extent. How do you compete with that? I'm involved with someone who is really secure in himself and is a great communicator—though isn't that always the key to a great relationship? His parents split up when he was eight, and his dad died when he was sixteen. He is intimately familiar with blending families and grief—it's almost a nonissue. We openly acknowledge the weirdness factor when it comes up. He once Snapchatted a picture of my kid at her dad's grave, and captioned it, "One of the weirder moments of my life." But he's 100 percent committed to putting her needs first and we work through the rest.

My boyfriend has straight-up told my daughter that he's not trying to replace her dad. He initiates conversations with her about her father to make it clear he's comfortable talking about it, and that she doesn't have to choose between the two of them. Once we got serious, he started taking her out for one-on-one time to make it clear that he wasn't just in it for me. When we move in together in a few months, we will keep the urn and other dad stuff in my daughter's room. But it doesn't bother him at all.

To make her father more real, and to temper that pedestal, I try really hard to let conversation of her dad come up naturally, good and bad. For example, I recently told my daughter, "Your dad drove me crazy when he slurped his soup like you're doing!" Once she caught my boyfriend and me bickering and later I said, "Your dad and I used to argue, too. We still loved each other; it's just part of life." Many widows feel the deceased dad is every bit as much a member of their family as anyone else.

Kids have to re-grieve the death at each developmental stage, so it comes up in new ways over and over again. I don't think there is anything that will make the pedestal thing go away completely. Just talking about it a lot, not taking things personally, and never ever shaming or blaming a kid for feeling a certain way. Feelings aren't good or bad, they just are, and they're always healthier to deal with when they're out in the open. Hiding only makes them more powerful.

In-laws are another challenge. I had one guy dump me when I mentioned having dinner with my husband's family because he thought that was too weird. But my in-laws are my family, not to mention my daughter's.

I've heard of in-laws who cause problems because they think the mom should have mourned longer, shouldn't date until the kids are grown up, or whatever nonsense they come up with. One friend's in-laws told the kids that mom must not really have loved their dad since she was dating a year after he passed. Those kinds of stories are common, and you may feel like you can't win. Be prepared to hear, "He would have wanted you to be happy, and you need to get back out there and find love again! Stop letting yourself get carried away with this grief nonsense and move on!" as well as, "You're moving on too fast; it's not healthy for you/the kids/whoever and you need to take more time before you start dating again!" But the truth is, there's no right way to date as a widow. There's just your way, and sometimes you have to tell people to mind their own business.

The key is to know that people are going to judge you no matter what you do. So many people think they know the "right" way to grieve and move forward. So decide what you're going to do, then commit to doing it, and be prepared to enforce boundaries along the way as necessary. You are also entitled to change your mind as you see fit.

Widows tend to either keep their in-laws as beloved family or cut them off completely. Widows have to remember that your in-laws are processing a huge loss, too, and be quick to forgive. But also be quick to stand up for yourself and your kids as needed. Be open and kind, and address issues directly and quickly before they fester. It may take your in-laws longer than you think to get comfortable with a new guy, and bringing him around will absolutely raise some grief and sadness they will have to process. My sister-in-law cried for an hour after the first time I brought my boyfriend around. But because we had talked

248 The Kickass Single Mom

about it, she didn't feel ambushed and we didn't take it personally. I didn't adjust my dating plans to accommodate my in-laws. But I did adjust the way they were exposed to it while they got used to the idea. We took my current boyfriend on a big family vacation with my in-laws a few months ago and it went great. I'm lucky that they welcome him unconditionally (they don't want to lose time with my kid, so they keep me happy!).

Conclusion

W E OFTEN SAY that as parents, we learn far more from our children than they do from us.

That is how I feel about my work with single moms. For five years I have been blogging about, and communicating every day with, single mothers around the world. It has been an incredible journey, one that humbles and inspires me daily. When I am feeling especially overwhelmed or lonely (yes, it happens to me, too . . . I'm human!), an email or Facebook message will appear from a mom who will share her journey. Sometimes the story is one of a woman in a very dark place, who has found some comfort or inspiration in something I've written or from the Millionaire Single Mom community. I love those notes and am grateful for them.

However, more and more, the story is often a beautiful account of a woman who leaves a very bleak and scary place, and through a lot of fight—and at least a little magic—finds herself in a life that stuns her in its beauty. Women who take their children out of an abusive place and find a safe and happy one. Women who were broke, terrified, and alone, and claw their way to a good job and a home in a community with good schools. Women who were depressed and angry in their relationships but who created a new life where their children see them laugh and thrive. Women who were stuck and miserable but got unstuck and found love, success, and the very best of their motherhoods.

There are so many stories, yet, as has been said: There are no new stories. So, too, with the single mom story. It is an old story.

It is a story about a woman who was shut down.

It is a story of a woman who could not see her way out, who felt alone and very scared.

It is a story of a woman who fought for herself and her children.

It is a story of choosing risk and hope—and being rewarded.

Ultimately, single mom stories are of the most beautiful love stories of all time: A story about a mommy and her babies.

As I have shared in these pages, my default coping tool is gratitude, and there is no greater gift I can give to you on this journey than to urge you to count your blessings. Today, as I write this, it is 2017, and women in the Western world and beyond have accomplished such incredible things in business, the economy, education, and politics. Those before us have fought for and achieved rights and protection in government, law, human rights, and the workplace.

When your life isn't working out how you had planned, and you find yourself with fewer financial, familial, or logistical resources than it seems your friends and neighbors have, it can be easy to slip into a scarcity mentality and focus on getting through the day, scraping by financially, and accepting that your romantic and social lives will never be what you'd hoped.

Instead, I urge you to focus on your choices and the gifts at your disposal. We are living in a glorious moment for women. You have more legal and financial rights than women have enjoyed in all of modern history. Give thanks for your education (and access to more education) and that you live in a safe place, in a time of peace. Focus on the beauty of technology that connects you in seconds to the support and friendship you need and deserve. Honor your right to dream really, really, scarily big. Put energy into your ability to set incredible goals and to look around and be inspired by so many other women who have achieved their own goals.

Go for it and don't look back.

Then, when you are ready, I urge you to give back. One of the most powerful ways you can change the world is to live your fullest life.

However, with each of these rights comes new questions and challenges. (Yay on us that we can now earn as much as men and more—but how does that work in dating and marriage?! Hurray that we might lead in the office—but then why are women still doing most of the work at home?) The single-mom experience embodies and highlights the feminist journey—the good, bad, ugly, and brilliant. Like it or not, you are a warrior for all women. What you do matters. Your kids are watching. So are your friends, neighbors, and colleagues. The example we set today sets our daughters up to navigate a new world of work, money, motherhood, and romance. From us, our sons understand what true equality means and are organically comfortable with women who achieve. Decisions you make at work push the envelope for better policies for all families—changes will reverberate in progress for generations to come.

During the dark times—and we all go through those very dark times—these pressures can feel like a daunting and unfair burden.

It is worth it.

Recently, a single mom named Wendy shared with me one of her single-mom idols, who she secretly watched as Wendy contemplated leaving an unhappy marriage. "Our kids went to the same day care, and I didn't know much about her, except that she owned first one, then eventually three, hair salons in our town. From what I could tell, her kids' dad was not involved much if not at all. She was always put together, her kids were very well behaved, and she was always very nice to the day-care staff and seemed like a genuinely happy person. I'd see that she was involved in some community service organizations. She was not an ostentatious person, and had no idea how much I secretly looked up to her. But from watching her from afar I started to see what was possible for me and my kids. That was powerful."

You have that power. If I can leave you with one message, it is permission to unleash that power to live your greatest, truest, happiest life—no matter how you define that for you and your family. That, for you and for moms everywhere, is really what I hope the Kickass Single Mom legacy will be.

Gratitude

I am so thankful to the many people whose work and support made this book possible.

To my lovely agent Wendy Sherman and TarcherPerigee editor Sara Carder for believing in this project and giving it so much love and attention. To my wonderful children, Lucas and Helena, who are a constant source of hilarity and wisdom, and whose unconditional love always surprises and humbles me. To my mom, Camille Johnson, who is always my number one fan, and my grandma, Shirley Johnson, one of my early female role models. To those who have known me from way back, who are there in dark times and celebrate my successes as their own: Josh and Susan Johnson, Jac and Cindy Johnson, Kirsten Searer, Cynthia Ramnarace, Betsy and Kris Smith. Thanks to friends and colleagues Jennifer Barrett and Katherine Taconi. A shout-out to my family's special community at The Colony.

This book is really fueled by the countless single mom blog readers and social media followers who share their stories, insights, heartbreak, and joys both privately with me as well as with our community. You are warriors and activists in big and small ways, in your quiet moments, in your families, in business, your communities, and the world.

Resources

Dear Reader,

Thank you so much for your time here. As a note of gratitude, I'd like to point you to a couple of totally free resources that might offer support as you continue on your Kickass Single Mom journey.

Book Reader Freebies

Wealthysinglemommy.com/bookfreebies

This is a hidden link *only* for Kickass Single Mom book readers, where you can access online goodies.

Millionaire Single Moms Closed Facebook Page

This is a free community of professional single mothers from around the world passionate about building their careers and finances. No income requirements. All members must be committed to big dreams, positivity, taking action, taking full responsibility for their lives, and embracing or working toward financial independence. We talk about all things single mom: Work, money, parenting, dating, sex, travel, real estate, gender politics, and on and on. Lots of laughing, support, some tears, and countless friendships made. Whiners, victims, blamers, and bitching strictly prohibited. This is not a mommy group. It is something else. Something better. Come join the party!

xo,
Emma

☆

Notes

INTRODUCTION

xix   **an Allianz survey found:** The Allianz Life Insurance Company of North America, "The Allianz Life Women, Money, and Power Study: Empowered and Underserved," February 3, 2014, https://www.allianzlife.com/retirement-and-planning-tools/women-money-and-power.

YOUR SINGLE MOM IDENTITY

12   **then-Senate candidate Rick Santorum said:** Andy Kroll and Tim Murphy, "Santorum: Single Moms Are 'Breeding More Criminals,'" MotherJones.com, March 6, 2012, http://www.motherjones.com/politics/2012/03/santorum-single-mothers-are-breeding-more-criminals.

12   **Senator Marco Rubio . . . told his GOP colleagues:** Marco Rubio, "Reclaiming the Land of Opportunity: Conservative Reforms for Combatting Poverty," January 8, 2014, https://www.rubio.senate.gov/public/index.cfm/2014/1/rubio-delivers-address-on-50th-anniversary-of-the-war-on-poverty.

Single Mom Money Management

36   **57 percent of millennial moms are not married:** Andrew J. Cherlin, Elizabeth Talbert, and Suzumi Yasutake, "Changing Fertility Regimes and the Transition to Adulthood: Evidence from a Recent Cohort," Johns Hopkins University, June 25, 2014, http://krieger .jhu.edu/sociology/wp-content/uploads/sites/28/2012/02/Read -Online.pdf.

36   **Of the 64 percent of millennial moms:** Ibid.

The SAHM Fantasy That Holds Women Back

41   **A full 70 percent of mothers:** United States Department of Labor, "Employment Characteristics of Families—2016," April 20, 2017, https://www.bls.gov/news.release/famee.nr0.htm.

41   **40 percent of these moms are the family breadwinner:** Wendy Wang, Kim Parker, and Paul Taylor, "Breadwinner Moms," Pew Research Center, May 29, 2013, http://www.pewsocialtrends.org /2013/05/29/breadwinner-moms.

41   **A recent Pew Research Center survey found:** D'Vera Cohn, Gretchen Livingston, and Wendy Wang, "Chapter 4: Public Views on Staying at Home vs. Working," Pew Research Center, April 8, 2014, http://www.pewsocialtrends.org/2014/04/08/chapter-4-public -views-on-staying-at-home-vs-working.

41   **38 percent of full-time working mothers:** Pew Research Center, "Modern Parenthood: Roles of Moms and Dads Converge as They Balance Work and Family" March 14, 2013, http://www.pewsocial trends.org/files/2013/03/FINAL_modern_parenthood_03-2013 .pdf.

41   **A *Working Mother* poll found:** Ilisa Cohen, "The Anatomy of Working Mom Guilt," *Working Mother*, May 18, 2010, http://www .workingmother.com/node/182485.

41   **In 1960, 73 percent of families:** Gretchen Livingston, "Fewer Than Half of U.S. Kids Today Live in a 'Traditional' Family," Pew Research Center, December 22, 2014, http://www.pewresearch.org /fact-tank/2014/12/22/less-than-half-of-u-s-kids-today-live-in-a -traditional-family.

42   **the number of working mothers has ballooned:** "Nation's Working

Mothers Increase 800% Over Last 150 Years," Ancestry.com, May 8, 2014, https://blogs.ancestry.com/ancestry/2014/05/08/nations-working-mothers-increase-800-percent-over-last-150-years.

43 **moms in 1965 spent an average of ten hours:** Pew Research Center, "Modern Parenthood."

43 **Stephanie Coontz . . . shared in *Time* magazine:** Stephanie Coontz, "There Is No Such Thing as the 'Traditional Male Breadwinner,'" *Time*, September 23, 2013, http://ideas.time.com/2013/09/23/there-is-no-such-thing-as-the-male-breadwinner.

44 **In a *New York Times* op-ed, Coontz writes:** Stephanie Coontz, "When We Hated Mom," *New York Times*, May 7, 2011, http://www.nytimes.com/2011/05/08/opinion/08coontz.html.

45 **A Harvard Business School study:** Kathleen L. McGinn, Mayra Ruiz Castro, and Elizabeth Long Lingo, "Mums the Word! Cross-National Effects of Maternal Employment on Gender Inequalities at Work and at Home," Harvard Business School Working Paper, No. 15-094, June 2015 (Revised July 2015), https://dash.harvard.edu/handle/1/16727933.

45 **moms spend an average of 14 hours per week:** Pew Research Center, "Modern Parenthood."

45 **For 3- to 11-year-olds, mothers spend:** Brigid Schulte, "Why Mothers Should Not Feel Guilty about Spending No Time with Their Children," *The Independent*, March 30, 2015, http://www.independent.co.uk/life-style/health-and-families/health-news/why-mothers-should-not-feel-guilty-about-spending-no-time-with-their-children-10142207.html.

46 **University of Maryland's awesome meta-study:** M. A. Milkie, K. M. Nomaguchi, and K. E. Denny, "Does the Amount of Time Mothers Spend with Children or Adolescents Matter?" *Journal of Marriage and Family* 77: 355–372 (2015), doi:10.1111/jomf.12170.

46 **A recent study looked at families in the United States:** Caitlin McPherran Lombardi and Rebekah Levine Coley, "Early Maternal Employment and Children's School Readiness in Contemporary Families," *Developmental Psychology* 50(8): 2071–2084 (2014), doi:10.1037/a0037106.

47 **study by University of Akron sociologist Adrianne Frech and co-author Sarah Damaske:** Adrianne Frech and Sarah Damaske, "The Relationships between Mothers' Work Pathways and Physical and

Mental Health," *Journal of Health Social Behavior* 53(4): 396–412 (2012), doi:10.1177/0022146512453929.

The Kickass Single Mom Money Rules

61   **billionaire investor Warren Buffett said:** Chris Winfield, "This Is Warren Buffett's Best Investment Advice," *Time*, July 23, 2015, http://time.com/3968806/warren-buffett-investment-advice.

Build a Lifestyle You Can Afford—Today

73   **A 2014 survey conducted by the Manhattan-based marketing agency Current:** Britt Clark, "Survey: Moms Have Had Enough of Social Media," *Adweek*, September 29, 2014, http://www.adweek.com/digital/survey-moms-enough-social-media-infographic.

Get Out of Debt for Good

80   **According to Federal Reserve data:** Erin El Issa, "2016 American Household Credit Card Debt Study," Nerdwallet.com, https://www.nerdwallet.com/blog/average-credit-card-debt-household.

Commit to Frugality

96   **The typical American home has tripled in size:** Mark J. Perry, "Today's New Homes Are 1,000 Square Feet Larger Than in 1973, and the Living Space Per Person Has Doubled Over Last 40 Years," *AEIdeas*, February 26, 2014, http://www.aei.org/publication/todays-new-homes-are-1000-square-feet-larger-than-in-1973-and-the-living-space-per-person-has-doubled-over-last-40-years.

96   **1 in 10 still rent a storage unit:** Jon Mooallem, "The Self-Storage Self," *New York Times*, September 2, 2009, http://www.nytimes.com/2009/09/06/magazine/06self-storage-t.html.

96   **more televisions than people:** "Average Home Has More TVs Than People," *USA Today*, September 21, 2006, http://usatoday30.usatoday.com/life/television/news/2006-09-21-homes-tv_x.htm.

96   **throws away 65 pounds of clothes each year:** Steve Hargreaves, "Your Clothes Are Killing Us," CNN.com, May 22, 2015, http://

money.cnn.com/2015/05/22/news/economy/true-cost-clothing
/index.html.

96 **the average 10-year-old kid owns:** "Ten-year-olds have £7,000
worth of toys but play with just £330," *The Telegraph,* October 20,
2010, http://www.telegraph.co.uk/finance/newsbysector/retailand
consumer/8074156/Ten-year-olds-have-7000-worth-of-toys-but
-play-with-just-330.html.

ESTATE PLANNING FOR SINGLE MOMS

101 **The US Social Security Administration estimates:** Social Security
Administration, "Fact Sheet: Social Security," December 2016,
https://www.ssa.gov/news/press/factsheets/basicfact-alt.pdf.

COLLEGE SAVING FOR SINGLE MOMS

105 **financial giant Allianz found that:** Allianz Life Insurance Company
of North America, "College Savings Take Priority for Today's Single
Parents," August 4, 2014, https://www.allianzlife.com/about/news
-and-events/news-releases/Press-Release-August-4-2014.

106 **24 percent of adult children expect to help their aging parents:**
"Parents and Adult Children Not in Sync as Many Families Still
Struggle with Financial Conversations," BusinessWire.com, November 14, 2012, http://www.businesswire.com/news/home/2012111
4006016/en/Parents-Adult-Children-Sync-Families-Struggle
-Financial.

107 **A noted study published by Alan Krueger:** David Leonhardt, "Revisiting the Value of Elite Colleges," *New York Times,* February 21,
2011, https://economix.blogs.nytimes.com/2011/02/21/revisiting-the
-value-of-elite-colleges/?_r=0.

108 **The American Council of Trustees and Alumni (ACTA) released:**
American Council of Trustees and Alumni, "Education or Reputation?: A Look at America's Top-Ranked Liberal Arts Colleges,"
January 2014, https://www.goacta.org/publications/education_or
_reputation.

108 **36 percent of college students do not demonstrate:** Richard Arum
and Josipa Roksa, *Academically Adrift: Limited Learning on College
Campuses* (Chicago: University of Chicago Press, 2010).

108   **National Survey of Student Engagement found:** National Survey of Student Engagement, "Fostering Student Engagement Campuswide: Annual Results 2011," Indiana University Center for Postsecondary Research, 2011, http://nsse.indiana.edu/NSSE_2011_Results/pdf /NSSE_2011_AnnualResults.pdf.

109   **an education comes with a quarter-million-dollar price tag:** American Council of Trustees and Alumni, "Education or Reputation?: A Look at America's Top-Ranked Liberal Arts Colleges."

109   **One Harvard report predicts:** William C. Symonds, Robert B. Schwartz, and Ronald Ferguson, "Pathways to Prosperity: Meeting the Challenge of Preparing Young Americans for the 21st Century," Report issued by the Pathways to Prosperity Project, Harvard Graduate School of Education, February 2011, http://www.gse.harvard .edu/sites/default/files//documents/Pathways_to_Prosperity _Feb2011-1.pdf.

RETIREMENT SAVINGS FOR SINGLE MOMS

115   **divorced women have dramatically lower incomes:** Barbara A. Butrica and Karen E. Smith, "The Retirement Prospects of Divorced Women," *Social Security Bulletin*, Vol. 72, No. 1, 2012, https://www.ssa.gov/policy/docs/ssb/v72n1/v72n1p11.html.

115   **a recent Fidelity survey of married couples found:** "2013 Couples Retirement Study Executive Summary: Disconnect between Couples; Women Less Engaged," Fidelity Investments, 2013, https://www.fidelity.com/static/dcle/welcome/documents/Couples RetirementStudy.pdf.

ON ALIMONY AND CHILD SUPPORT

120   **marital rape didn't become illegal:** Jennifer A. Bennice and Patricia A. Resick, "Marital Rape: History, Research, and Practice," *Trauma, Violence, & Abuse* 4 (3): 228–246 (July 2003), https://www .ncjrs.gov/App/Publications/abstract.aspx?ID=201457.

121   **Banks wouldn't allow:** Rose Eveleth, "Forty Years Ago, Women Had a Hard Time Getting Credit Cards," Smithsonian.com, January 8, 2014, http://www.smithsonianmag.com/smart-news/forty-years -ago-women-had-a-hard-time-getting-credit-cards-180949289.

121 **A woman in the United States:** "The Pregnancy Discrimination Act of 1978," US Equal Employment Opportunity Commission, October 31, 1978, https://www.eeoc.gov/laws/statutes/pregnancy.cfm.

121 **Women are breadwinners in 40 percent of households:** Wendy Wang, Kim Parker, and Paul Taylor, "Breadwinner Moms," Pew Research Center, May 29, 2013, http://www.pewsocialtrends.org/2013/05/29/breadwinner-moms.

121 **are the majority of undergraduate students:** Mark Hugo Lopez and Ana Gonzalez-Barrera, "Women's College Enrollment Gains Leave Men Behind," Pew Research Center, March 6, 2014, http://www.pewresearch.org/fact-tank/2014/03/06/womens-college-enrollment-gains-leave-men-behind.

137 **low-income noncustodial fathers were more likely to contribute:** Jessica Firger, "Low-Income Fathers More Likely to Give Gifts, Not Money," *Newsweek*, June 21, 2015, http://www.newsweek.com/low-income-dads-more-likely-give-gifts-not-money-345409.

PARENTING AND THE SINGLE MOM

154 **one study of 1,700 children by Cornell University researchers:** Henry N. Ricciuti, "Single Parenthood and School Readiness in White, Black, and Hispanic 6- and 7-year-olds," *Journal of Family Psychology* 13(3): 450–465 (September 1999), http://dx.doi.org/10.1037/0893-3200.13.3.450.

154 **What does matter, found the study:** Jennifer E. Lansford, et al., "Does Family Structure Matter? A Comparison of Adoptive, Two-Parent Biological, Single-Mother, Stepfather, and Stepmother Households," *Journal of Marriage and Family*, 63: 840–851 (2001), doi:10.1111/j.1741-3737.2001.00840.x.

156 **Sarah S. McLanahan, of Princeton University, found:** Sara S. McLanahan, "Family Stability and Parental Investments in Children Are Key to Reducing Childhood Inequalities," *Child & Family Blog*, October 3, 2014, https://childandfamilyblog.com/family-stability-parental-investments-education-key-reducing-childhood-inequalities.

The Argument for Equally Shared Parenting

159   **According to the most recent survey from Pew Research:** Gretchen Livingston and Kim Parker, "A Tale of Two Fathers," Pew Research Center, June 15, 2011, http://www.pewsocialtrends.org /2011/06/15/a-tale-of-two-fathers.

159   **African American fathers of separated (and married) families spend:** Charles M. Blow, "Black Dads Are Doing the Best of All," *New York Times,* June 8, 2015, https://www.nytimes.com/2015/06/08 /opinion/charles-blow-black-dads-are-doing-the-best-of-all.html.

161   **There are forty-three academic papers that support shared parenting:** Richard A. Warshak, "After Divorce, Shared Parenting Is Best for Children's Health and Development," *STAT,* May 26, 2017, https://www.statnews.com/2017/05/26/divorce-shared-parenting -children-health.

161   **which are nearly always the fathers:** Edward Kruk, "Discontinuity between Pre- and Post-Divorce Father–Child Relationships: New Evidence Regarding Paternal Disengagement," *Journal of Divorce & Remarriage* 16: 195–228 (1992), http://dx.doi.org/10.1300/J087v16n 03_03.

161   **One book on this subject:** Edward Kruk, *The Equal Parent Presumption: Social Justice in the Legal Determination of Parenting after Divorce* (Montreal: McGill-Queen's University Press, 2013).

Co-Parent Like a Pro

174   **Robert Emery, PhD, author of the excellent:** Robert E. Emery PhD, *The Truth About Children and Divorce: Dealing with the Emotions So You and Your Children Can Thrive* (New York: Plume; Reprint edition, 2006).

Finding Your Parenting Style

189   **Research on children's play suggests that:** Michelle Stevens, "The Wrong Way to Keep Kids Safe From Predators," *New York Times,* April 14, 2017, https://www.nytimes.com/2017/04/14/opinion/the -wrong-way-to-keep-kids-safe-from-predators.html?_r=0.

189   **In a recent survey of more than a thousand US adults:** Kimberly Dishongh, "Study Finds Having Kids Do Chores Is a Good Thing," *Washington Times*, July 12, 2015, http://www.washingtontimes .com/news/2015/jul/12/study-finds-having-kids-do-chores-is-a -good-thing.

190   **I borrowed this from parenting expert Amy McCready:** Amy Mc-Cready, *The Me, Me, Me Epidemic: A Step-by-Step Guide to Raising Capable, Grateful Kids in an Over-Entitled World* (New York: TarcherPerigee, 2016).

Index

men (*cont.*)
  and single-mom identity, 15
  and stereotypes, 132
  See also dating as a single mother;
    fathers
millennial moms, 36, 73, 217
Millionaire Single Moms Facebook
  group, 3, 24–25
Mint.com, 74–75, 81, 83
modeling
  healthy dating attitudes, 8, 196–98,
    232
  professional ambitions, 45
  success, 9, 57–58
money and finances
  abundance formula, 37, 50, 54,
    60–61, 148
  and affordable lifestyle, 37, 54, 71–73
  bankruptcy, 80, 84, 85–86, 93
  budgeting, 73, 74–79, 81
  control over, 38
  and co-parenting, 166
  and credit reports, 85, 86, 87
  and credit scores, 80, 83, 84–89
  and dating, 140–41
  debt, 80–83, 85–87, 88, 89
  and decision making based on family
    status, 47
  and dependence, 126–27, 133 (*see
    also* alimony; child support)
  and divorces, 80
  and downsizing, 72
  earnings, 36, 37, 47, 54–61, 74
  and emotional decision making,
    93–95
  estate planning, 100–104
  and financial advisers, 116–17, 119
  financial independence, xx–xxi, 8,
    35–36, 140–41
  financing options, 87–88
  frugality, 54–56, 70, 96–99
  and guilt, 117
  holding back on earning potential,
    58–60

  and housing, 85, 86, 90–95
  and investing in outsourcing, 63–70
  and marital tension, 38, 72
  mind-sets surrounding, 49–52
  prioritizing, 35–36
  saving for college, 105–10
  saving for retirement, 88, 105–6,
    114–19
  and stereotypes about single moms,
    50–51
  struggles with, 6
  and weddings, 117
  and women as breadwinners, 59–60,
    116, 121
  See also credit cards; poverty
monikers of single moms, 16–18
mortgage payments, 86, 91
mother-daughter relationships, xxii
motivation, motherhood as, 56–57
Ms. SingleMama blog, 203

National Foundation for Credit
  Counseling, 82
National Student Loan Data System,
  81
networking, 24–25, 109–10
New York City, 23
nontraditional families, 42

Obama, Michelle, 14
one-on-one time with kids, 190–91
online dating sites, 226–29
outsourcing household labor, xxi,
  63–70

parenting style, 186–91
pay gap, 36, 40, 45, 125
peers, influence of, 22–23
phone bills, 76
PolicyGenius, 77
politicians and policy makers, 12

About the Author

EMMA JOHNSON is an award-winning business journalist and former Associated Press reporter, best known as founder of the world's largest platform for single mothers, Wealthysinglemommy.com, and host of the award-winning podcast *Like a Mother*. As an expert, Emma has appeared on CNN, Headline News, TIME, FoxNews.com, Oprah.com, the *New York Times*, the *Wall Street Journal*; has won *Parents* magazine's "Best of the Web"; and is cited as a host of a *US News* "Top 15 Personal Finance Podcasts." Emma frequently speaks on women's issues and has presented at the United Nations' Fund for Gender Equality. She is founder of the Kickass Single Mom Grant, which gives $1,000 monthly to an amazing single mom doing incredible things. Emma lives in Astoria, New York, with her children.